Renowned textile artist and tutor Hannah Lamb frequently uses and is inspired by old fabrics in her work, from age-worn cotton and linen sheets to delicate lace collars, vintage patchwork to snippets of colourful printed silk. In this book, she explores many creative ways to incorporate historical textiles into your own work, from tracking down historical textiles in shops, markets, museum collections or your own family scrap bag to designing and planning your work, starting with mood boards and sketchbooks and progressing to practical creative experimentation.

Unfolding Cloth also covers the practicalities of using old and fragile materials in your work, and how to use them to create pieces that tell powerful stories. Hannah also presents alternative ideas, such as digital printing, that allow you to import the fabric's essence but leave the original piece intact.

Illustrated throughout with inspirational examples of the author's own work and that of other leading textile artists, this thoughtful, imaginative book provides a valuable introduction to working with historical textiles to enhance your own pieces of textile art.

Unfolding Cloth

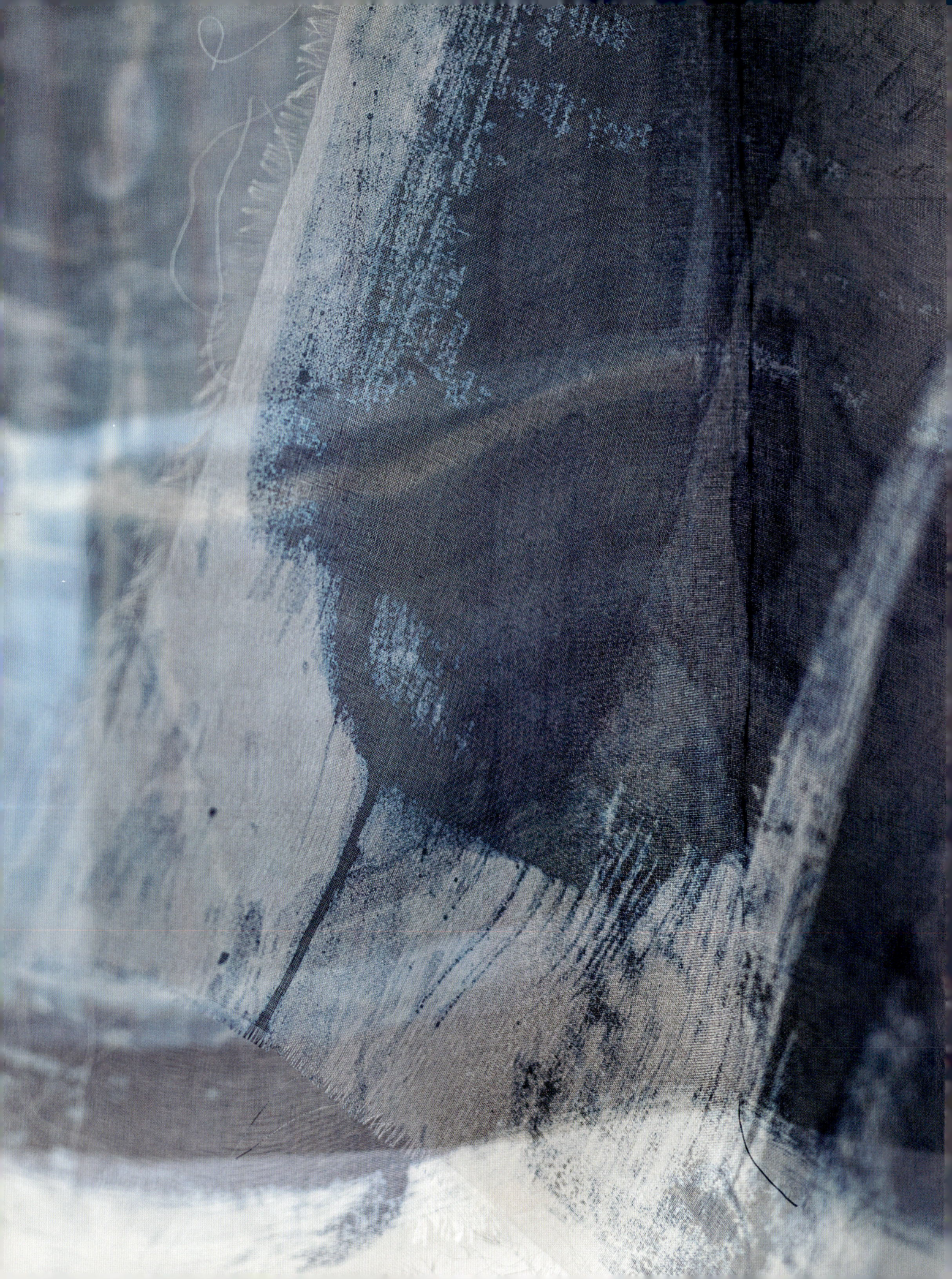

Unfolding Cloth

INSPIRATION FROM HISTORICAL TEXTILES

BATSFORD

Hannah Lamb

CONTENTS

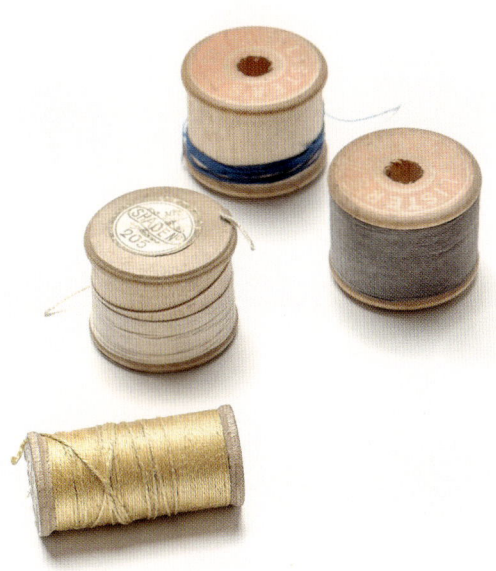

INTRODUCTION

I have always loved old things. From a young age, my summer holidays were spent visiting museums, castles, stately homes and working textile mills. I was fascinated by displays of curious tools, exquisite costumes and all kinds of historical artefacts. Perhaps I'm a little bit odd, but the musty smell of old things really excites me. There is something magical about opening the lid of an old trunk, or unwrapping layers of crisp, archival tissue paper, to rediscover objects from past times.

I have cherished memories of rainy Sunday afternoons spent sorting through Grandma's button tin; pressing to my cheek cold glass buttons, smooth wooden wartime buttons, or spidery Dorset thread buttons. As I arranged and sorted them into groups, Grandma would reminisce about the tiny buttons from the boots she wore to school, the linen ones from Liberty bodices, or the black imitation-jet buttons from her own Victorian grandmother. Invariably the stories would meander, and I would learn so much more about our family, and what people wore or what life was like in the past. What I learned at my grandmother's knee was the power of historical objects to tell stories.

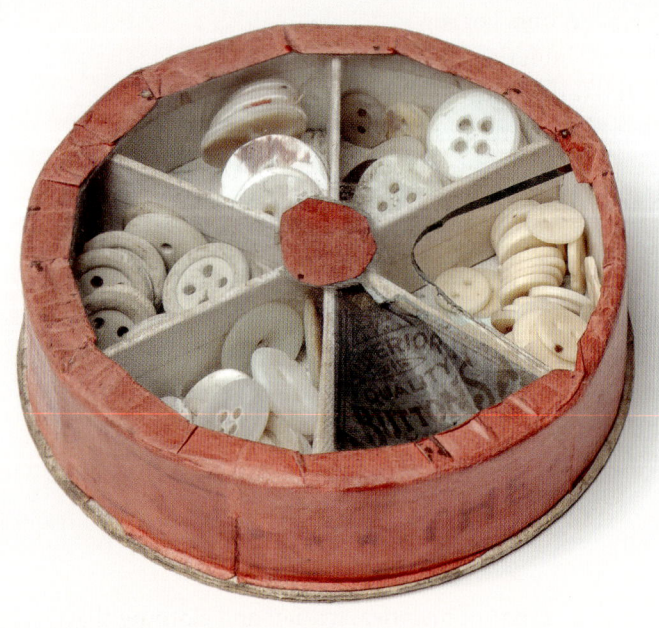
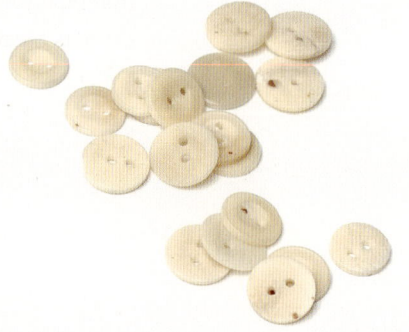
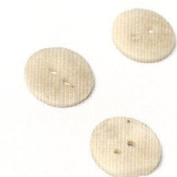

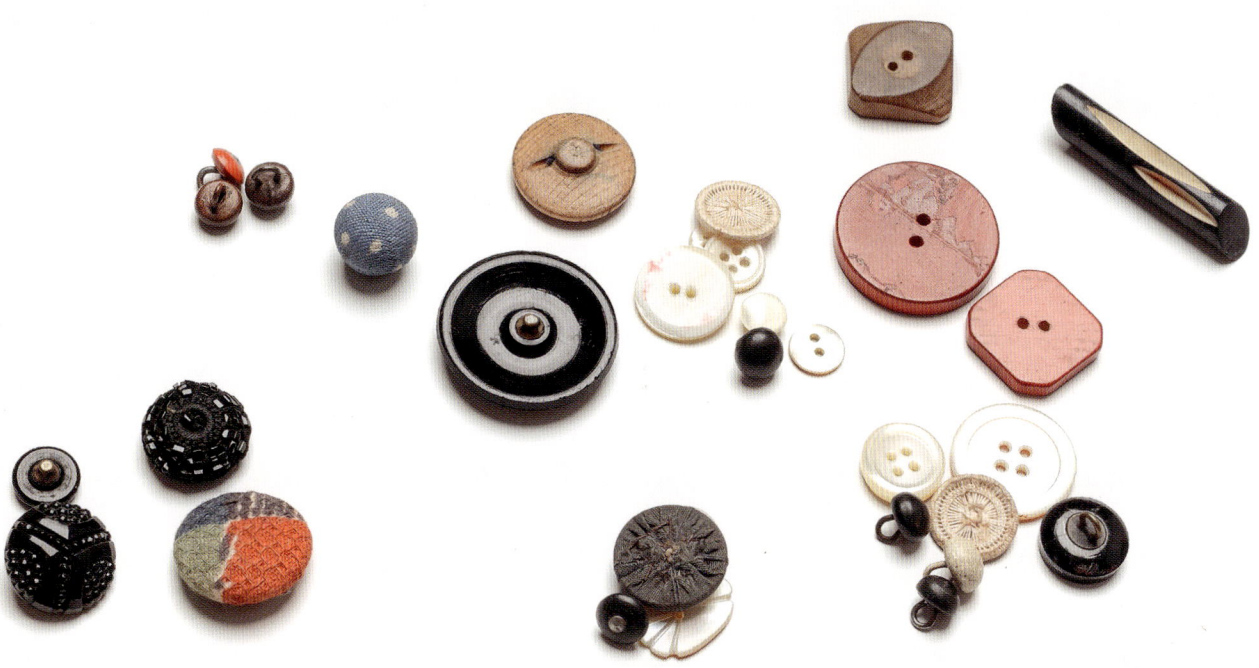

As textile artists and textile lovers, we can enjoy old textiles and clothing for their sheer beauty, admire the quality of making and marvel at the intricacies of their construction. For some of us, our emotional response to textiles might be more important: how they make us feel and the memories they evoke. But even if we don't have a personal connection, textiles can transport us to other times, places and cultures, allowing us to stand in someone else's shoes – sometimes, perhaps, even literally! All of these responses can offer creative inspiration.

Whether you are a student, a professional textile artist, or just someone with a collection of lovely old fabrics, this book provides inspiration and practical techniques to inspire your own projects. Throughout the book there is a strong focus on using research as part of the creative process, taking a slow approach to seeing, and exploring historic pieces through drawing, mark-making, print and collage. You will find the suggestions open-ended, with plenty of scope to explore and develop ideas in your own way.

We'll start by looking at the range of historical textiles and clothing that might inspire you, and how and where you might find them, as well as some practical approaches to discover more about them. In the chapters that follow, I introduce some creative techniques, using embroidery and cyanotype to create beautiful responses. While this isn't a project book, you will find lots of advice about how to develop your own original ideas to create thoughtful and meaningful textile art.

OPPOSITE AND ABOVE
A selection of vintage buttons from my own collection.

A TO Z OF CLOTH AND CLOTHING

This is not a definitive list,
but some thoughts to get you started...

Antimacassars, aprons, armour

Badges, bags, bandanas, banners, baskets, beadwork, bed hangings, bedspreads, blankets, bonnets, burqa, buttons

Capes, caps, carpets, caskets, children's clothes, chintz, christening gowns, collars, corsets, crinolines, cuffs, curtains, cushions

Dance costumes, dashiki, denim, doilies, dolls' clothes, drapery, dresses

Eiderdown, embroideries, evening dress

Fancy dress, fans, fishing nets, flags, flour sacks, football jerseys

Gloves, goldwork, gowns

Handbags, handkerchiefs, hats, Hawaiian shirts, headdress, hijab, hot pants, housecoat, huipils, huswifs

Ikat, indigo dyeing

Jackets, jeans, jerseys, jumpsuits

Kaftans, kanga, kente cloth, kilts, kimono, kippa, knitwear, kurta

Lace, lappets, lingerie, long johns

Mantilla, mantua, mats, mittens, moquette, mourning dress, muffs

OPPOSITE *The top section from a child's silk dress, with hand-stitched smocking and embroidery.*

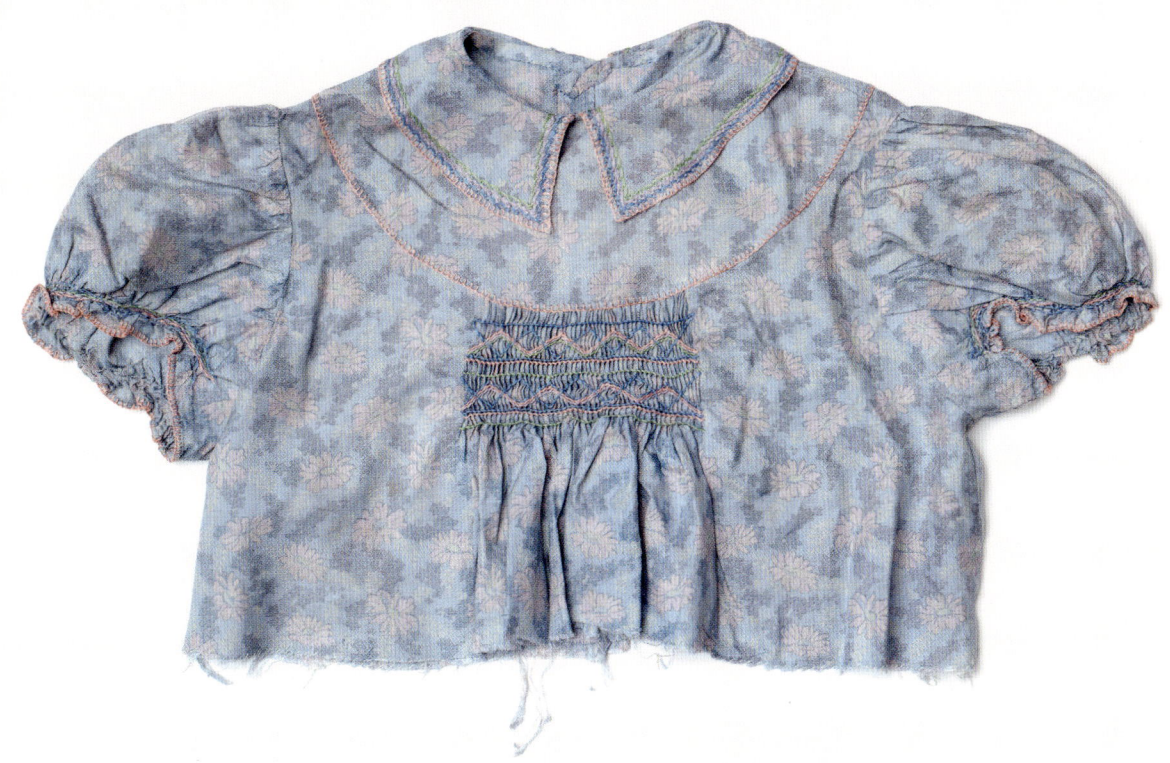

National costumes, neckties, needlework, nightdresses

Obi, overalls, overcoats

Palampores, parachutes, parasols, passementerie, pelmets, petticoats, pillows, pincushions, pockets, ponchos

Qipao, quilts

Rag dolls, reticules, ribbons, rucksacks, ruffs, rugs

Sample books, samplers, saris, sarongs, screens, shawls, sheets, shirts, shoes, shrouds, skirts, socks, sportswear, stockings, suits, swimwear

Tablecloths, tapestries, tea cosies, tents, theatrical costumes, toys, trousers, T-shirts, tunics, turban cloth

Underwear, uniforms, upholstery

Veils, velvets, vestments, vests

Waistcoats, wall hangings, wax cloth, wedding dresses, whitework, workwear

X-ray skirt

Yarmulkes, yashmaks

Zoot suit

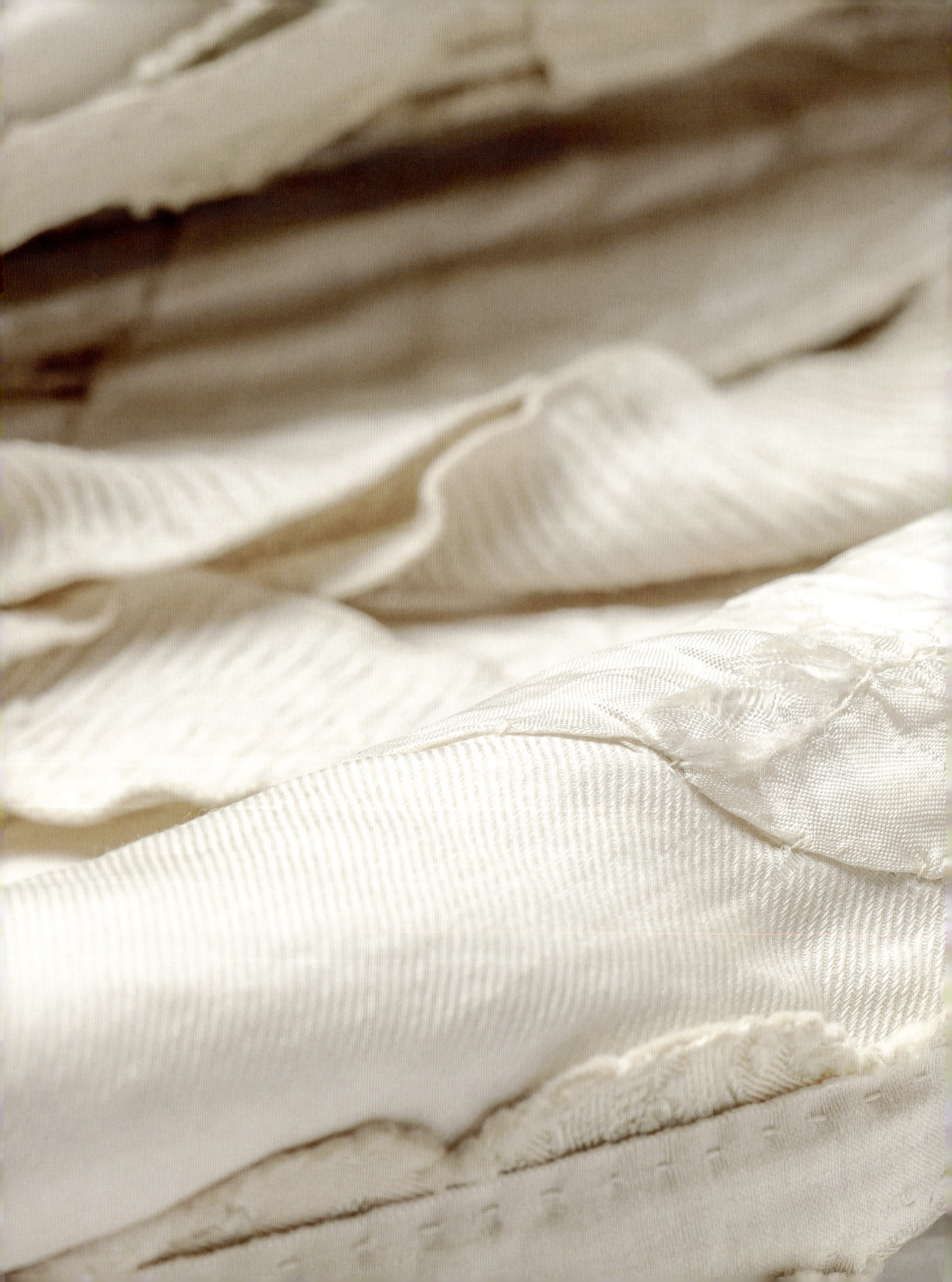

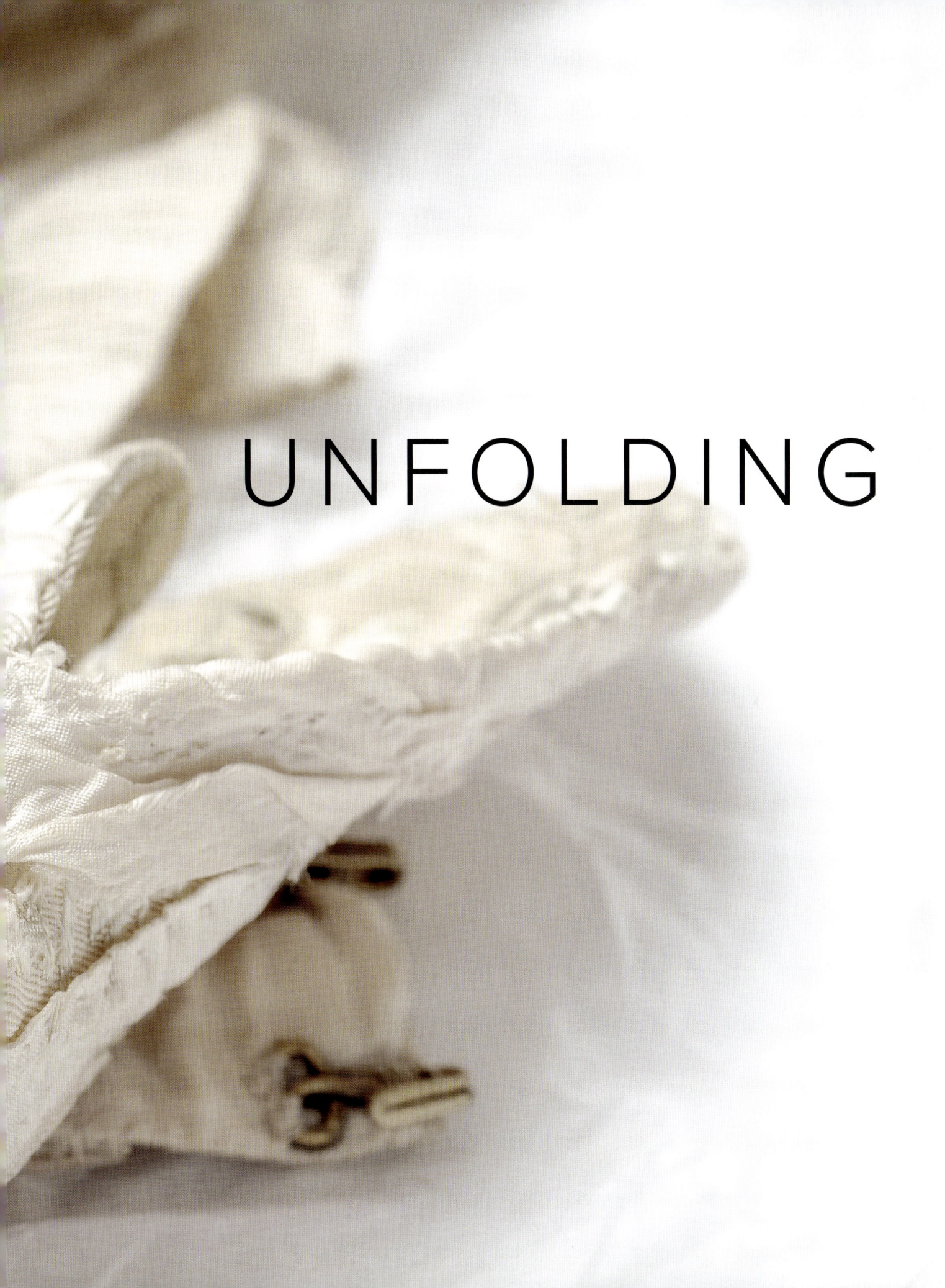

UNFOLDING

LOCATING SOURCES

Historical textiles can be found in many different places, from grand pieces in stately homes and national museums, to humble everyday items in our own homes. Historic textiles don't have to be ancient, exotic, expensive or rare, but from a creative point of view, they do need to be interesting. When starting a project, I'm searching for what grabs my attention and resonates with my current obsessions. I also look for pieces that tell a story, things that I feel a connection to. Where might you begin?

CLOSE TO HOME

It can be surprising what is available in our own homes and communities, and it's well worth chatting to friends and family to see what treasures they may have. Often, we overlook everyday things, or even forget about precious textiles tucked away.

For decades an old wooden trunk stood at the top of my grandma's stairs. We passed it all the time without a second thought. One day, in searching through commonplace sheets, old nightdresses, tablecloths and antimacassars, we noticed a small bag labelled 'the Prince's Shirt' in my grandmother's curling handwriting. After much research, I discovered it was an early 19th-century men's shirt that had very likely belonged to a British prince. How it came to be in our humble family we may never know, but it is remarkable that it was overlooked for so long.

Many fascinating textiles lay forgotten in attics, wardrobes and at the back of drawers. These range from items made for special occasions (wedding dresses, christening robes, saris, commemorative sports strips, etc.) to more everyday pieces. Yet sometimes it can be the commonplace things that hold particularly poignant memories for us and are just as worthwhile as a creative stimulus. When it comes to research, having ready access to historical textiles is hugely beneficial because you can spend as long as you like studying them up close.

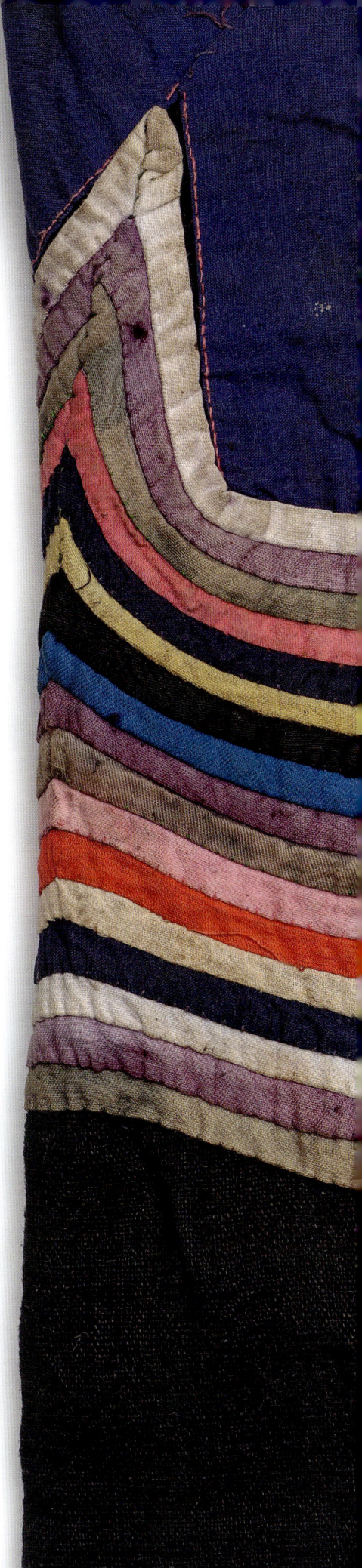

BUYING ANTIQUE AND VINTAGE

Antique textiles and costumes can be purchased at auction, in antique shops and at specialist fairs and markets. You may even find treasures in your local charity shop or thrift store. There are also an increasing number of dealers selling online, direct to the public. As with any purchase, it pays to be cautious. Always check the item's condition and ensure you are aware of any issues. If you are spending a lot of money, try to buy from dealers or auction houses with a track record.

I like to buy smaller, more affordable textile items. Often these are incomplete or not in perfect condition, but they make great study pieces. Items in pristine condition and those that are particularly rare can fetch big prices. Fortunately, this is where museums come into their own.

MUSEUMS

Depending on where you live, the chances are there is some kind of museum local to you. Even tiny museums have interesting collections, often with relevance to the local community. While they may not have the big budgets and blockbuster exhibitions of the national museums, regional collections are often full of weird and wonderful artefacts.

While a collection that is on your doorstep can be much quicker and easier to access in person, national museums generally hold more extensive collections, often with better-quality or rarer artefacts. However, don't overlook specialist museums. Collections of transport, military, industrial or rural life can all include fascinating examples of textiles and clothing for specific uses and settings. For a list of some of my favourite museums and collections, see Resources for Research on page 125.

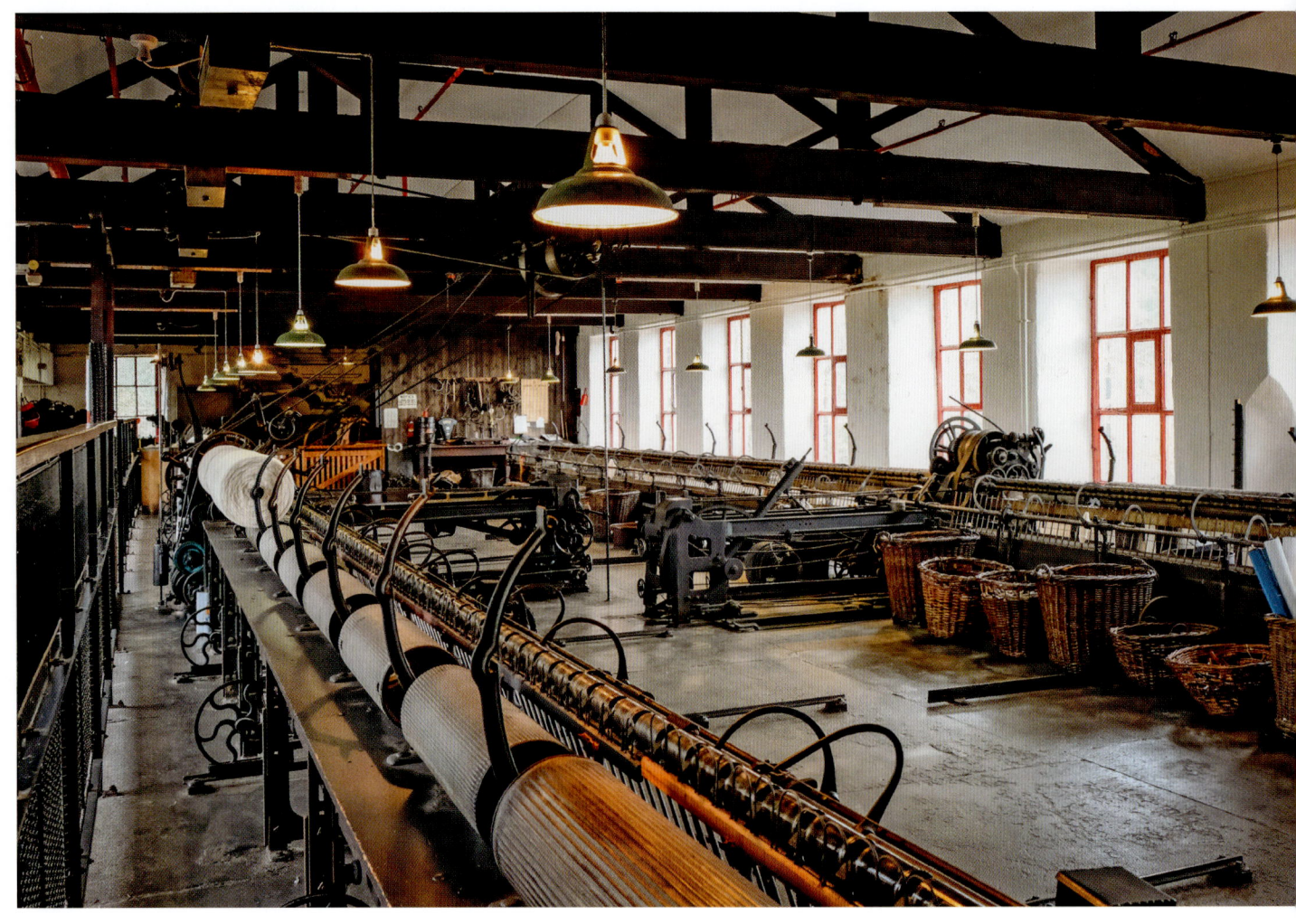

HISTORIC BUILDINGS

Ranging from privately owned historic houses to stately homes and castles looked after by charitable organisations, places such as these can provide access to a wide range of textiles, often displayed in period room settings. Typically, we might see examples of domestic textiles, such as curtains, bed hangings, carpets, quilts and upholstery. Sometimes we may be lucky enough to discover more intimate pieces created, used or worn by former residents, such as samplers, needlework objects or costumes.

HERITAGE INDUSTRIAL SITES

Industrial museums help us to understand historical textile manufacturing, with some still having working machinery. Their collections typically focus on items directly connected to the mill or manufacturer and sometimes the community associated with it. This might include tools, promotional materials, fabric samples, photographs, ledgers or logbooks. Similar kinds of artefacts can also be found at regional museums with a textile heritage.

ABOVE *Spinning machinery at Leeds Industrial Museum.*

OPPOSITE *Printer's notebook from the Society of Dyers and Colourists collection.*

ARCHIVES AND LIBRARIES

Archives provide a different kind of collection as they were never intended to become part of a museum, but are the product of the normal working activities of an organisation. In the late 20th century, when textile manufacturing declined rapidly in Great Britain, many companies folded or were bought up by international firms. A great many business records were lost, including textile sample books, dye recipe books and ledgers. However, many of the most beautiful textile pattern books were saved and preserved as archives within larger collections in regional museums, libraries, universities and colleges.

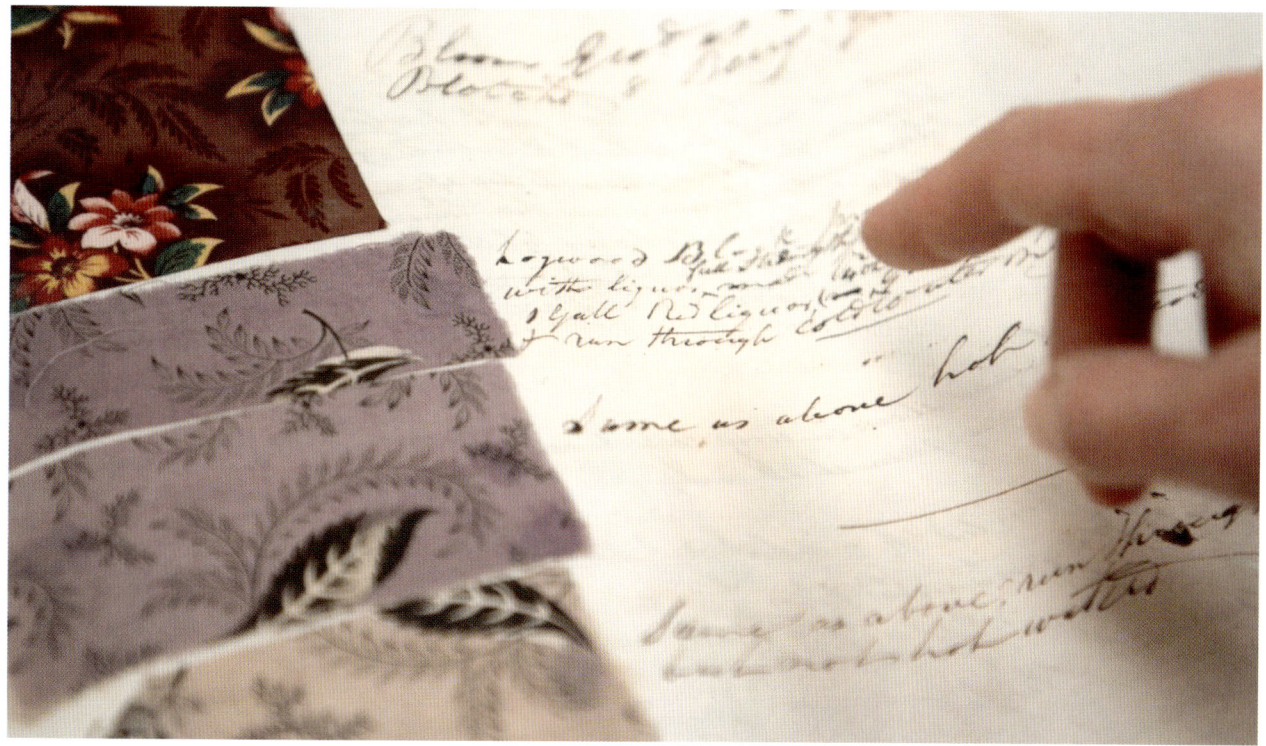

Looking for inspiration

In my teaching role I have spent a lot of time thinking about the different ways we search for inspiration. As individuals, we all think differently, but in my own practice I identify strongly with education-thought-leader Guy Claxton's description of how our brains handle information. He says, 'Attention runs along a continuum from a tight focus, like a spotlight, to a low focus, like a floodlight.'[1] I like to imagine a lamp that can be adjusted, focused in to illuminate a small area brightly or spread outwards to cover a wider area more softly. Imagine your attention doing the same and you get the idea. These two ways of looking are useful for thinking about how we can use museums and collections for creative inspiration.

At the start of a new project, or when looking for new ideas and connections, I really enjoy the 'floodlight' mode. Activities I associate with this include browsing library shelves, flicking through books, or wandering through a gallery or museum. This gentle, soft focus allows me to notice things as they catch my eye, seeing patterns and connections without actively searching for them. This approach is great if you are unsure what you want to look at, especially when it's a new subject. To take a 'floodlight' approach, remove limitations: set aside time without other distractions, be gentle on yourself, and cast aside expectations of a 'solution'.

At the other end of the continuum, the tighter focus of the 'spotlight' is something I associate with more focused research and learning. When I am in spotlight mode, I feel myself getting quite obsessive about a particular topic. This kind of attention is great when you need to gather specific information on a subject. Try to define what you want to know by writing yourself a brief or a question, the more specific the better, as there is less chance then of getting distracted.

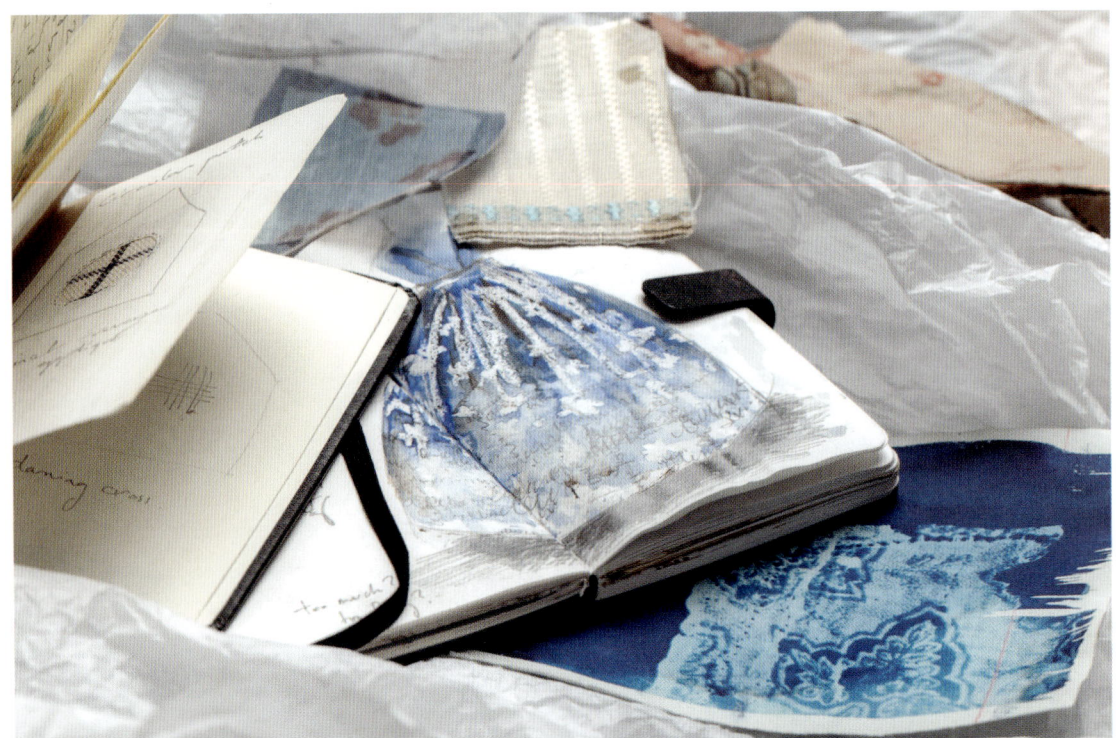

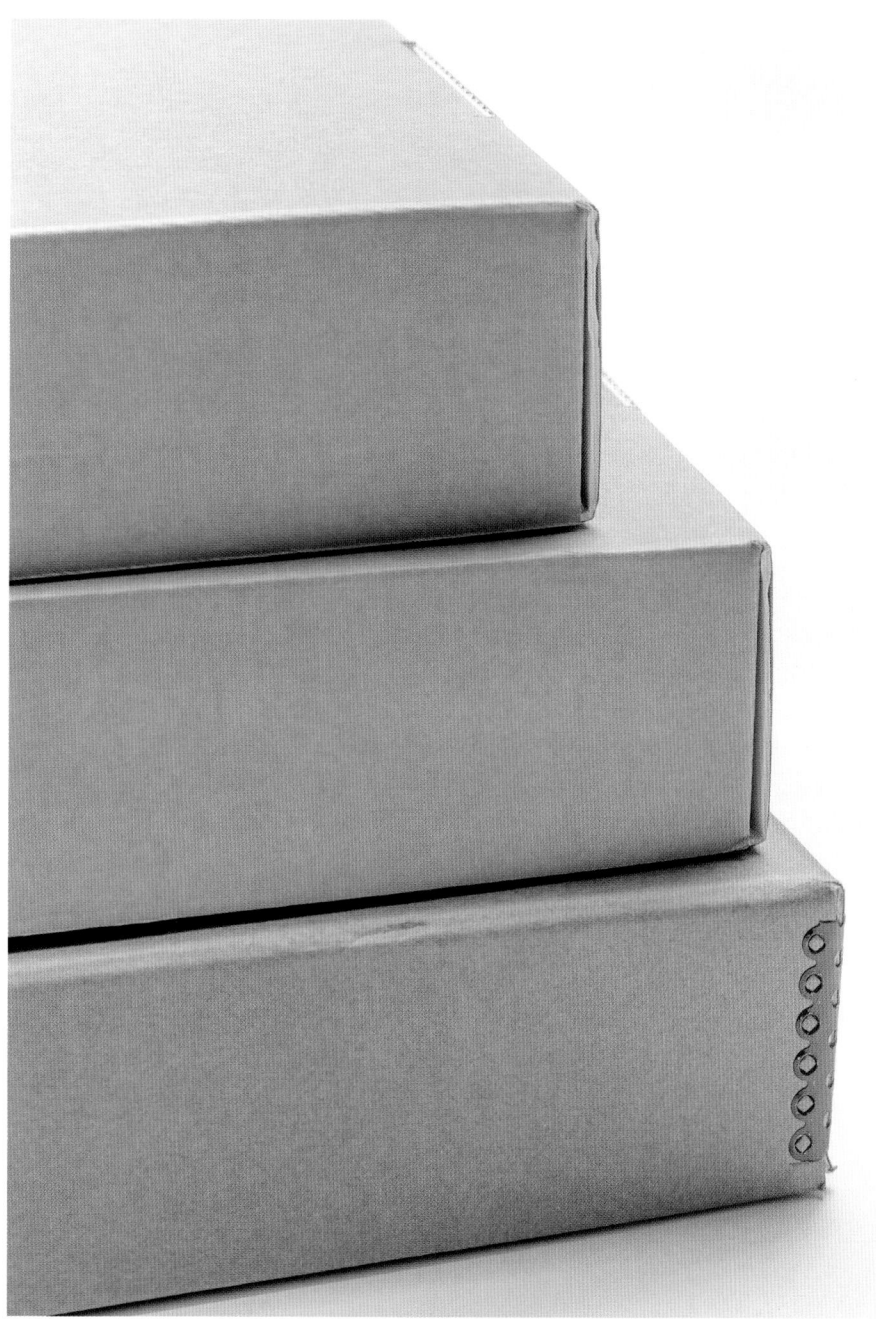

SEARCHING DIGITAL CATALOGUES

Many major collections now have online catalogues that enable the public to easily search for items from anywhere in the world, 24 hours a day. While viewing objects on a screen is never a substitute for seeing and handling the real thing, it can allow us to quickly see examples; it enables us to get an overview of a collection and compare items in different collections around the world. If you want to spend some time browsing, it can be fun to just scroll through a catalogue (think 'floodlight' mode); however, many collections are extensive and easier to use if you first define what it is you are looking for. You can either do this with a light touch and choose a single search term, e.g. 'quilts', or define more specific criteria.

STEP 1: IDENTIFY IDEAS If my research question is, 'How have Asian textiles influenced British fashion?', I could search for 'Asian textiles' and 'British fashion'. These are big subjects, so consider narrowing this to a specific era, for example '1970s' or '20th century'. Do some quick surface-level reading to gain a general understanding of the topic to help you define your research question.

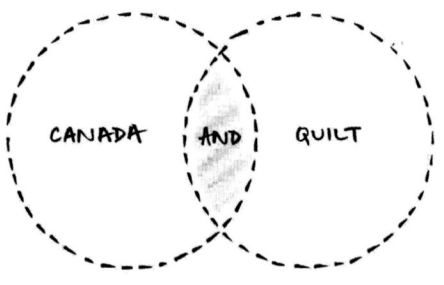

STEP 2: IDENTIFY KEYWORDS We could just search for 'Asian textiles' or 'British fashion' and get good results; however, we might miss entries that use different words or phrases. Consider synonyms and related terms to describe your subject. For example, instead of 'Asian' try 'India' or 'Pakistan'; instead of 'British', try 'UK'.

STEP 3: IDENTIFY WHICH CATALOGUES TO SEARCH You can usually find a summary of each collection's holdings on their website. If you are unsure where to begin, the big national museums often have broader collections, which can be a useful starting point.

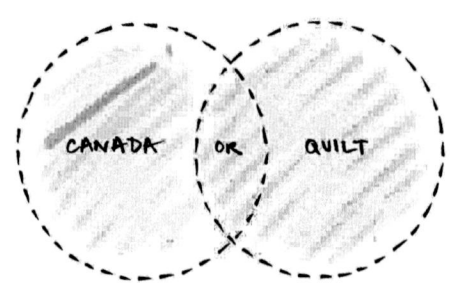

STEP 4: TEST YOUR KEYWORD SEARCH Try typing your keywords into the search facility on your chosen catalogue. Make a note of the different keywords you try, and which are most successful. If your results don't give you what you want, try changing the keywords. If you get too many results, try using more specific keywords, or limit your search using specific fields. Examples may include:

- Type of object
- Material or technique
- Date range
- Place of origin*
- Artist/manufacturer

*Remember that place names and political boundaries continue to change throughout history.

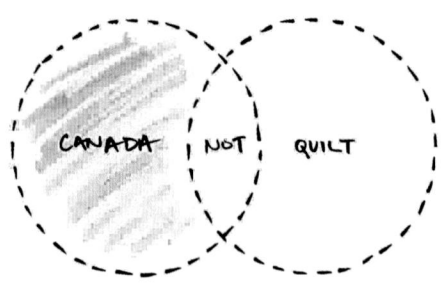

STEP 5: TRY AN ADVANCED SEARCH The following hints will help you to hone your search terms:

- Use the asterisk symbol where you are unsure of a spelling or to find words with a variety of endings (e.g. 'quilt*' will find quilted, quilting, quilter, etc.).
- Use double quotes to search for a specific phrase, e.g. "Red Cross".
- Use AND to search for catalogue entries that include both fields, e.g. Canada AND quilt.
- Use OR to bring up any record that includes either of the search terms.
- Use NOT to exclude records, e.g. Canada NOT quilt.

Each catalogue will be slightly different, so it is best to consult any instructions or guidance provided by the host organisation. If you need more help with catalogues or databases, try asking a librarian.

ARCHIVE AND MUSEUM RESEARCH

Museums and archives provide us with incredible access to rare and precious artefacts. While books and online sources are wonderful, there is no substitute for seeing the real thing in a historic setting. Studying an object up close, being able to move around it, perhaps see it from different angles, makes a huge difference to how we understand it. How often have you seen a photo of an object and then discovered it is much smaller or bigger than expected in real life? Public museums can be inspiring, but they can also present some creative challenges; crowds of people, low lighting and glass cabinets can all get in the way. If you are making a special trip, it is worth checking a few things before you go.

MUSEUM VISIT CHECKLIST

- What are the opening times?
- What are the access arrangements? Especially important if you have particular access needs.
- Is photography permitted?
- What do you hope to find out or explore? Consider writing some questions to help you stay focused.
- Is what you want to see on display? Displays change and sometimes items are removed for conservation, or loaned to other museums.

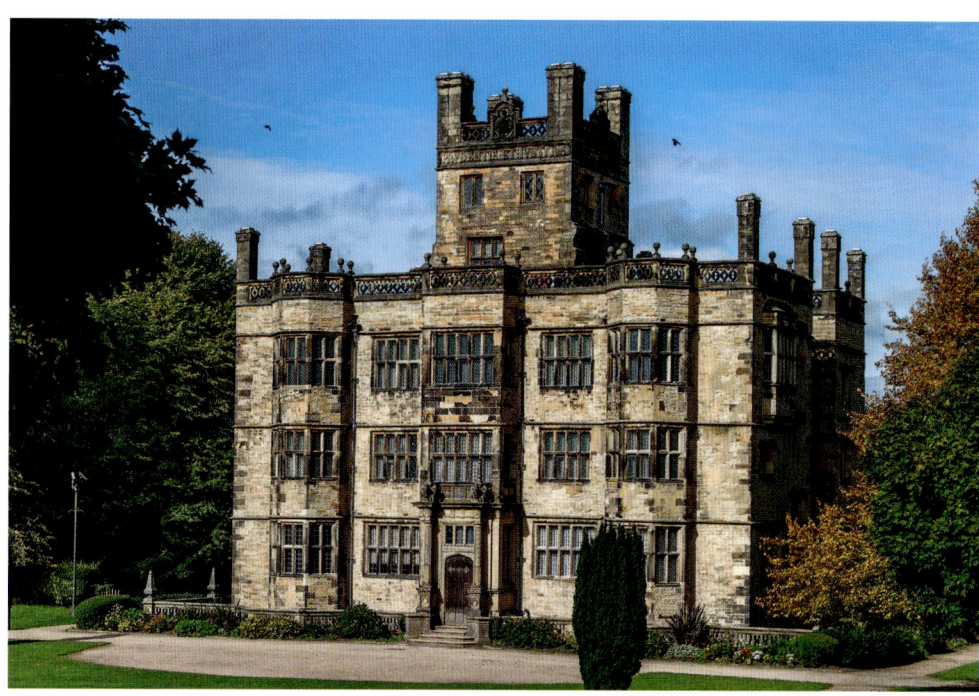

RIGHT Changing displays from the Gawthorpe Textiles Collection can be viewed at Gawthorpe Hall, near Burnley in Lancashire, but this represents a very small proportion of the main collection.

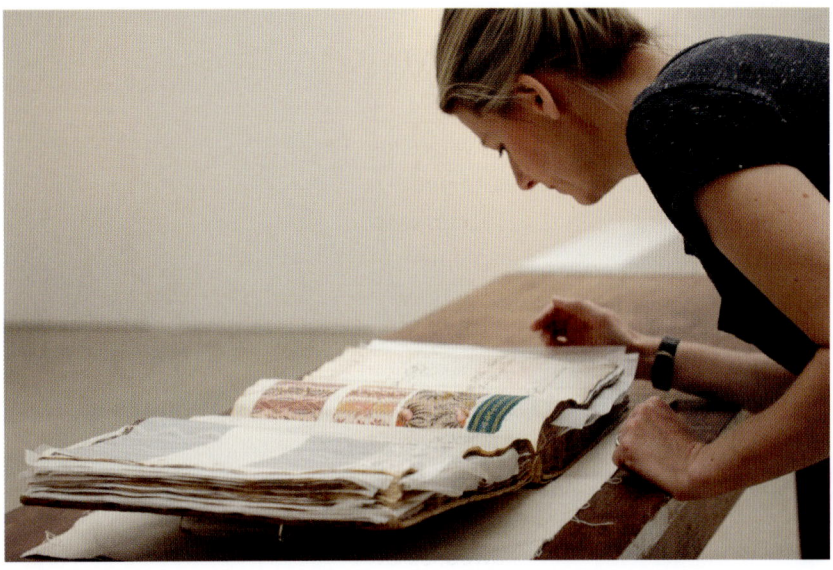

Museum stores

The exhibits on display in a museum tend to represent only a tiny percentage of the overall collection, and the remaining objects will be kept in the museum store or reserve collection. The display of historic textiles needs to be balanced with their conservation. By rotating the exhibits, the museum can show different objects, while allowing others to rest and be cleaned. In some cases, artefacts will simply be too fragile to be displayed at all.

When viewing a reserve collection I always get a little thrill, because it feels like a privileged 'backstage' view. There's something very special about opening archive boxes and unwrapping precious antique textiles ensconced in layers of tissue paper. The particular benefit of viewing objects in this way is that you get to have unparalleled sensory access. Sometimes (although not always) you may be able to carefully handle items, to inspect them up close, turn them around and look inside. You can feel their weight in your hands, notice the texture and the details of construction, hear the sound of the material as it moves, even smell it! This kind of tactile, visual and sensory experience is wonderful for sparking creative inspiration.

If you want to view items not currently on show, you will need to book an appointment, and timescales will vary. While some specialist collections are only open to academic researchers, the majority are open to anyone with a specific request, and it never hurts to ask. Look on the website or phone the museum to check what the process is for booking a visit. Usually, you will need to request to view a specific type of object, e.g. '19th-century christening robes', so it's important to do your research beforehand. If possible, use online resources to check what the museum holds in their collection. If you have a very specific request, you can even give the accession number for an individual item you would like to view.

ABOVE AND OPPOSITE
Viewing historic dye recipe books from the collection of the Society of Dyers and Colourists.

Visiting a reserve collection

Museum stores and study areas vary enormously, from purpose-built, high-spec conservation spaces, to poorly lit, cramped cellars in historic buildings. If you have specific access needs, always make sure you mention this to ensure appropriate arrangements can be made wherever possible.

Each library, archive or reserve collection will have its own visitor rules. Some may require you to leave your possessions in a locker and only allow you to bring in limited items in a transparent bag, while others may take a more relaxed attitude. Below are some pointers to make your visit run smoothly.

- Double-check that photography is permitted.
- Often just pencils are allowed, so do check if there are any media restrictions.
- Don't bring food or drink into the collections.
- Wash your hands.
- Avoid wearing heavy, dangly jewellery or scarves that could damage museum artefacts.
- Put any bags or coats well away from the study area.
- If allowed, handle objects with care and respect.
- If gloves are provided for handling, wear them.
- If in doubt, follow the lead of the heritage professional.

One additional bonus of viewing reserve collections is the opportunity to speak with specialist curators. Often they are a fount of knowledge and can provide additional context to the artefacts, or even suggest other avenues for you to research. However, this does vary and sometimes the person you meet may not be a specialist in your subject. In general, curators and archivists are very keen to help but often overstretched.

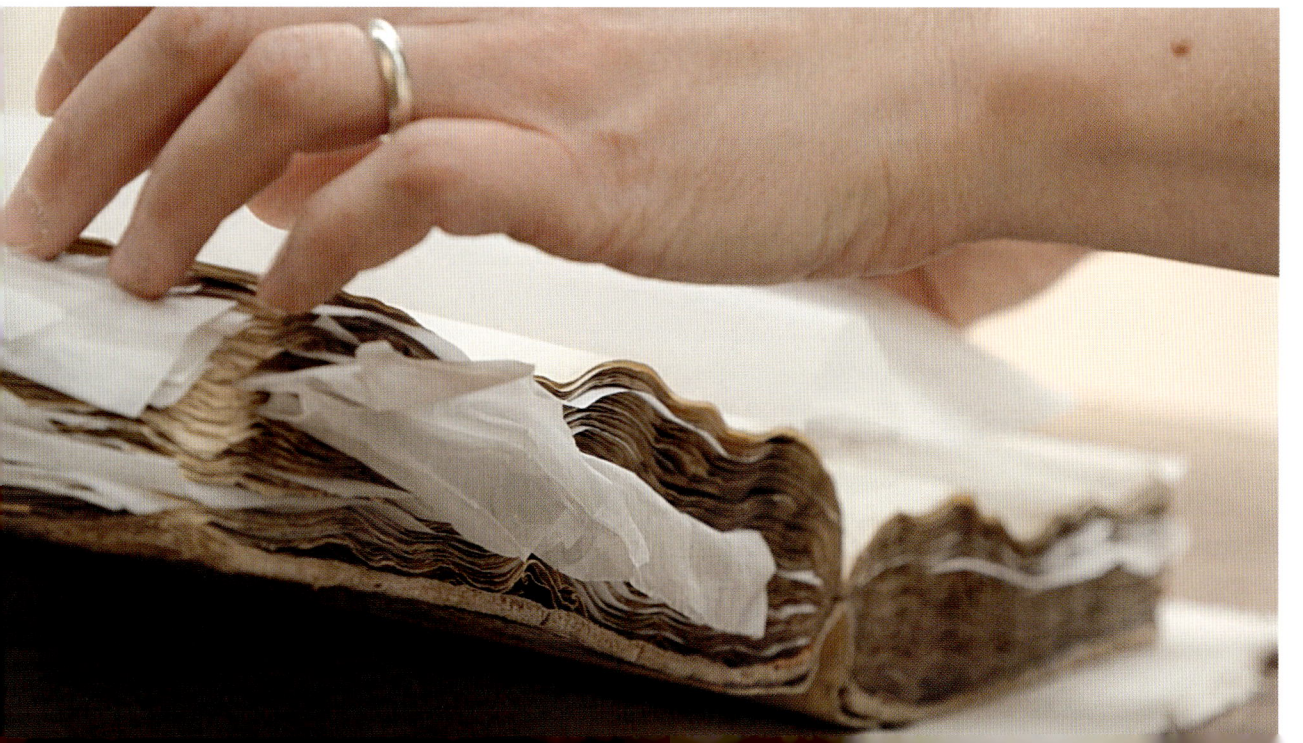

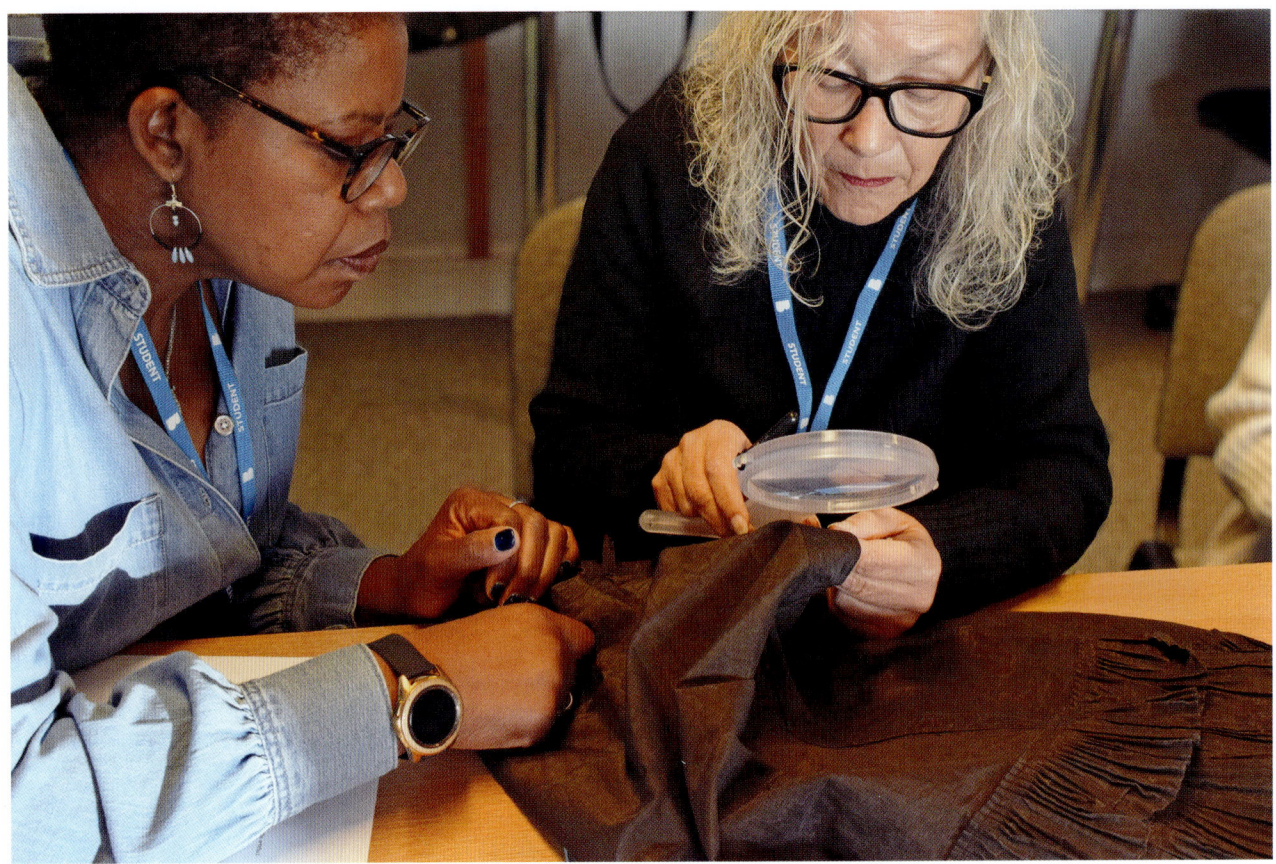

Sketching in museums

Museums don't always feel like inviting places to draw, and sometimes it can be a bit intimidating. We might think other people are judging us or that we are in the way, so there is an enormous temptation to reach for a camera instead of a sketchbook. But for conservation reasons, textiles are often kept in dark rooms or behind glass, making it difficult to take good-quality photos. It can also be challenging to adequately capture construction details or embellishment. This is when drawing really comes into its own.

Along with these practical considerations, drawing has an important role in helping us to look more carefully. There is a slowing down that happens when we stand in front of an object and start to draw it. We notice more about its construction – how different components are joined, how a pattern repeats across the piece – and we notice details of embellishment and subtleties of colour. I also find that it gives me creative thinking time and headspace to be inventive or imaginative. If I am visiting an exhibition, I like to challenge myself to choose one item to spend time with and sketch. I just focus on the bits that interest me and I don't worry about these being 'good' drawings; it's what's happening in my head that really matters.

ABOVE *Students study the construction of a 19th-century underskirt.*

OPPOSITE *Items from my travelling research kit.*

A travelling research kit

When making a research visit to a museum reserve collection or archive, regardless of whether I plan to do any serious sketching, there are a few basic items I find handy to have with me. Most archives and museum stores restrict visitors to pencil only – no pens or wet media – and erasers and pencil sharpeners are also frowned upon, as they make a lot of mess. My basic kit includes:

- Pencils – several pre-sharpened or a propelling pencil.
- Small notebook.
- Soft fabric tape measure.
- Camera (check you know how to turn off the flash).
- Magnifying glass or eye loupe.
- Torch (or use the one on your phone).

In less restricted museum settings, I tend to use whatever I have to hand. Washi tape, fine-liner drawing pens and watercolour pencils are all useful.

OBSERVATION

Studying material artefacts from real life is referred to as 'primary research' because it is a first-hand experience that puts us in touch with the people who made, wore or owned that object. Taking our time to carefully observe and study historical textiles can reveal a wealth of hidden information and creative potential.

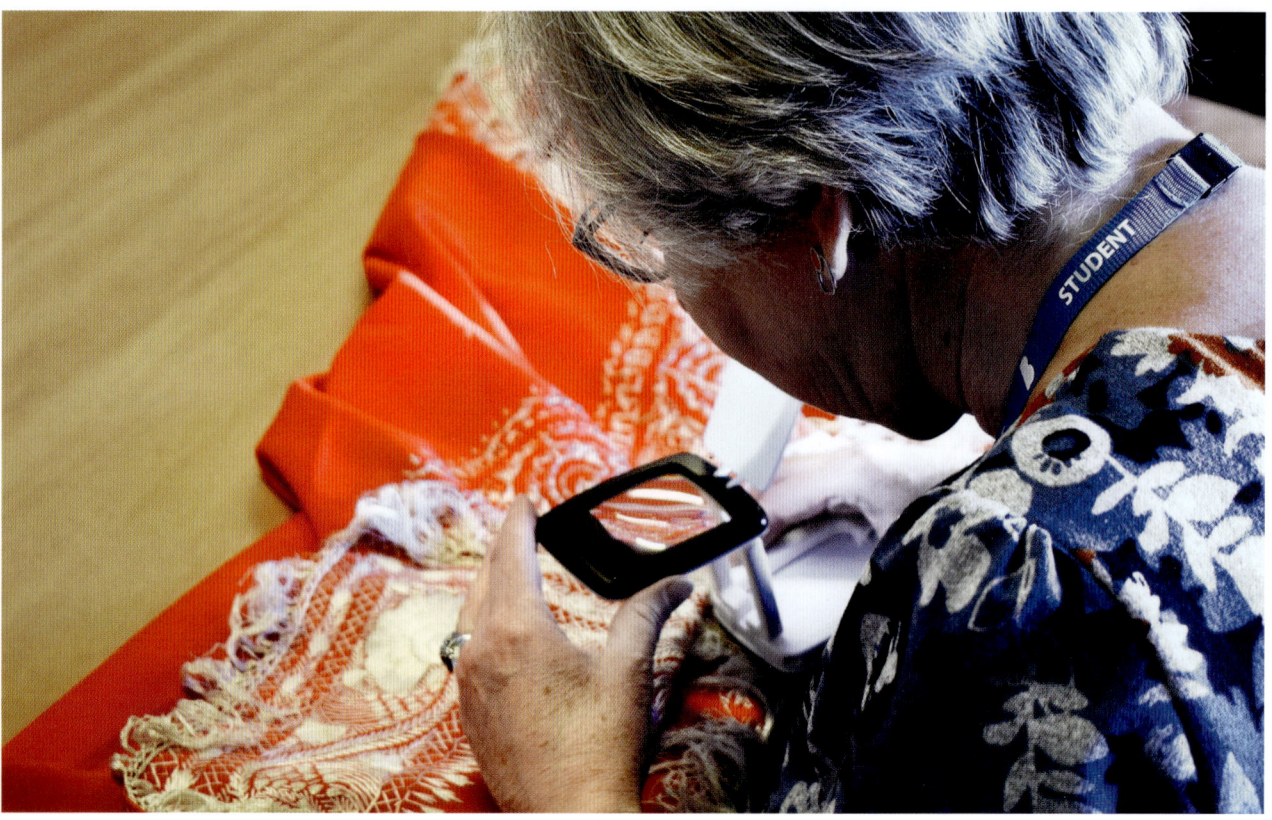

ABOVE *Careful observation of old textiles can reveal hidden information and offer creative inspiration.*

An introduction to slow seeing

In their book *The Dress Detective*, Ingrid Mida and Alexandra Kim refer to a 'slow approach to seeing'. This involves taking your time to carefully observe historical artefacts, working in a thoughtful, patient and methodical way, as they explain:

'Before commencing an examination of a dress artefact, the researcher must resolve to be mindful and present... pause, turn off other distractions, and mentally commit to slow down.'

This slow approach to seeing means focusing all of the senses to observe and notice the subtle clues a material object might be concealing. This immediately resonated with me as an artist. I recognised the mental slowing down and the way my mind slips into a different state, losing itself in the detail of observational drawing.

When studying historical costume and textiles, it can be tempting to simply take some quick photos. Drawing can feel like too much trouble but, in fact, taking the time to draw will help you to more carefully observe. When you draw, you have to go through a process of looking, analysing what you see, puzzling over it and so understanding it better. This is not about making perfect drawings; it is all about the process of looking itself. I try to think of the drawing as a by-product, albeit one that you might actually find useful at a later date.

On the following pages I introduce a step-by-step process of drawing for slow seeing (or 'slow looking' as I often call it). This is based on a classic art school technique that I return to time and again with my students. It's an invaluable method for training our brains to look more carefully. If you are new to observational drawing, or haven't done it for a while, practise this at home. Don't worry if you don't have any historic textiles at hand; you can use an item from your wardrobe to practise on – something fairly small that you can hold in your hand is ideal, such as a glove, sock or handkerchief.

A slow seeing exercise

This is an activity to do in a quiet space, when you aren't feeling rushed or distracted. Gather just the things you need: your textile object, paper, pencil or pen (choose just one drawing medium). Clear everything else from your work surface and remove distractions (set your phone to silent). Make yourself comfortable, settle your mind and your breathing. You may find it helpful to use a sketchbook that opens flat or tape a loose sheet of paper to your table.

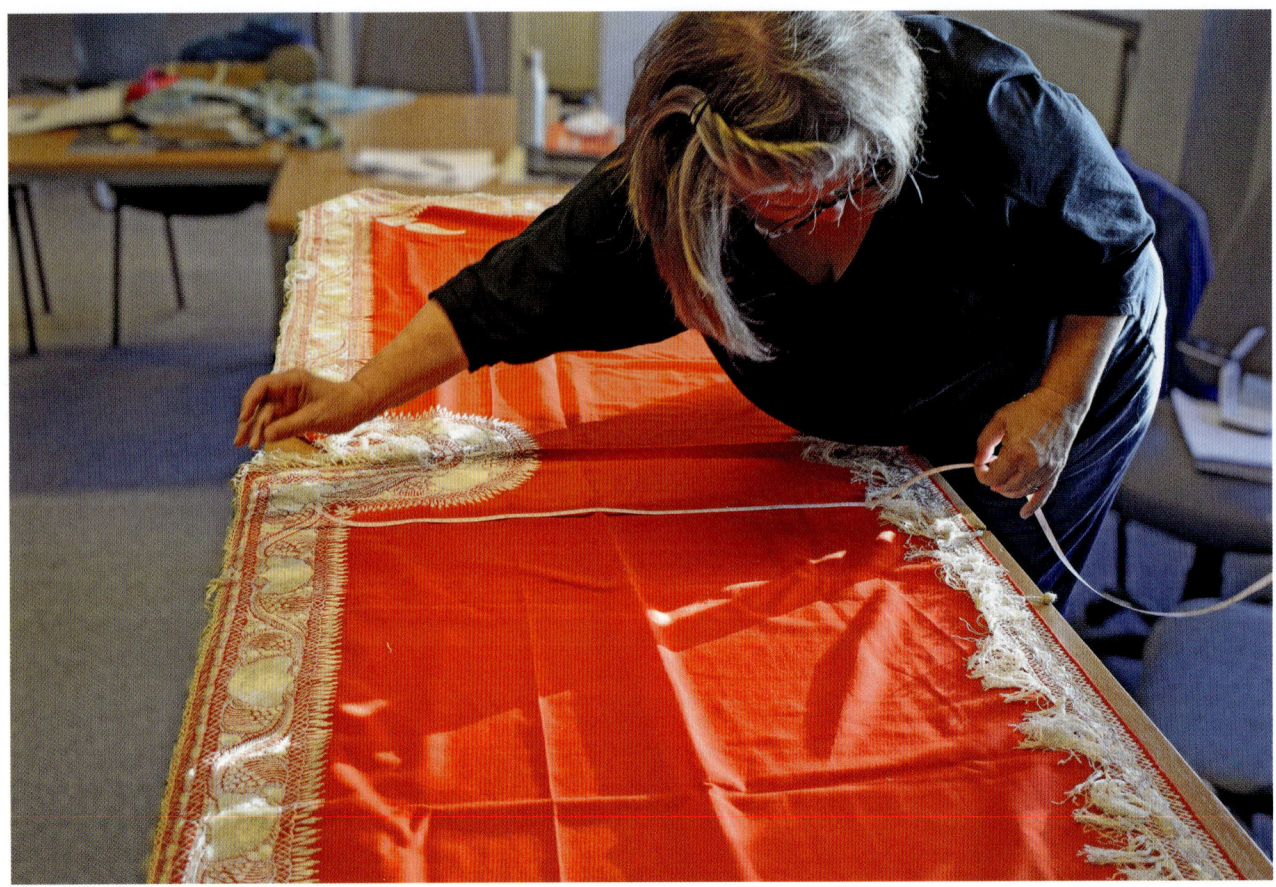

STEP 1 Begin not by drawing but by just quietly observing your textile object. Set a timer for two minutes and spend all of that time actively looking at and focusing on your chosen item. Don't talk, write or take photos – just look! Really take the time to study every tiny detail, each thread, fold and stitch. Notice how it is constructed.

STEP 2 When the time is up, stay present in your 'slow looking'. Set your timer for a further two minutes. Pick up a pen or pencil and rest your drawing hand on the paper. Holding your object in your non-dominant hand, turn your head and body away from the paper and look towards your object. This might mean rearranging your chair. Your focus should be on looking at the object throughout; **DON'T LOOK at the paper at all**. Focus your attention on a detail of your object, perhaps an edge or a line of stitching. As you look carefully, rest your pen or pencil on the paper and start to make a mark. Continue looking in detail at the contours of the object and, as your eyes move around it, just allow your drawing hand to follow. At this stage, don't attempt to draw the whole shape or outline, just focus on details. If you find it helpful, you can keep your pen or pencil on the page to make a continuous line drawing. Don't worry if your pencil falls off the edge of the paper; just continue wherever you like on the page.

STEP 3 When the time is up, stop drawing and look at your page. You might be surprised by what you have drawn. At first glance it might appear to be nothing like your object, but if you look carefully you may see some distinctive marks and shapes from your artefact. Try not to worry about how closely your drawing resembles your object and focus instead on the process and how it felt. As you were drawing, did it help you to study your object more carefully? Did you observe anything new about it? Notice how it felt to sit and look for that period of time. Some people can feel a bit tense after concentrating like this. If you do, have a good stretch and shake it out.

STEP 4 Regardless of how your first drawing went, the important thing is to repeat the exercise multiple times. Repetition is the key to improving your observational skills. Do a minimum of three slow-looking drawings in a row, to warm up.

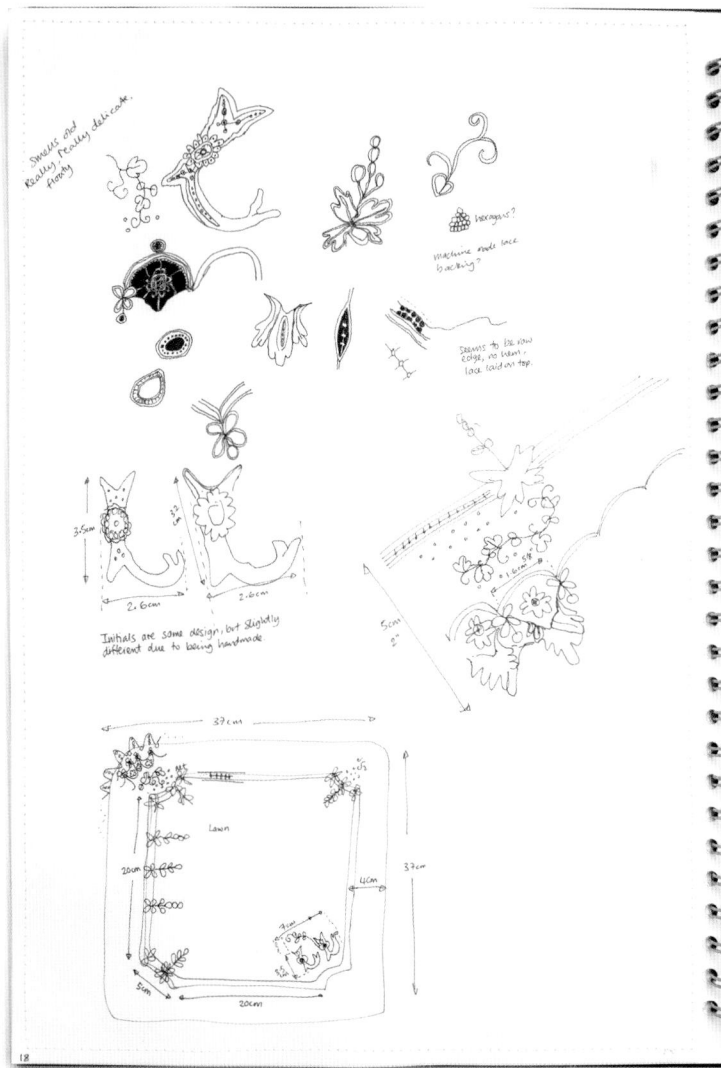

You might like to repeat this exercise a few times each day to improve your observational skills. As you get more confident with looking and observing, you can glance at your page occasionally to get your bearings and maintain proportions. Once you allow yourself to start looking at the page, however, it is important to still spend most of your time observing from the object, just glancing to check your position on the paper.

Putting slow seeing into practice

The slow seeing exercise is intended as a way to develop your slow looking skills. In the museum setting you might adapt this as part of your creative research process. Some key things to focus on:

- Take time to observe, focusing on the details.
- Make quick sketches to establish the main shapes and areas of detail.
- Establish the proportions of the piece you are working from.
- Annotate your drawings with measurements and further observations.
- Make drawings of different views of the item (front, back, inside, underneath).
- If you make any mistakes, or your understanding changes while you are drawing, don't worry. Make a note, so that you can return to it.

It is unlikely that you will be able to include all of the information in one image, so take your time to think about what it is you want to capture in each drawing. You may need to make multiple sketches to understand different aspects of the artefact.

CONSTRUCTION DETAILS How do the different parts go together? Annotate to help you understand the drawing when you get home.

COLOUR Use coloured pencils, or write detailed colour notes and revisit your sketches on your return home to add colour.

PATTERN AND SURFACE EMBELLISHMENT Look carefully from both sides to ascertain how the pattern has been made. If it is a repeating pattern, just draw a section, noting how it continues (e.g. in a border or around an opening).

THE BIGGER PICTURE Use your senses to notice other characteristics, such as:

- Weight – is it heavy or light?
- Texture and movement – does it rustle or drape in a particular way?
- Size – is it bigger or smaller than other similar pieces? Would it fit you?
- Does it have a distinctive smell or sound?
- Note any distinguishing labels or markings.

As you draw you will probably find yourself understanding new things about the item, or thinking of further lines of enquiry. Make notes alongside your drawing so you don't forget. It is important to keep an open mind while drawing, questioning your assumptions. The level of detail you explore will depend on time and how complex your item is.

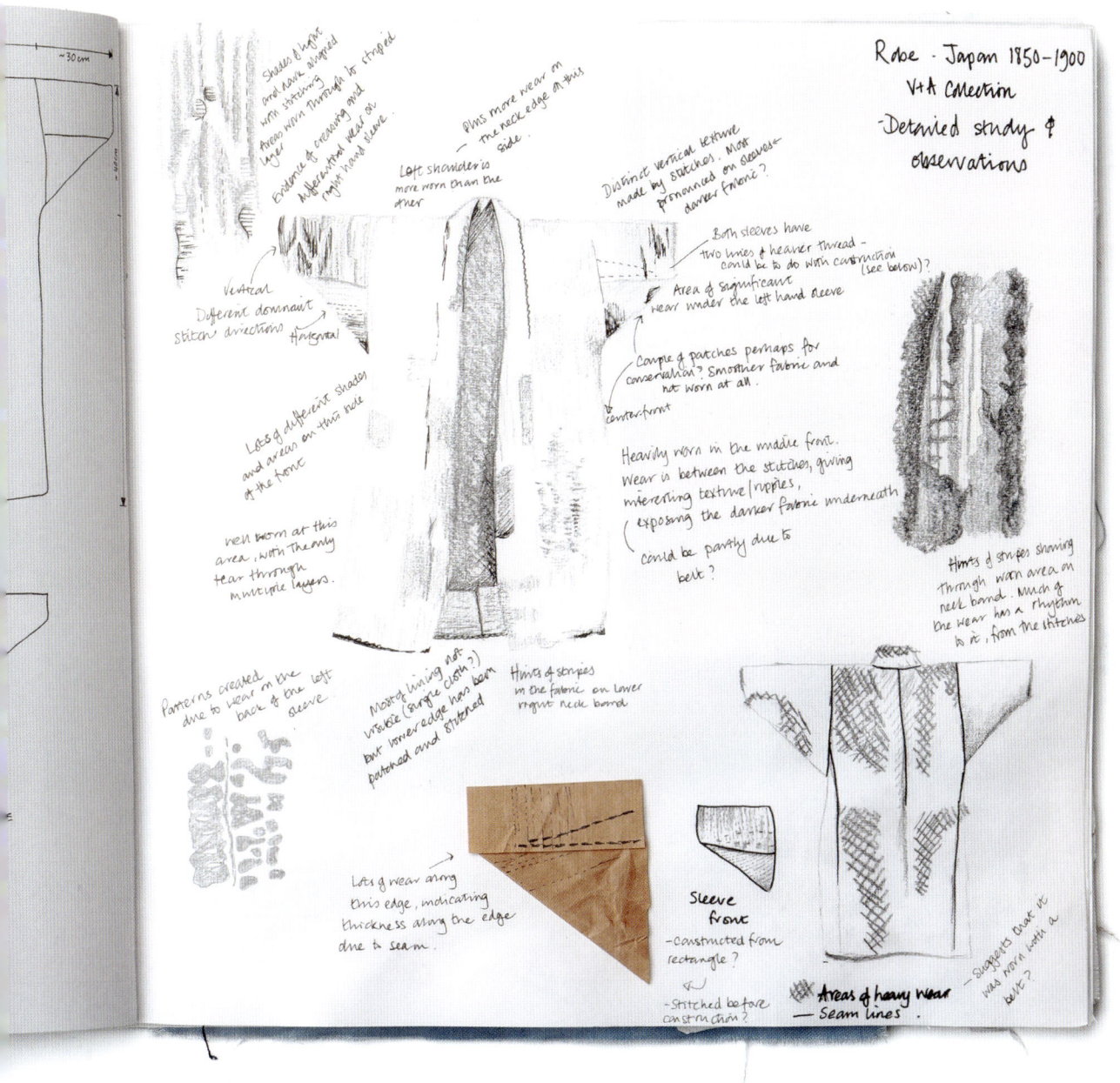

The sketchbook page contains numerous handwritten annotations around the drawings:

Robe · Japan 1850–1900
V+A Collection
· Detailed study & observations

Shades & lights and have aligned with stitching. Areas worn through to striped lines. Evidence of creasing and differential wear on right hand sleeve.

Has more wear on the neck edge on this side.

Left shoulder is more worn than the other.

Distinct vertical texture made by stitches. Most pronounced on sleeves - darker fabric?

Both sleeves have two lines of heavier thread - could be to do with construction (see below)?

Area of significant wear under the left hand sleeve.

Couple of patches perhaps for conservation? Smoother fabric and not worn at all.

← centre front

Heavily worn in the middle front. Wear is between the stitches, giving interesting texture/ripples, exposing the darker fabric underneath. Could be partly due to belt?

Vertical. Different dominant stitch directions. Horizontal.

Lots of different shades and areas on this side of the front.

Well worn at this area, with the early tear through multiple layers.

Patterns created due to wear on the left back of the sleeve.

Most of lining not visible (orange cloth?) but lower edge has been patched and stitched.

Hints of stripes in the fabric on lower right neck band.

Hints of stripes showing through worn area on neck band. Much of the wear has a rhythm to it, from the stitches.

Lots of wear along this edge, indicating thickness along the edge due to seam.

Sleeve front
- constructed from rectangle?
- stitched before construction?

Areas of heavy wear
— Seam lines.

— Suggests that it was worn with a belt?

REFINING SKETCHES

I often find there are mistakes with the quick sketches I make in a museum setting. Things are often out of proportion, or I realise while I am drawing that I have missed something. Try not to worry too much. Back at home you can check against any photos, and refine and improve on your original drawings. Using tracing paper over the top of your initial sketches, you can trace the bits you want to keep and adjust the bits you want to fix, such as lengthening a sleeve, for example. Working in this way, you can make multiple drawings until you are happy with the result.

Items with complex surface decoration or patterning may require a lot of time and different 'layers of looking' to fully describe and analyse. You may find it helpful to make one drawing (or use a photo) of the pattern and trace or photocopy it. Alternatively, graph paper can be used to accurately plot a design.

ABOVE *This annotated sketchbook page by Vicky Poulson shows detailed observation of a heavily worn and mended Japanese robe, c.1850–1900.*

29

Techniques beyond the museum setting

Museums and archives are often quite restrictive in terms of the way we can use media and handle objects. If you have access to historical textiles from your own collection, the possibilities can be more expansive. In the following pages I explore cyanotypes (see pages 34–42) as a way of capturing exquisite details from textiles. Another option is frottage, the process of taking a rubbing from the surface of an item. This is a great way to capture the details and tactile qualities of material objects. As well as the more obvious surface textures of embroidery and embellishments, it can be excellent at showing subtle hidden layers and construction details, and the effects can be quite beautiful.

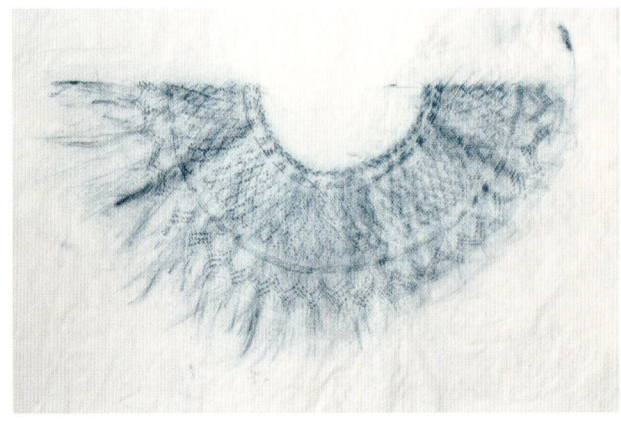

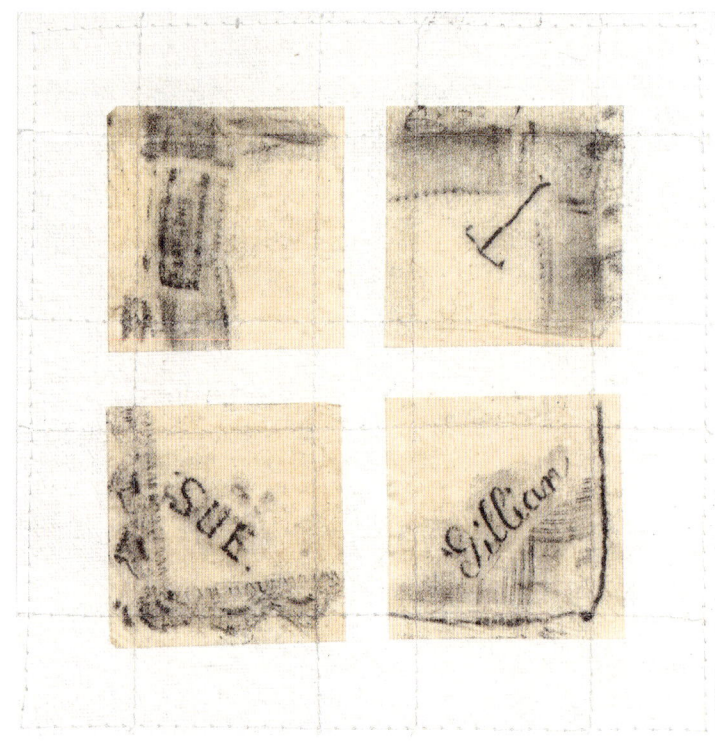

ABOVE *Rubbing from a child's smocked dress by Diana Spoors.*

RIGHT *Rubbings from a selection of embroidered handkerchief corners by Pippa Wardman. Graphite on tissue.*

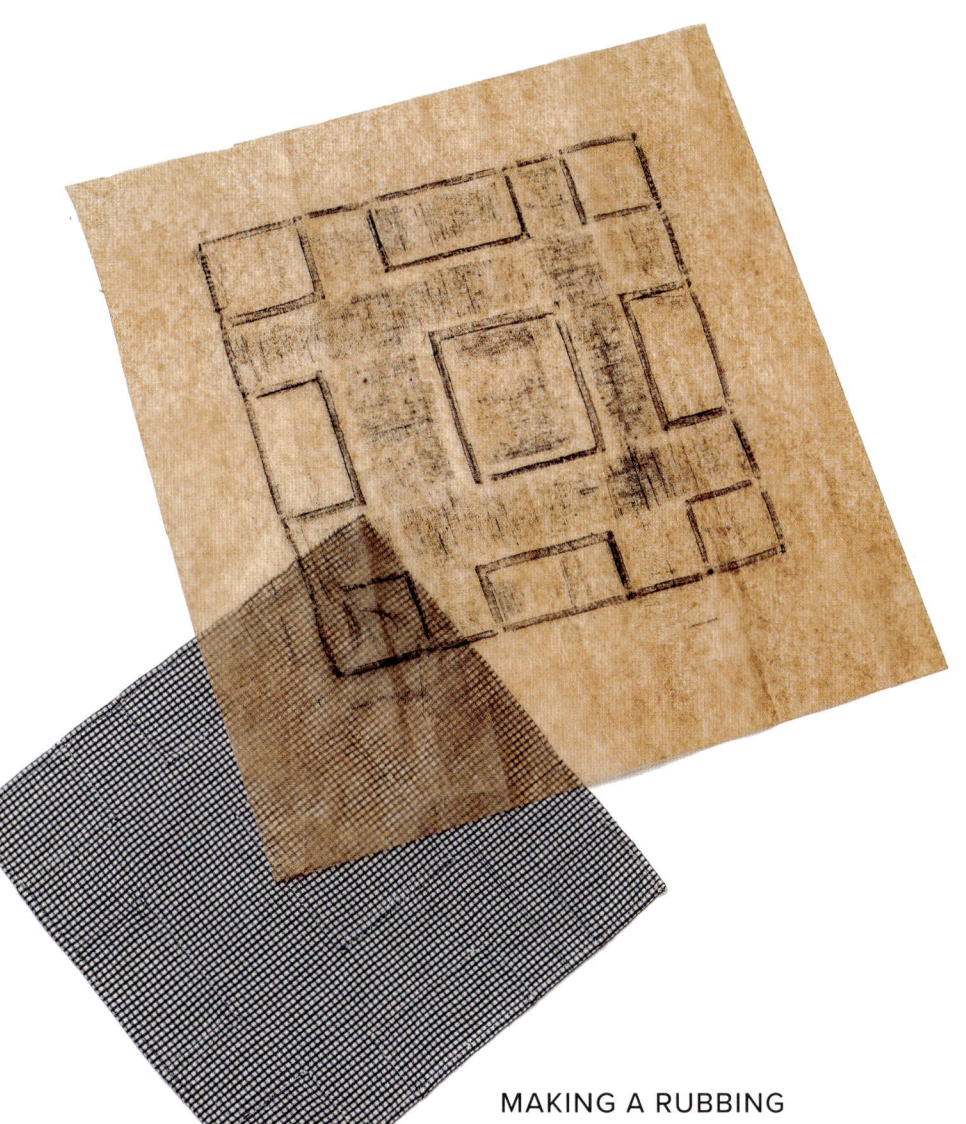

MAKING A RUBBING

Before you consider making a rubbing of a textile object, always check that it is robust enough to cope with being squashed and manipulated. Be careful using messy art media near pale or white textiles, to avoid staining.

To make a simple rubbing, or frottage, lay paper over your textile object, hold it steady and use the side of a graphite stick or wax crayon to rub over it. Aim to capture as much detail as you can. It is a good idea to start gently and build up the pressure if needed. If you rub too vigorously, you may tear the paper and media could go onto your cherished textile.

Experiment with different papers, such as tissue paper, tracing paper, printer paper or newsprint, together with different media. Here are a few ideas:

- Graphite on white tissue paper works well for objects with subtle textures, such as seams.
- Wax crayon or oil pastel is good for more robust textures.
- Use a white wax candle and then paint black ink over the rubbing to get a reverse image.
- Try different combinations of coloured wax crayon/pastel and coloured inks.
- Tissue and tea-bag fabric are more flexible to shape around 3D objects.

31

SARAH CASEY

Absent Presence

Sarah Casey is a UK artist primarily engaged in making drawings that 'flirt with the limits of visibility and material existence'. She is interested in how drawing might be used as a way of capturing material memory, recording and preserving something of the fragility of fading historical garments. She often uses drawing as 'an act of careful, patient looking' to capture and record archival objects, noticing the tiny details that point towards the item's construction, wear and decay.

Sarah starts with sketches made in her sketchbook from direct observation, before translating this experience into presentation drawings. For example, for the *Absent Presence* series she recounts how, back in the studio, she 'chose to transcribe these drawings onto newsprint, thinking of the garments that many of us may have inherited in our own families and stored folded up in newspaper, packed safely away. I coated the newsprint with wax, thinking of it as a medium for preservation, for sealing up specimens. I then drew into this delicate wax surface by inscribing the surface with a dressmaker's pin to leave a ghostly white mark.'[2] While the process of creating these careful drawings is painstaking and immensely time-consuming, the result is fragile and subtle.

Beyond the physical presence of the garment, Sarah's drawings seem to capture the haunting absence of a garment's previous owner. Costume curator Ingrid Mida says, 'Sarah Casey sees clothing as a metaphor of the ephemerality of human presence. Her life-sized wax drawings depict the haunting absent presence that clings to historic garments.'[3] The human scale of her drawings and choice of media hint at the presence of a person, but also have a ghostly, ethereal quality. As Sarah herself says, 'drawing has spectral presence, it brings something into being, creating an image from a blank page'[4].

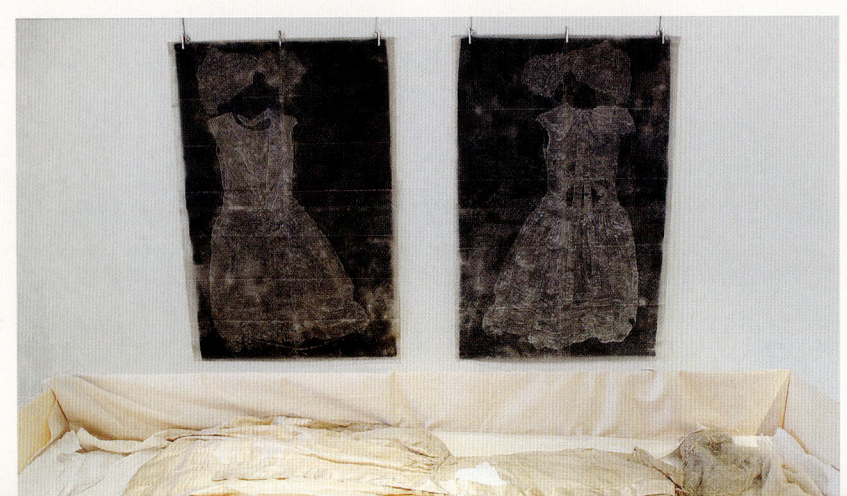

LEFT Absent Presence
Wedding Recto and
Verso, *Installation view
at MLC Gallery, Toronto
(2019) by Sarah Casey.*

OPPOSITE Absent
Presence: Yolande
(2019) by Sarah Casey.

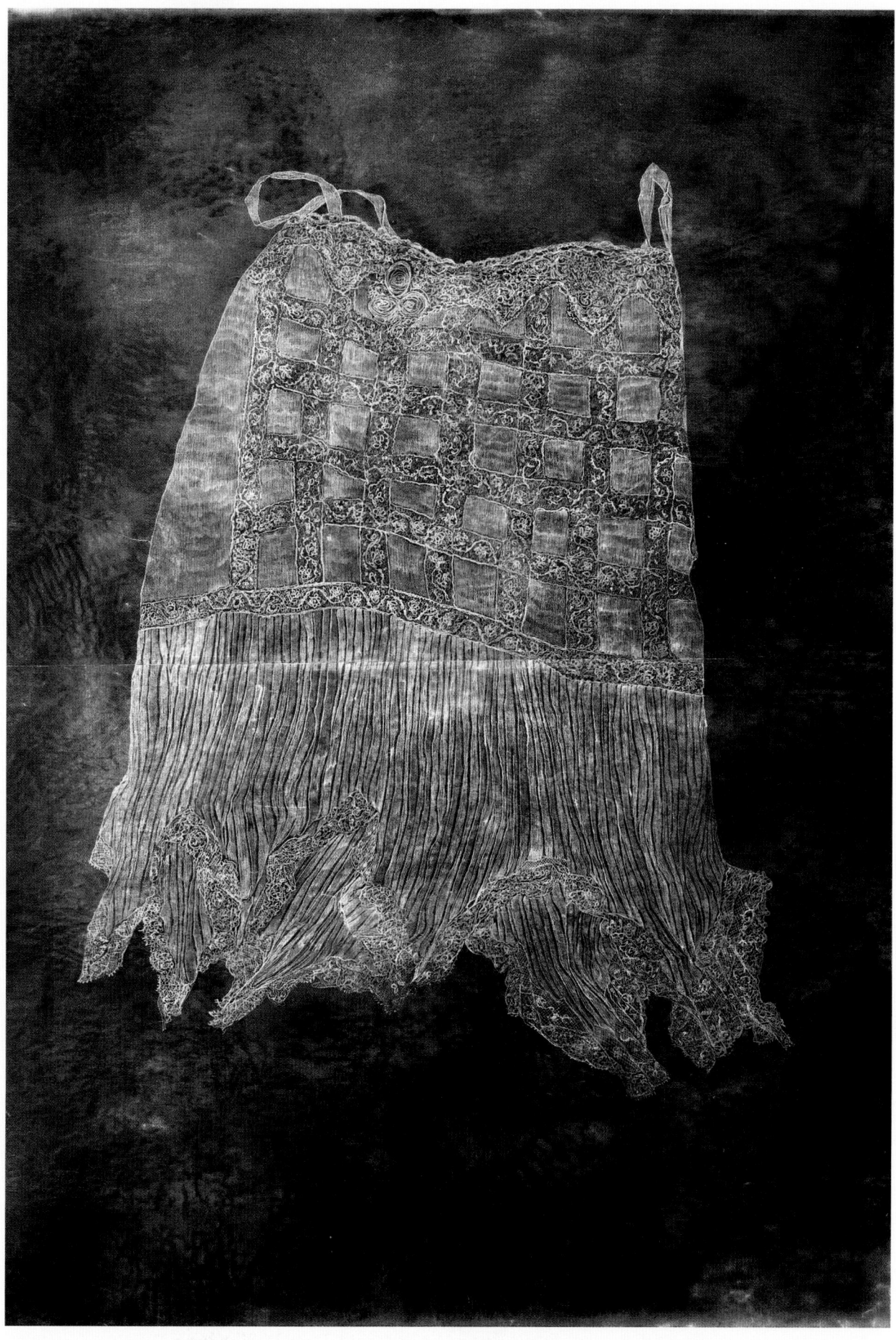

TEXTILE BLUEPRINTS

Characterised by its striking Prussian blue colour, cyanotype is a
photographic process dating back to the 1840s. It is an effective way of
printing stencil-like photograms from real objects onto paper or textile,
without damaging the original, as I explored in my first book, *Poetic Cloth*.
When observing and capturing historical textiles, cyanotype can create
some beautiful results with an incredible level of detail. In some cases,
this can allow us to see hidden details, almost like an X-ray. These textile
'blueprints' can be used as part of an observation process, to learn more
about a historic piece, or they can become artworks in their own right.
Cyanotype can be successfully combined with embroidery or other textile
processes to create layered effects.

You can buy ready-prepared blueprinting paper and textiles from craft
suppliers, but I always prefer to make my own because I love to see the brush
marks and imperfections of the handmade mark. Coating your own materials
also gives you far greater choice. Cyanotype will work well on paper, silk,
cotton, linen, viscose or any cellulose-based fibre, but not on wool.

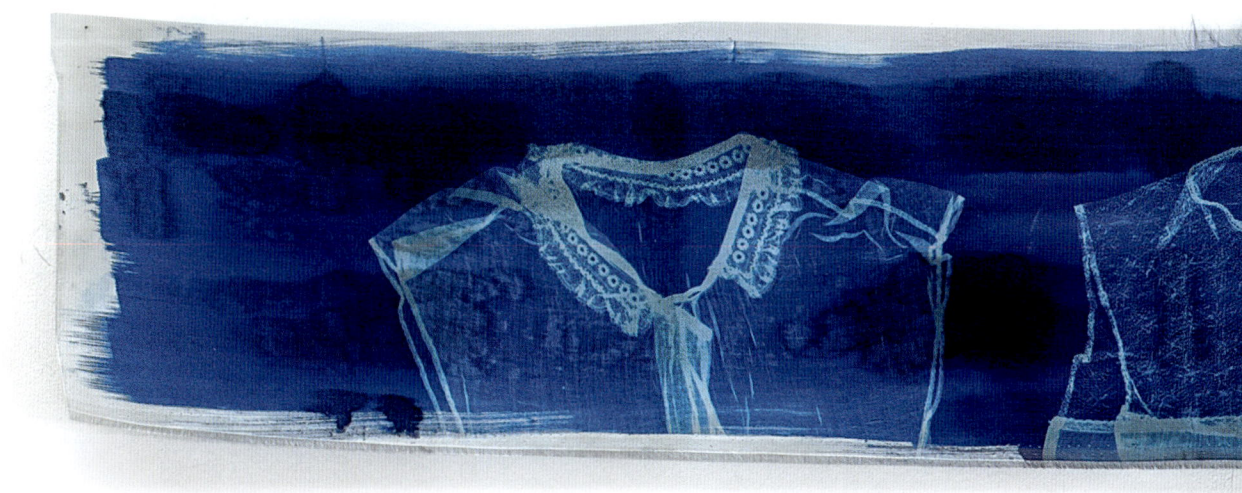

Cyanotype health and safety

Before you get started there are a few rules to be aware of to keep yourself and your environment safe, as follows:

- Never use cyanotype equipment for food preparation.
- Avoid working in your kitchen or food prep area.
- Always label cyanotype chemicals and store them out of the reach of children.
- Wear protective gloves (surgical gloves are ideal).
- When working with powdered chemicals, avoid inhalation; wear a dust mask when measuring and mixing.
- Avoid contact of the chemicals with the skin and eyes; if contact occurs, rinse immediately with water.
- Always wash your hands after handling chemicals.
- Wash-out water (i.e. diluted chemicals) can be disposed of in normal household waste water. Never pour waste chemicals directly into rivers or streams.
- Never mix potassium ferricyanide with strong acids such as hydrochloric acid, as this can create a chemical reaction resulting in toxic cyanide gas.

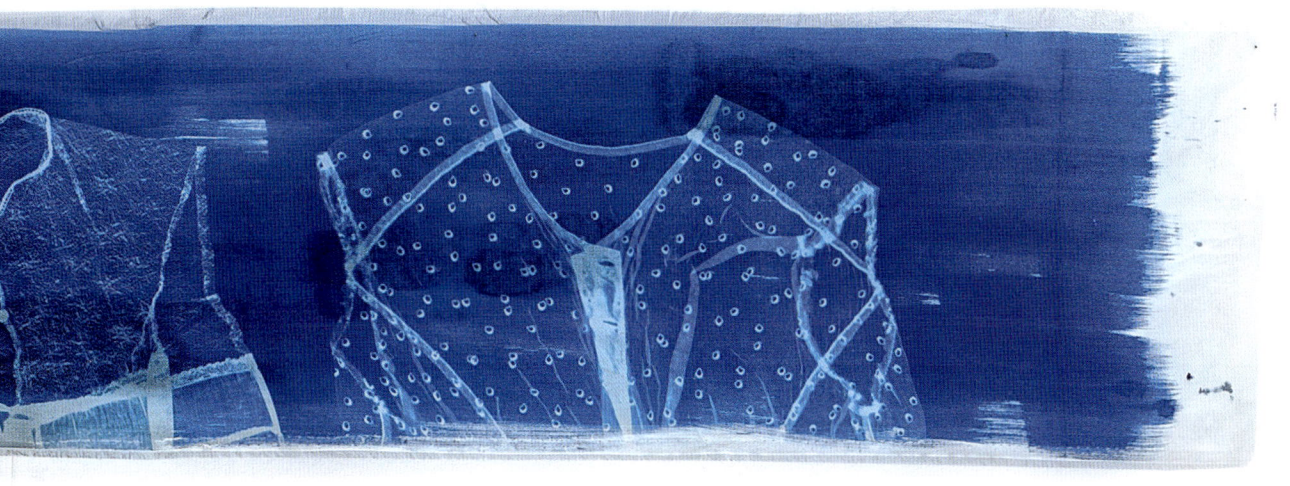

Preparing the materials for cyanotype printing

When preparing the chemicals for the cyanotype solution and coating your materials with the mixed solution, work in a room away from sunlight (UV light). I work in my studio, which has blackout blinds, with the electric lights on. Protect work surfaces with plenty of newspaper or plastic dust sheets, and wear a dust mask while measuring out the powdered chemicals.

FOR THE CYANOTYPE SOLUTION YOU WILL NEED:

- 30g (1oz) ferric ammonium citrate (green)
- 15g (½oz) potassium ferricyanide
- 250ml (8½fl oz) warm water

PREPARING THE SOLUTION

Wearing a dust mask, place both of the powdered chemicals into a measuring jug. Add warm water up to 250ml (8½fl oz). Stir until completely dissolved into a lime-green solution, ready for coating your chosen paper or textile substrate. You can take the mask off at this point.

COATING METHOD

I like to use a broad, flat paintbrush to coat my materials. A decorator's brush works well, although a traditional hake brush avoids any risk of metallic contamination. Spread your fabric or paper on a protected surface. Dip the brush into the solution and then against the side of the container to remove any excess. Paint the solution onto the fabric or paper. Wherever you paint the solution will be your sensitised area for printing. Try not to oversaturate the fabric; you are looking for a nice even coverage, not a puddle. Leave the painted material in the dark (away from UV light) to dry completely. I like to coat a whole batch of items one evening, allowing them to dry overnight, ready to print the following day.

Any leftover solution can be placed in a glass jar, labelled and dated. Stored in a cool, dark place, it can be kept for several months, although it is always most effective when fresh.

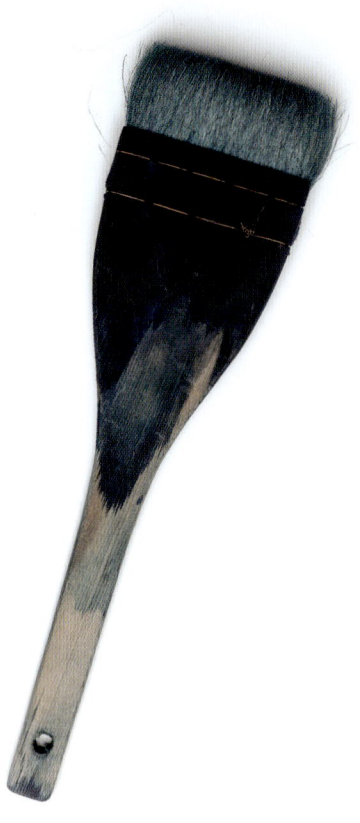

ABOVE *A soft-bristled hake brush with wooden handle.*

OPPOSITE *Various lace fabrics make ideal subjects for cyanotype prints.*

The cyanotype printing method

CHOOSING YOUR HISTORICAL TEXTILES

When choosing old textile items to use as stencils, there are three main characteristics that make for particularly exciting prints:

LACY EFFECTS These can include lace, drawn-thread and pulled work, and open lacy knitted, crochet or woven structures.

TRANSLUCENCY Very sheer fabrics, such as cotton lawn, silk organza or even nylon, can be stunning when printed, especially where there are multiple layers, pleats or gathers.

UNUSUAL SILHOUETTES Artefacts with particularly intricate edges or unusual shapes can make striking images.

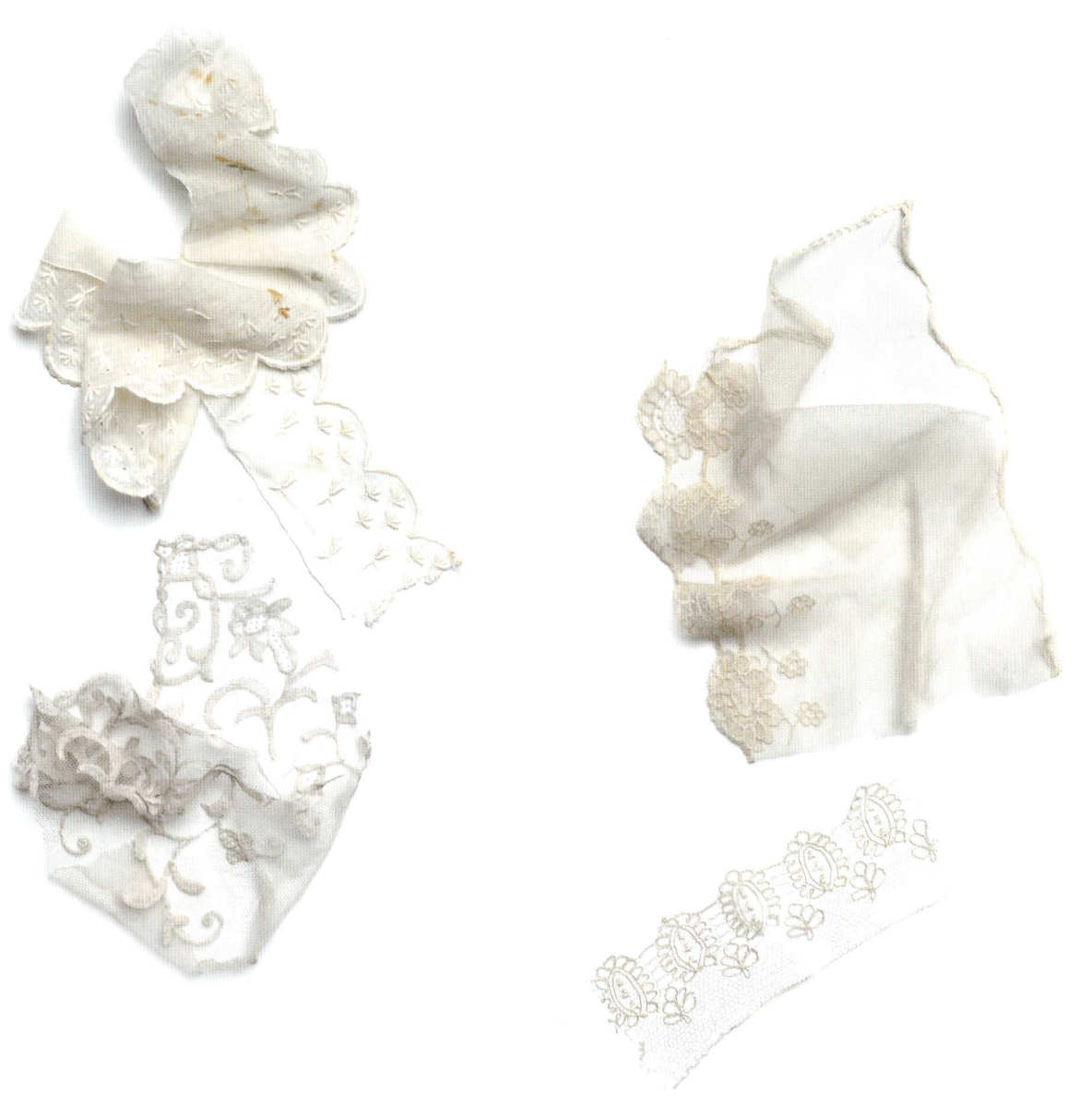

PREPARING TO PRINT

Always ensure your coated material is completely dry before printing, to avoid the chemicals transferring to your precious historical artefact. If done with care, the process is low risk; but if you do have concerns, a very thin sheet of archival plastic can be put between coated material and historic textile to avoid contamination.

PRINTING METHOD FOR FLAT MATERIALS

The easiest way to create small prints with flat materials is to sandwich them between a backing board and a piece of glass. A simple shop-bought clip (picture) frame is an affordable and easy-to-use option. Alternatively, you can make your own with a piece of glass or clear acrylic sheet, a firm backing board and a set of clamps or clips.

Working in a room away from sunlight, lay your coated (sensitised) paper or textile right side up on the backing board. Then place the stencil objects (textile items you want to print with) onto the coated surface. Put the glass on top and clip or clamp in place. It is important to create tight contact between the objects and the printing surface. The cyanotype method makes a negative print: the areas that are exposed to UV light will turn blue while the areas that are covered by the object will remain white; if light leaks underneath the object, your print won't be clear.

PRINTING METHOD FOR 3D OBJECTS

If your object is 3D or can't be squashed flat, a little ingenuity is called for. A cork noticeboard or sheet of recycled polystyrene foam can be used as a base. Place your coated fabric on the base, stretch it flat and pin it at the edges. Position the stencil object or garment, and pin it in place.

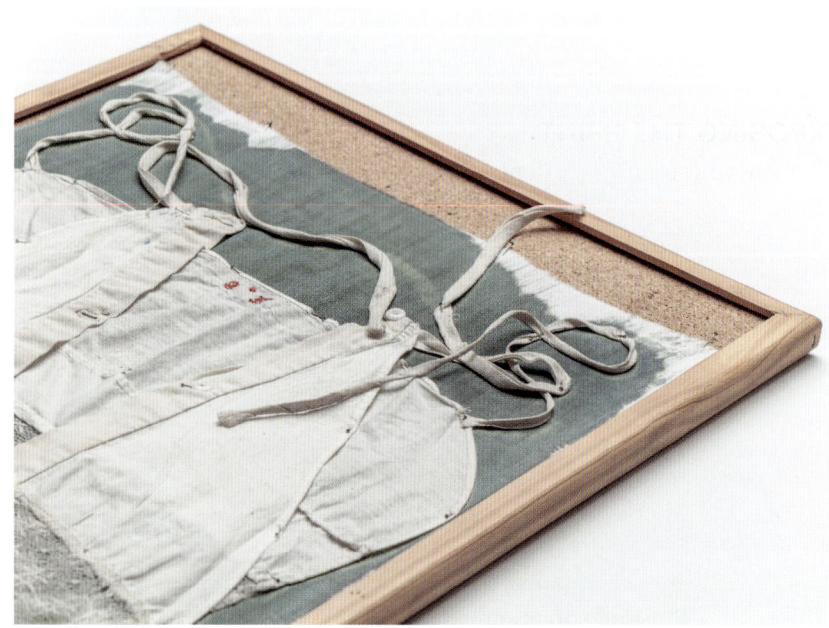

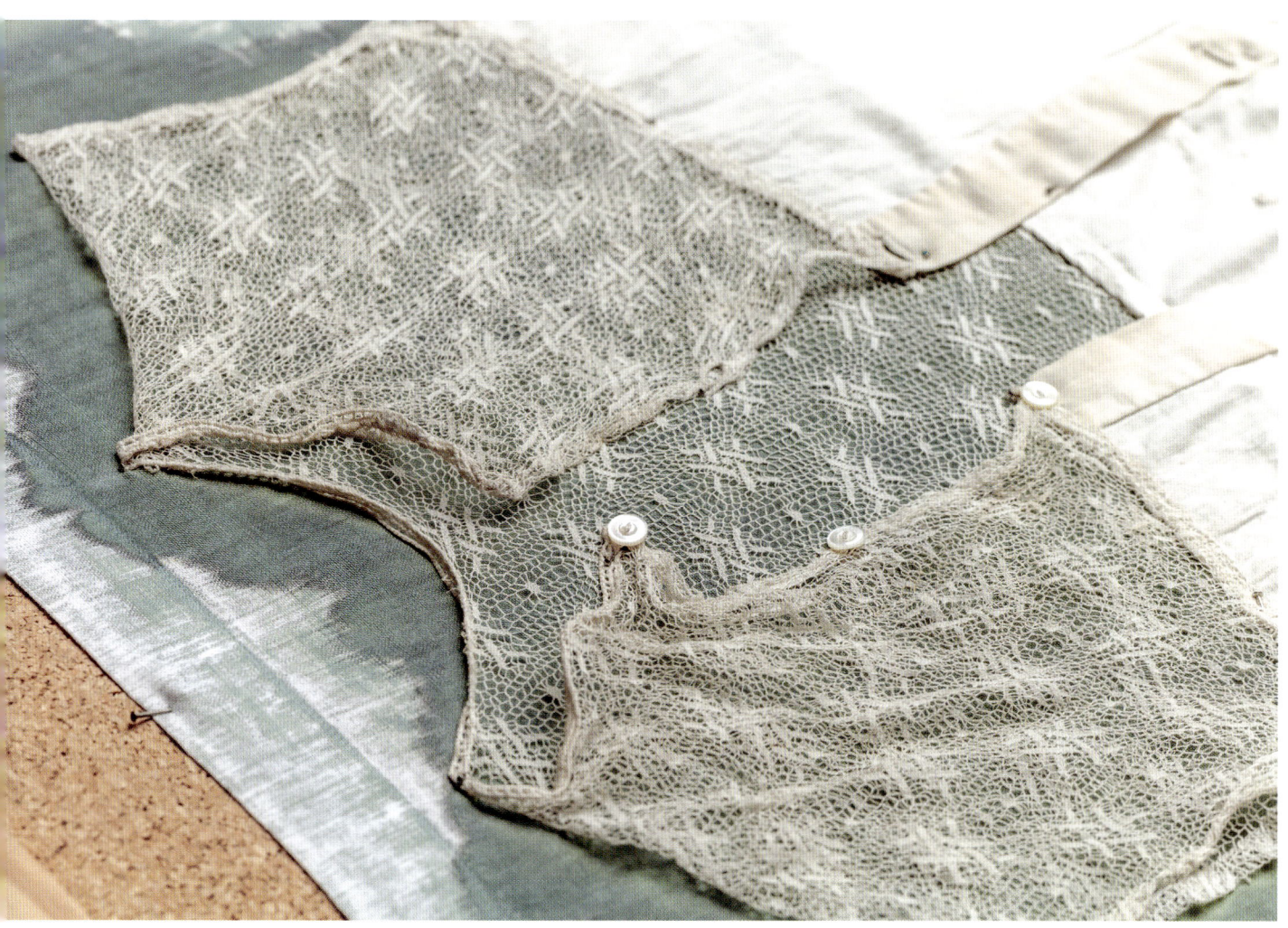

Do remember that the pins themselves will block the light, leaving white marks, so try to put them where they will be least conspicuous. I like to be quite thorough in pinning objects so that they won't move during the print exposure time.

EXPOSING THE PRINT

To create your print you will need to expose it to UV light. On a bright sunny day this can be done outside. Timings will vary depending on the season and where you are in the world. In my home county of Yorkshire, in the northeast of England, on a bright midsummer day, I would be looking to expose a print for 8–15 minutes. With experience, I have come to judge this by eye, but it is a good idea to do some test samples with different timings if you want to be sure of the results.

If you don't have bright sunshine, a UV tanning lamp or grow light can be used. Daylight replacement lamps do not work because they do not emit UV light. For my very large prints I use a print exposure unit (usually used for exposing silk screens); this type of equipment can be found in professional print workshops and artists' studios.

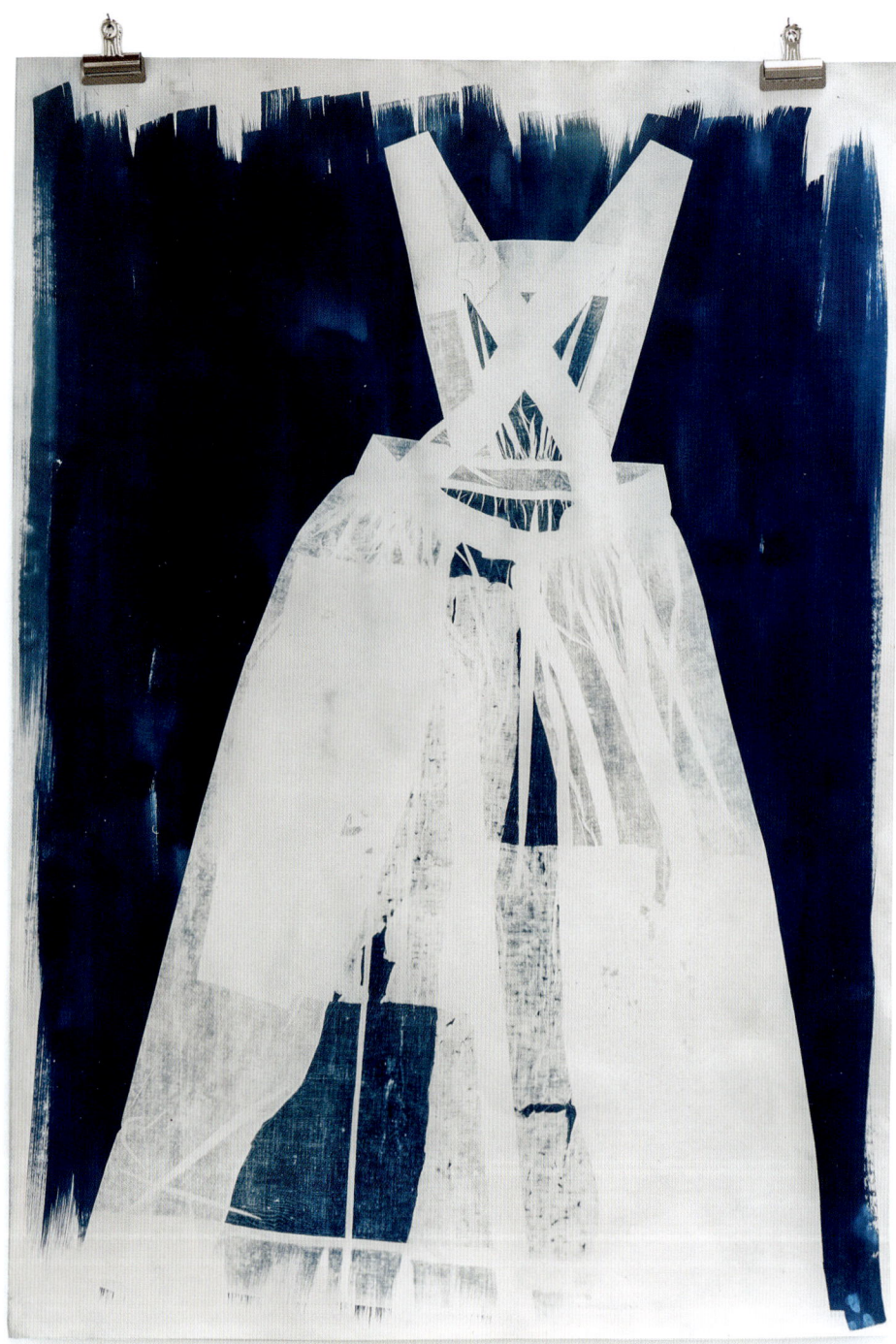

FINISHING THE PRINT

When you feel your print has had sufficient exposure, bring it inside away from sunlight and carefully remove the stencil objects. At this stage, the print may look greyish-green in colour. Fill a bucket with water (the temperature doesn't matter) and rinse your print. Change the water and continue rinsing until the water runs clear and no yellowish-green tinge is seen in the white areas of the print. Textile prints can be squeezed and wrung out, but for paper-based prints use only gentle agitation.

Leave your print to dry. Fabrics can be hung on a washing line or airer. Papers are best left to dry flat. After drying, the prints can be ironed from the reverse.

ABOVE Saturdays Child – Ghost Print (2021) by Hannah Lamb. Cyanotype on watercolour paper. 140 x 100cm (55 x 39⅓in).

Toning cyanotypes

If the vivid Prussian blue of a traditional cyanotype is too strong for your project, you might wish to consider toning. This is a photographic term, referring to the way a print is recoloured with a tint or stain. To create a vintage, sepia-like effect, cyanotypes can be toned to shades of brown with tannic acid. Tannin is a natural substance found in different concentrations in plant material. Useful sources include oak galls and tree barks, but perhaps the easiest and most readily available is tea, which makes a great toning solution. Tannic acid can also be purchased in pure form from photographic and natural dye suppliers.

It may seem counterintuitive, but if you want to make a brown print, you must first make a blueprint as already described. A solution of soda ash (sodium carbonate) is used to remove the blue, leaving a yellow and white print. Your print may even seem to disappear altogether, but don't worry as it will reappear once the tannin reacts with the print. You will need to use a clear blueprint with strong contrast, as subtle tonal areas can lose definition in the toning process.

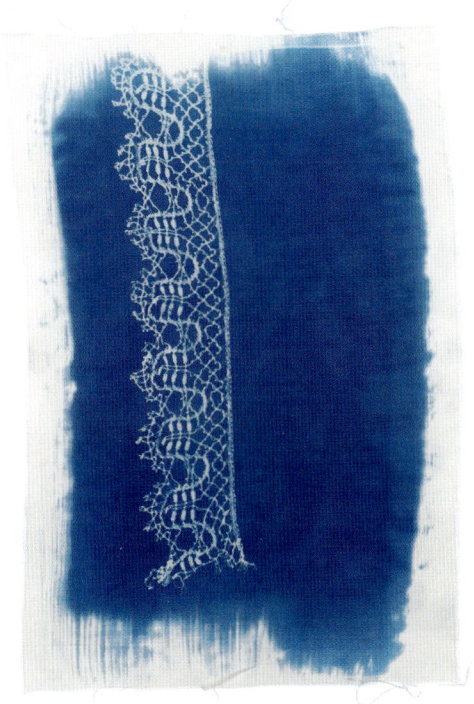
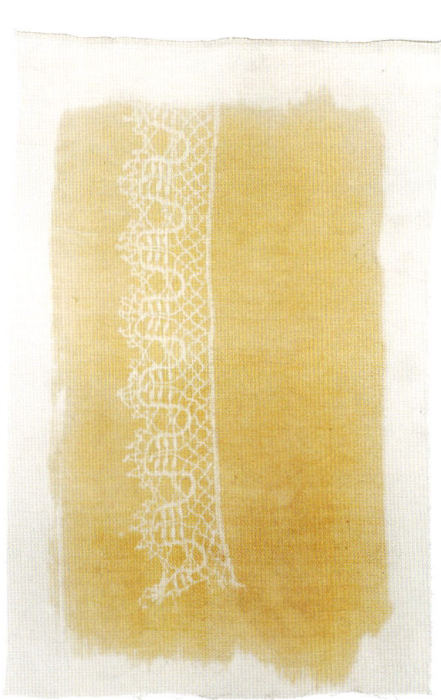
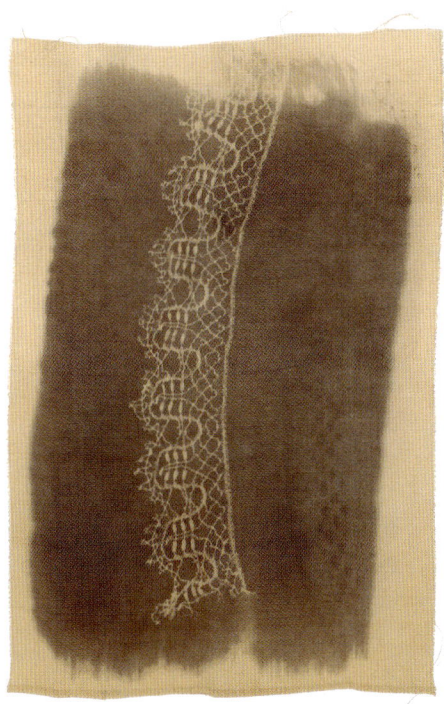

YOU WILL NEED

- Cyanotype blueprint on natural fibre fabric
- Soda ash (sodium carbonate or washing soda)
- Water
- Tea bags (standard tea, nothing fancy!)
- Surgical or washing-up gloves
- Plastic or non-reactive measuring jug*
- Stainless steel or plastic spoon*
- For toning larger pieces you may need a larger vessel, such as a plastic bucket or washing-up bowl*

* I always keep a separate set of equipment for toning, to avoid accidentally stripping the colour from other blueprints. Never use food preparation equipment.

SAFETY NOTE: Soda ash is mildly caustic and should be treated with caution, as you would with any household cleaning product. Use in a well-ventilated area and avoid contact with the eyes. To avoid skin irritation, it is advisable to wear protective gloves.

METHOD

1. Put one tablespoon of soda ash into a jug. Add 500ml (18fl oz) of warm water per tablespoon of soda ash and stir until dissolved. You will need enough solution for your print to be submerged.

2. Wearing gloves, submerge your blueprint in the soda ash solution – you will be able to see the blue disappear.

3. Remove the stripped print and rinse in several changes of water.

4. Make up a tannin bath using tea bags and boiling water. I use about three or four tea bags in approximately 500ml (18fl oz). The more tea bags you use, the stronger the tannin solution will be.

5. Submerge your stripped print in the tannin solution and agitate to ensure even coverage. Remove when you are happy with the depth of colour.

6. Rinse thoroughly and dry away from sunlight.

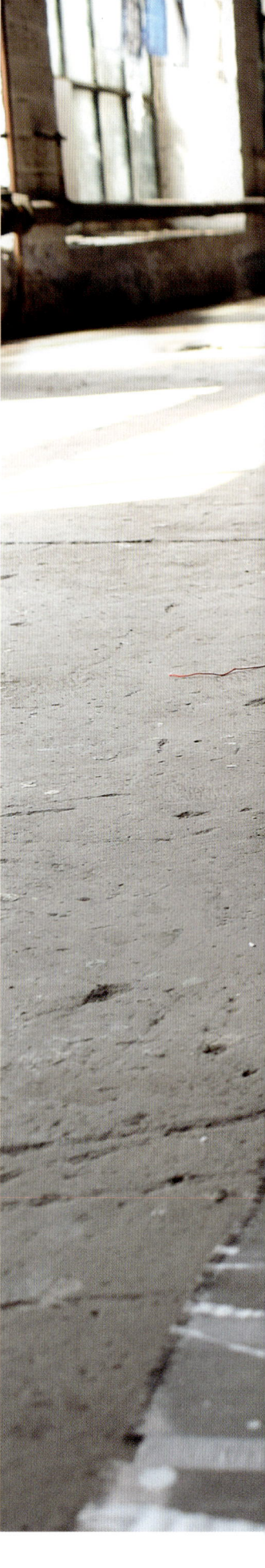

RIGHT [De]Constructed Cloth *(2019) by Hannah Lamb. In this piece I selected areas of the cyanotype to tone, creating shifting areas of colour.*

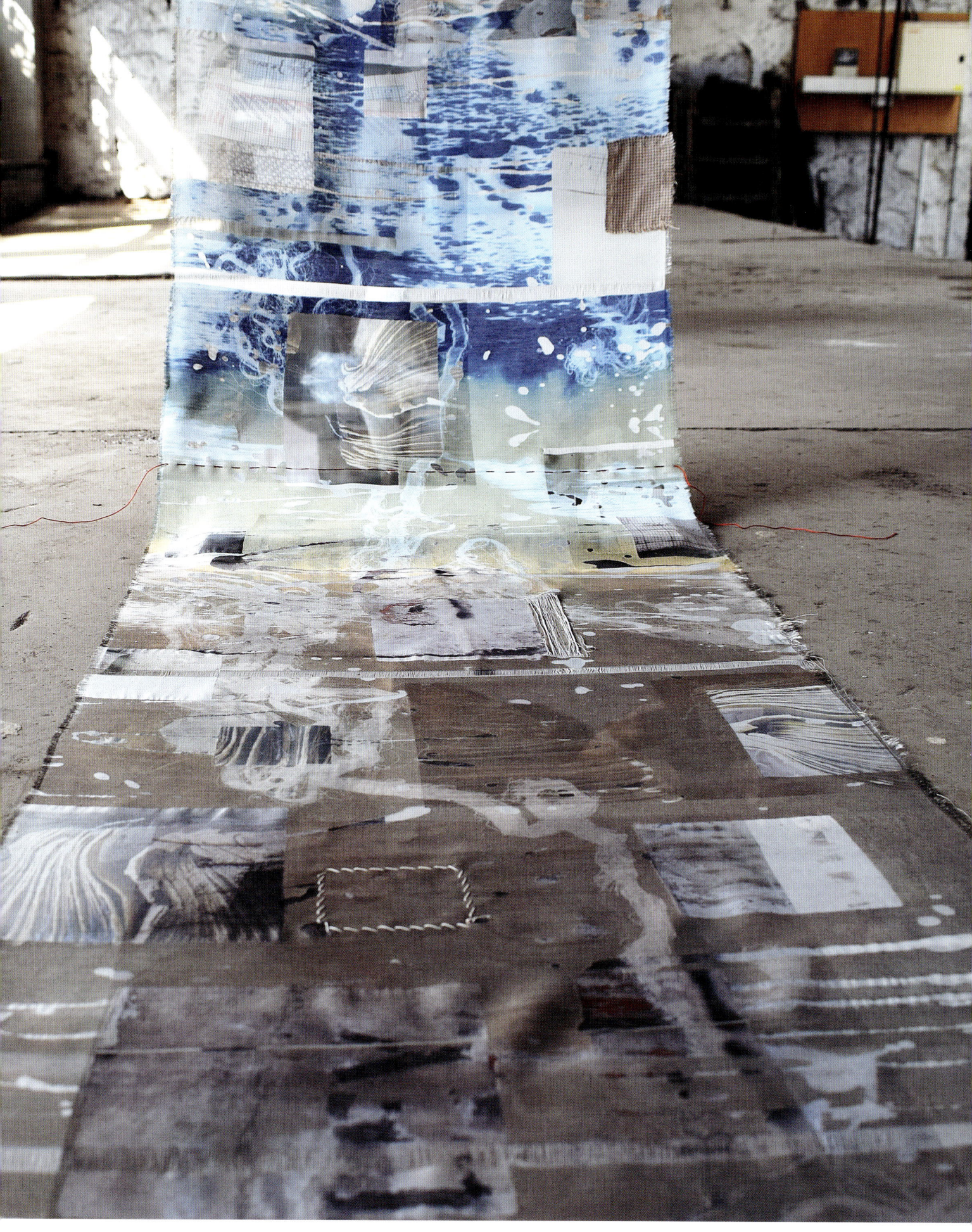

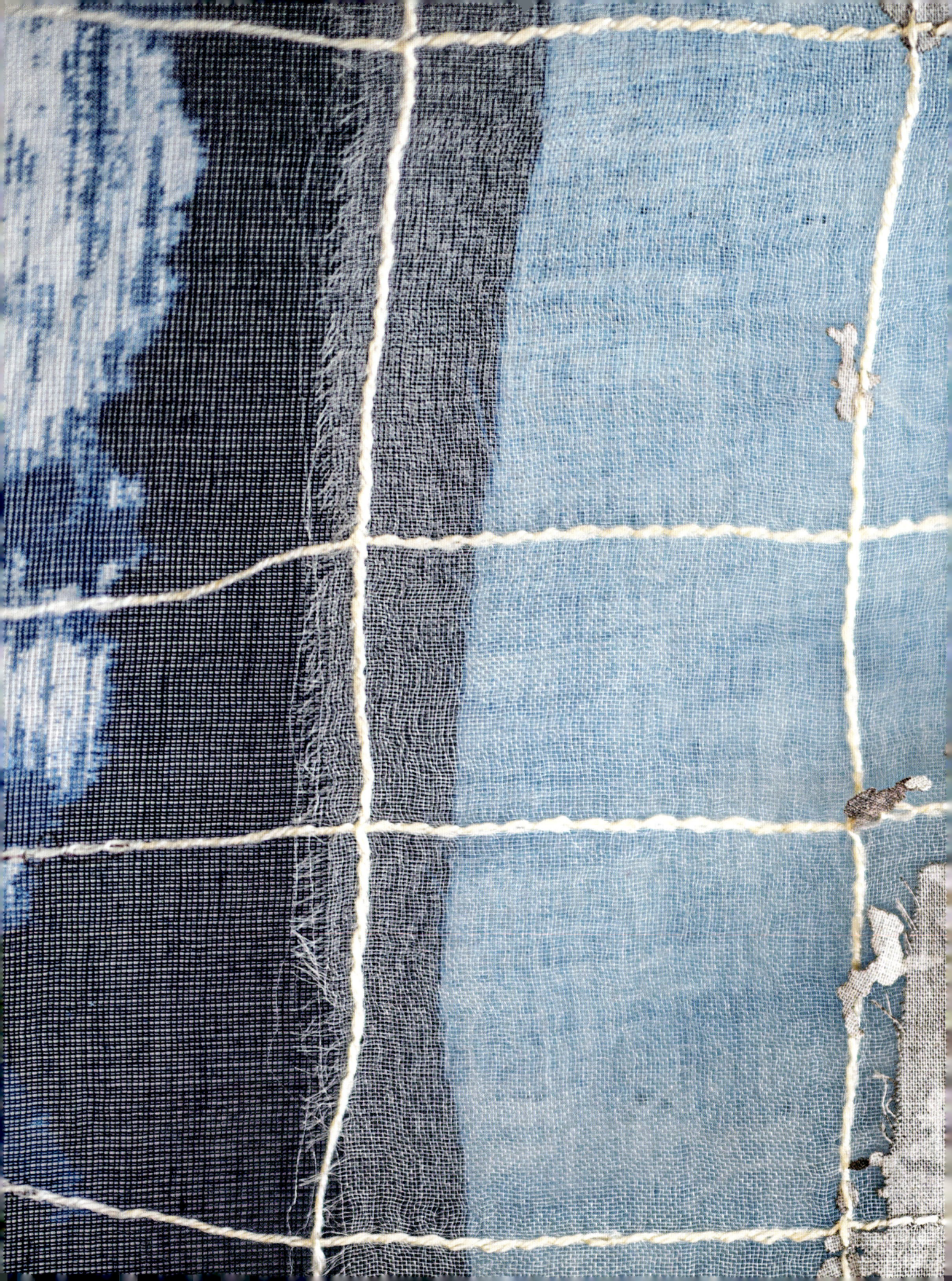

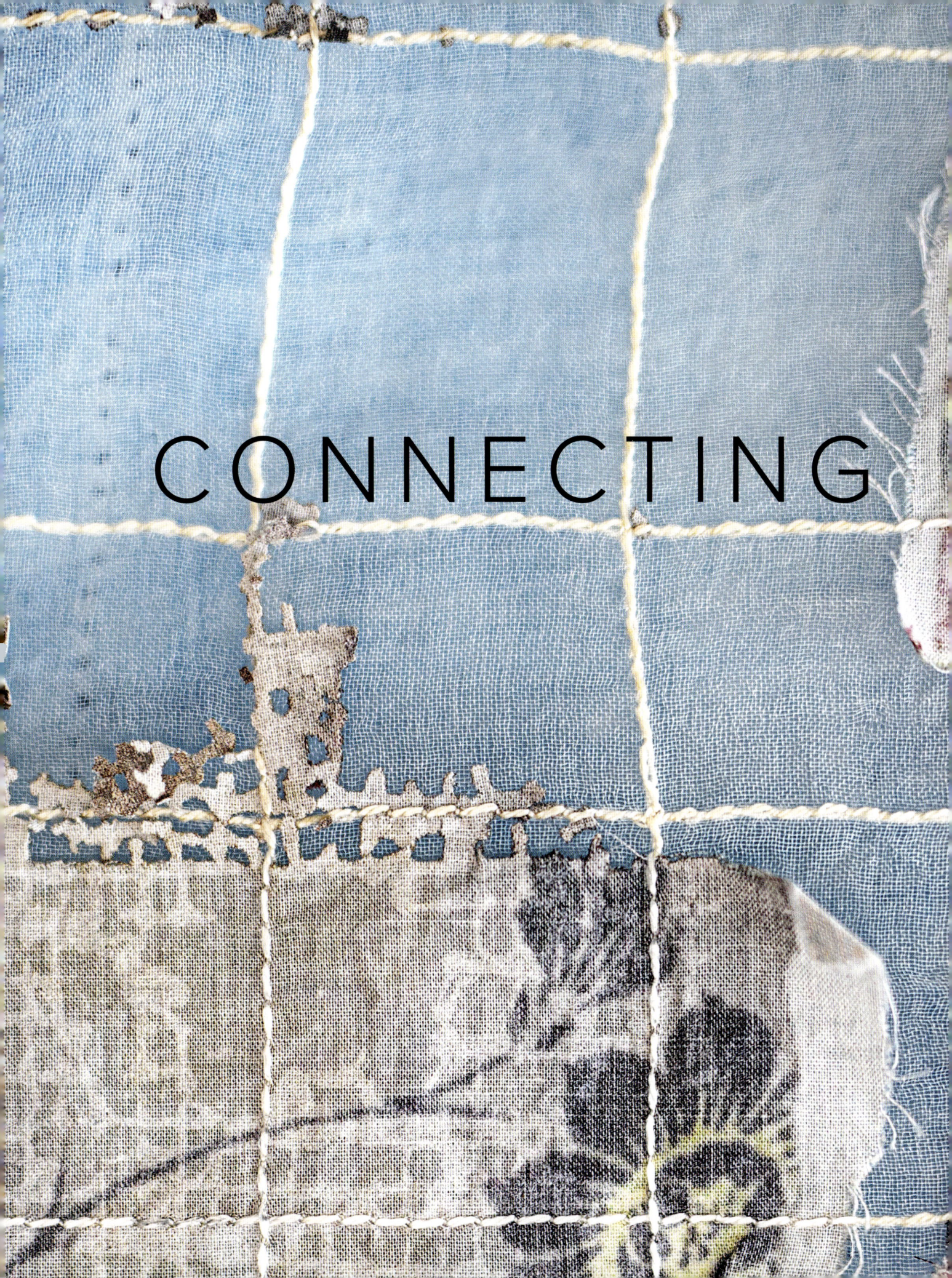

CONNECTING

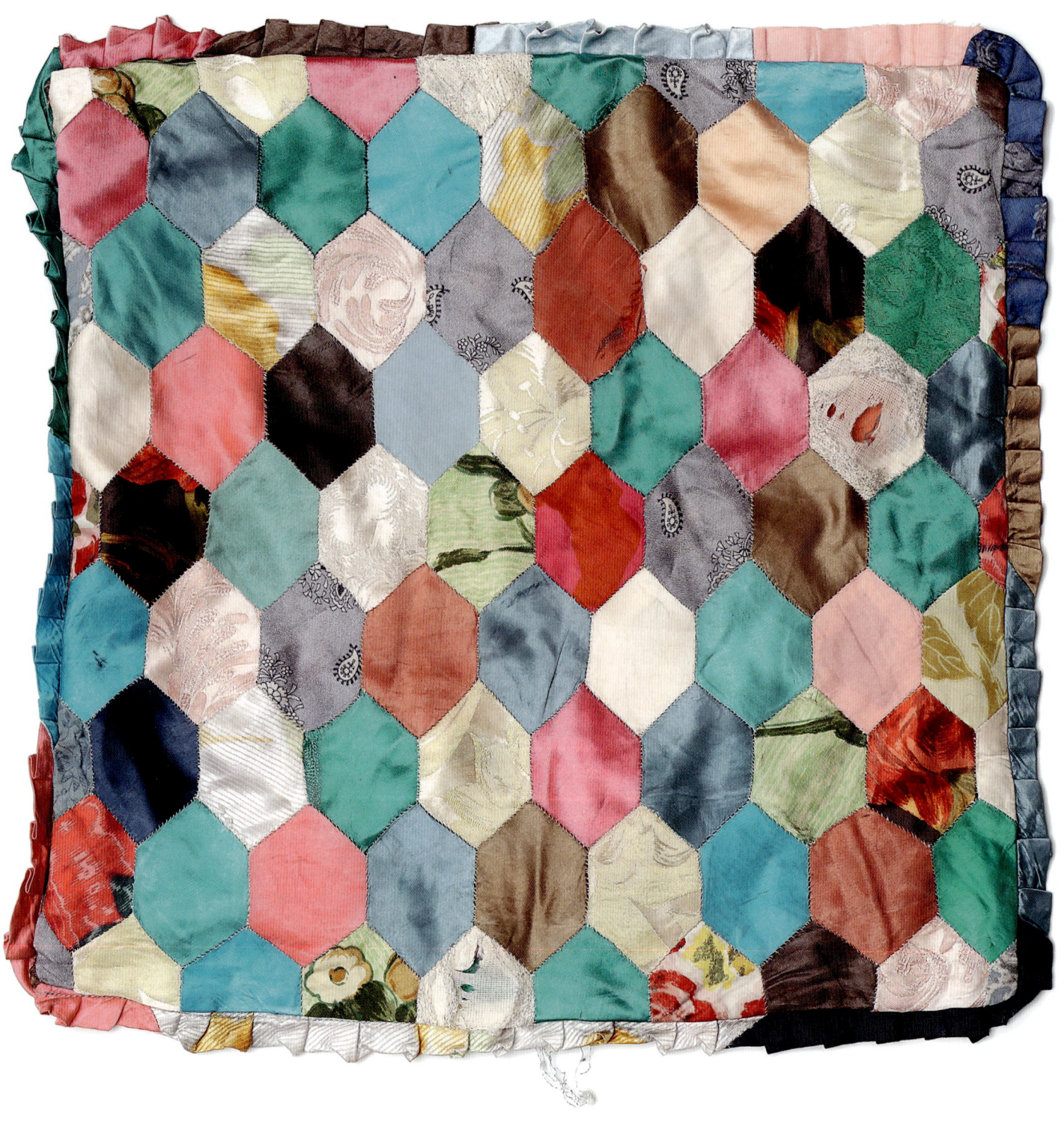

BACKGROUND RESEARCH

After our initial first-hand research, we might want to dig a little deeper. Often the act of slow seeing and observing historical pieces throws up further questions, or makes us aware of gaps in our knowledge. Additional research can provide further clues, setting the item in a particular place, time or social location. It can also give us a richer story to inspire creative responses.

Dating historic textiles

Hand or machine stitch? Machine stitching as we know it today started to become widespread from the late 1850s, and sewing machines were available for home sewers from the 1860s. Machine stitch is recognisable from hand stitch by the regular stitch length and lock stitching (interlocking top and bottom threads). Look out for machine stitching to indicate an item dates after 1850.

Synthetic dyes began with mauvine, also known as aniline purple, invented by William Henry Perkin in 1856. This was swiftly followed by other aniline dyes in vivid shades of royal blue, green, etc. Aniline dyes were only used on silk, and this created a fashion boom in colourful silk dresses, ribbons and accessories. This is useful for dating recycled fabrics in patchwork and quilting.

Manmade textile fibres were invented around the turn of the 20th century with cellulose-based silk substitutes (i.e. artificial or 'art' silk), although they did not gain in popularity until the mid-1920s, when they were marketed to the public with the names 'viscose' and 'rayon'. Nylon followed in 1939, Dacron in the 1950s and Lycra in 1959. Zips became prevalent in clothes from the 1930s onwards.

Patchwork and appliqué items can be made from materials from a range of different dates or made over a long time period. Although not all patchwork items were made from repurposed materials, a typical sewer might expect their scrap bag to contain old clothes and offcuts from their family spanning up to 20 years.

OPPOSITE *This patchwork cushion cover incorporates silk, viscose and even lurex fabrics, recycled from clothing from the 1950s to the 1970s.*

LABELS AND MARKINGS

If you are lucky, your textile item might have a label or identifying mark. Labels in garments can provide information about makers, manufacturers and place of manufacture. If you find a company name you are unfamiliar with, a quick internet search can often provide more details and dates. Unfamiliar logos and badges can be hard to pin down. Fortunately, the internet can also help here. By using a reverse image search, you can upload an image of your badge or logo to reveal other similar items online. Some search engines have this facility built in, but otherwise type 'reverse image search' into your web browser.

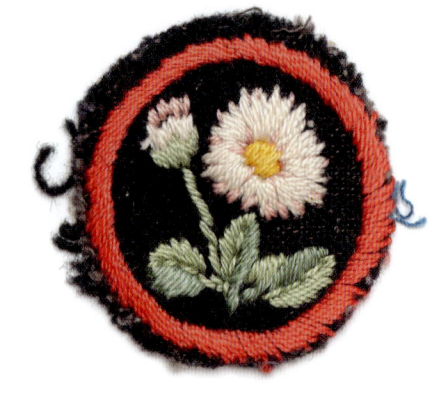

If you are *very* lucky you might even find a label that identifies the owner or wearer of an item. These can vary from exquisite embroidered monograms to more humble hand-sewn laundry marks and woven name tapes more typical in school uniforms. These types of labels give us an intimate contact with the original owner and a sense of what the item meant to them.

We can also sometimes find clues in additional ephemera that accompany an item. While items that are not a physical part of the original garment are less reliable, they can provide additional context. In our family collection, a white cotton baby's bonnet wrapped in a parcel of tissue contains a slip of paper with the words '*Dad's own baby bonnet*' in my grandma's handwriting. While this kind of information is always fascinating, if you want to be sure of its validity, you'll need to confirm dates and provenance through your own background research.

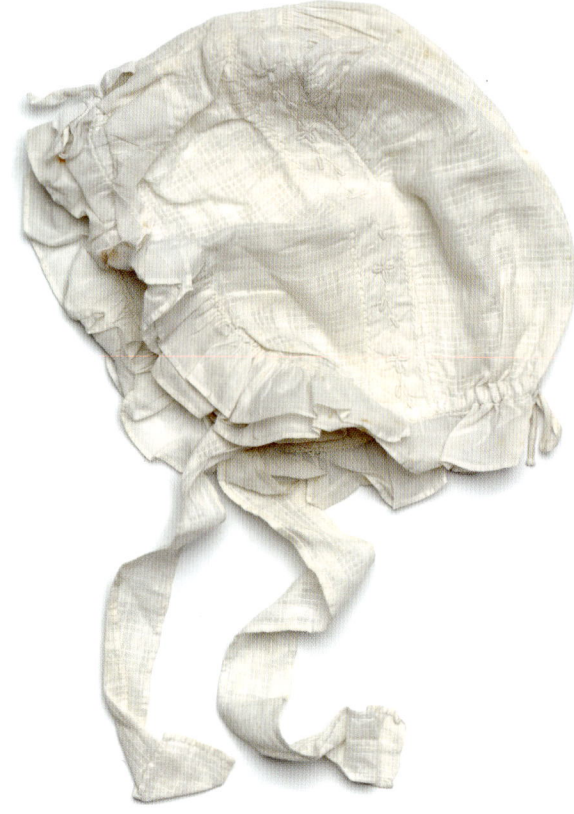

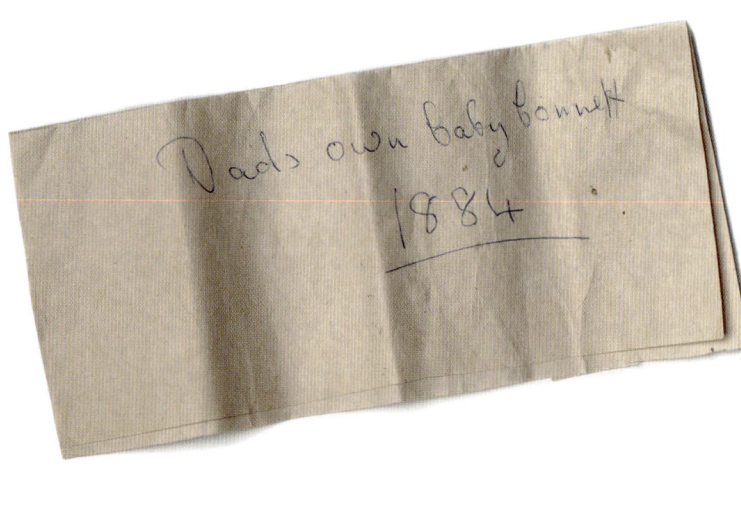

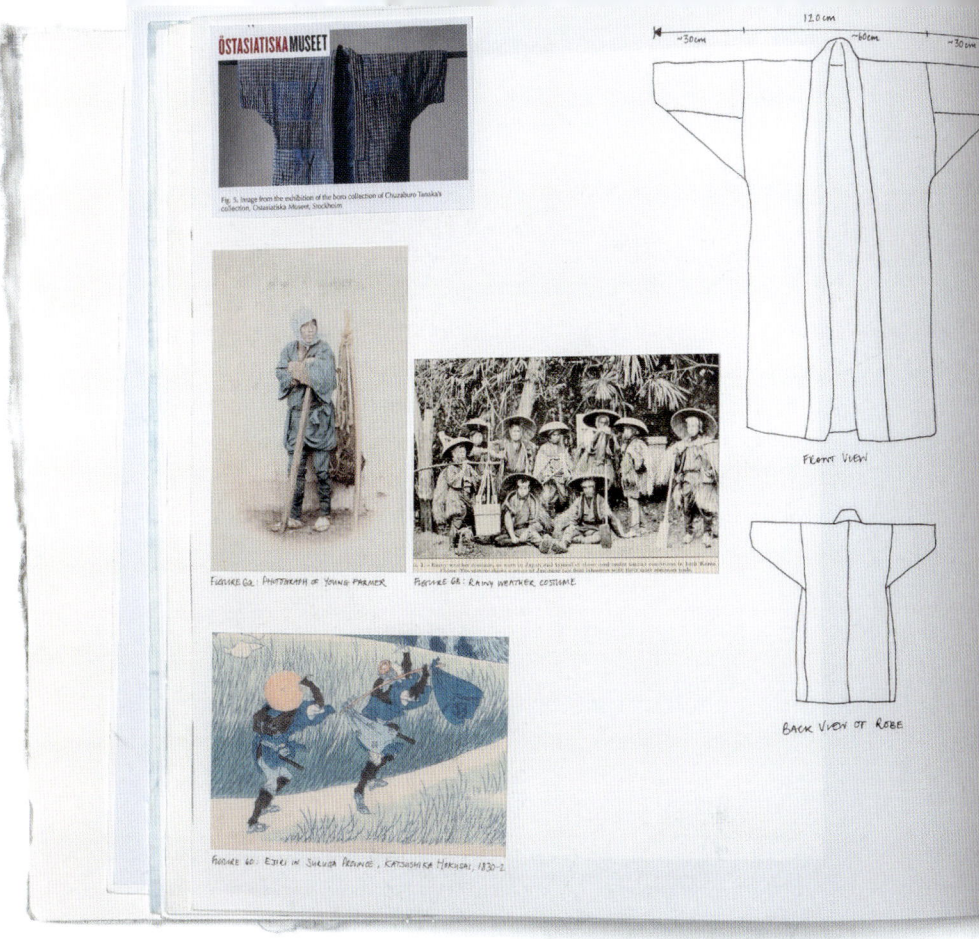

SECONDARY SOURCES

To help date and contextualise an item, it is useful to look for similar examples, or to research the background of specific makers, designers or global traditions. If you are fortunate to have access to a good library, look for specialist books. Online museum databases can also be a useful source. Collect images and details of visually similar items in a notebook or on an online pinboard, so that you can compare them.

As well as dating or placing an item in time, consider its function. How would it have been worn? What was it for? It can be helpful to look for contemporaneous images to help set the piece in context. Historic portraits in museum collections (or online catalogues) can provide a fascinating sense of how textiles were worn, represented or used in the past, and family photo albums might even show someone wearing a specific garment.

PERSONAL CONNECTIONS – DIGGING DEEPER

You may want to know more about the person who made or used your textile item. If you have a name and a rough idea of date, you might be able to find out more by searching public records. British census records show us where people lived and with whom, and some records also show where people worked. Records of births, baptisms, marriages and deaths can also provide further clues to our ancestors and their lives. Fortunately, these are now readily available through genealogy websites. Libraries or local studies services will be able to advise you about how to access these records.

OPPOSITE, ABOVE
An old Girl Guide patrol badge.

OPPOSITE, BELOW
A 19th-century baby's bonnet with handwritten label. This could be helpful in identifying the item's former owner.

ABOVE *This research journal by Vicky Poulson includes some background research, exploring the cultural context of the Japanese robe (see page 29).*

Family stories and personal narratives

While it's wonderful to be able to access online sources from around the world, it can be easy to overlook the people around us as a source of information. Family members can often help shed light on heirloom pieces and people from our local community might be able to expand on what we know about historic items in our locality. Whether it's an informal chat over coffee or part of a public event in a community setting, some prior planning can help you get the most from the experience.

Choose a mutually convenient time and place. If you want to chat with a group or as part of a family event, think about how you will manage the group dynamic. In-person conversations are often the best, but where that isn't convenient, arrange a suitable time for a phone call or online video call.

Either beforehand or at the beginning of your meeting, it is important to make it clear what the nature of your research is and how you will use any information. Is it just for personal interest or will it be shared publicly anywhere? Will you be recording the conversation, writing notes or taking photos? If so, how will you store that information?

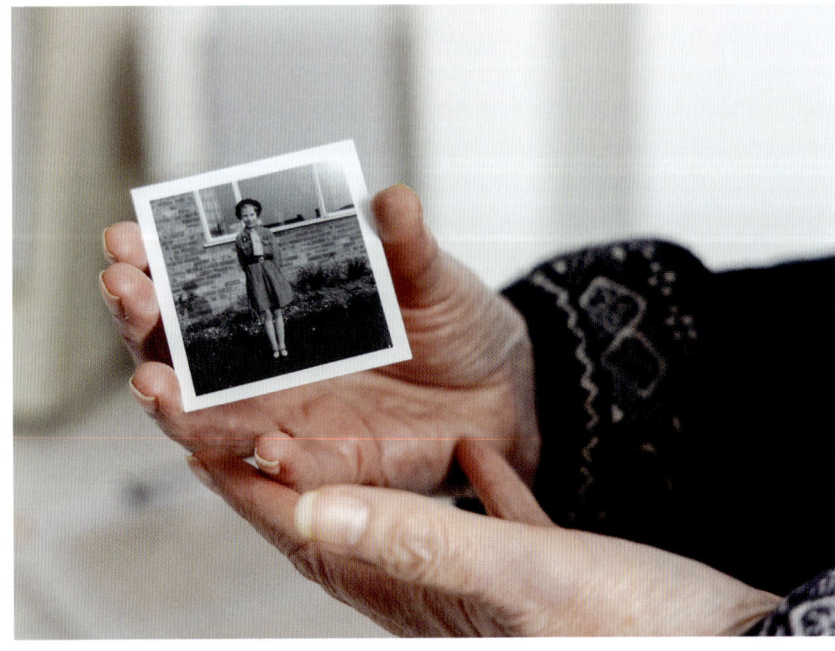

LEFT *Objects and photographs can trigger personal memories of textiles and clothing.*

OPPOSITE *A wool felt Brownie beret, yellow cotton Brownie tie and other ephemera accompanied by a photo of the owner proudly wearing her Brownie uniform in the 1950s.*

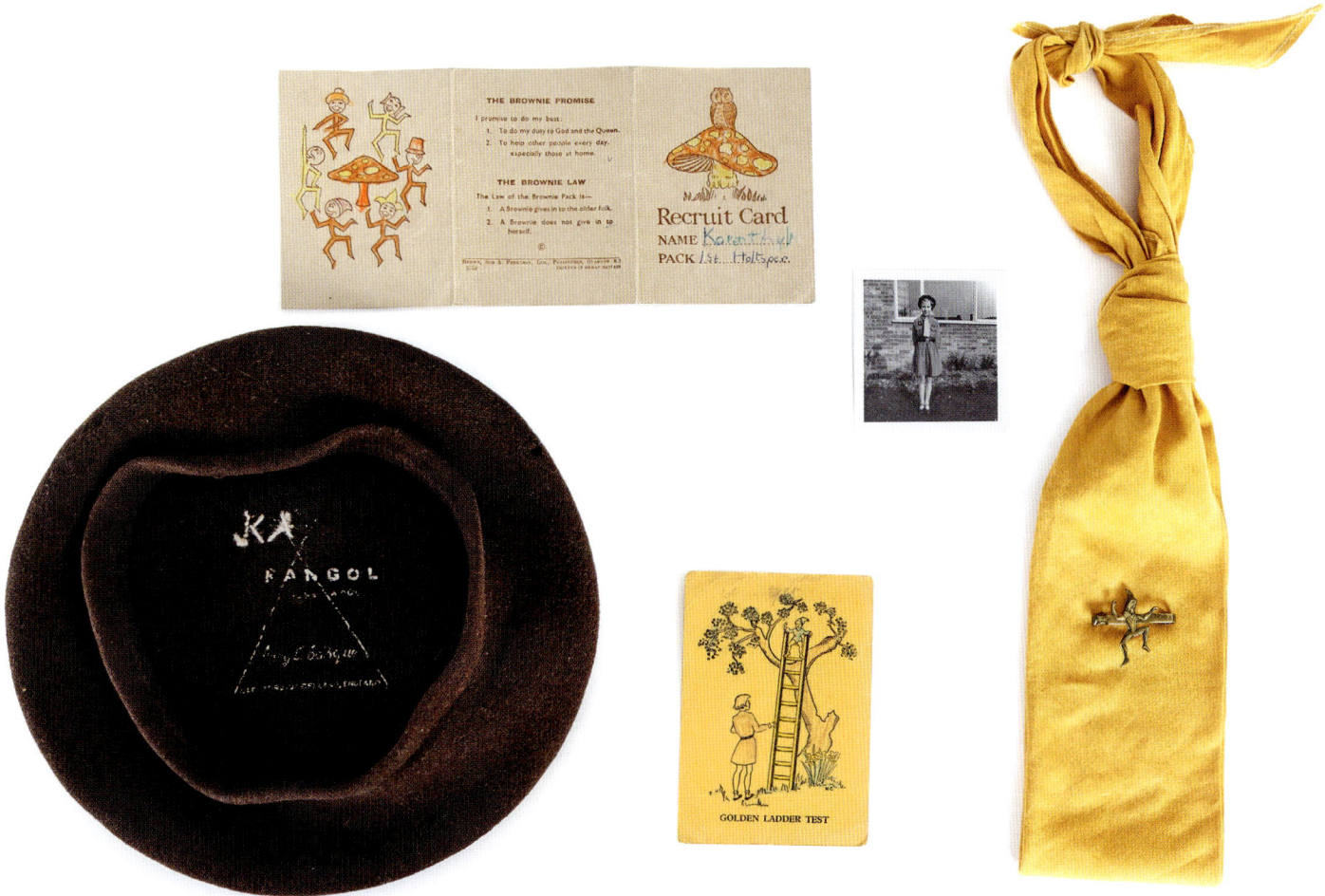

QUESTIONS TO ASK

Even if you are having a very informal chat with a family member, it can be helpful to think ahead about what information you would like to find out. While each project will need different questions, you might like to think about the following themes:

- What do they know about where the item came from? Who made it? Where was it purchased? How did it come to be here?
- Is the item connected with a specific event or person?
- What does this item mean to them personally? Do they like it? What memories does it evoke for them?

Focus on asking open questions to avoid influencing the answer. For example, rather than saying 'Did this dress belong to Aunt Susan?', try 'Who did this dress belong to?' Listen attentively and try to avoid interrupting too much; you never know what unexpected information you might learn.

As well as noting down the responses to your questions, you might like to ask if they have any other material relating to any particular pieces, such as family photos, documents or other related artefacts. This can open up further discussion and creative inspiration. On a final note, it's nice to ask people if they would like to be kept up-to-date with how your project develops. Perhaps you could show them work-in-progress or invite them to an exhibition.

As an alternative to verbal questions, it can also be productive to ask people to share written responses. This works particularly well when you want to engage with lots of people over a longer period of time, or if the respondents would prefer to be anonymous. I used this approach for the *Fragment of a Dress* project at the Brontë Parsonage Museum (see page 117).

BELOW *A handwritten personal narrative about a special and memorable item. Part of my* Fragment of a Dress *project for the Brontë Parsonage Museum (see page 117).*

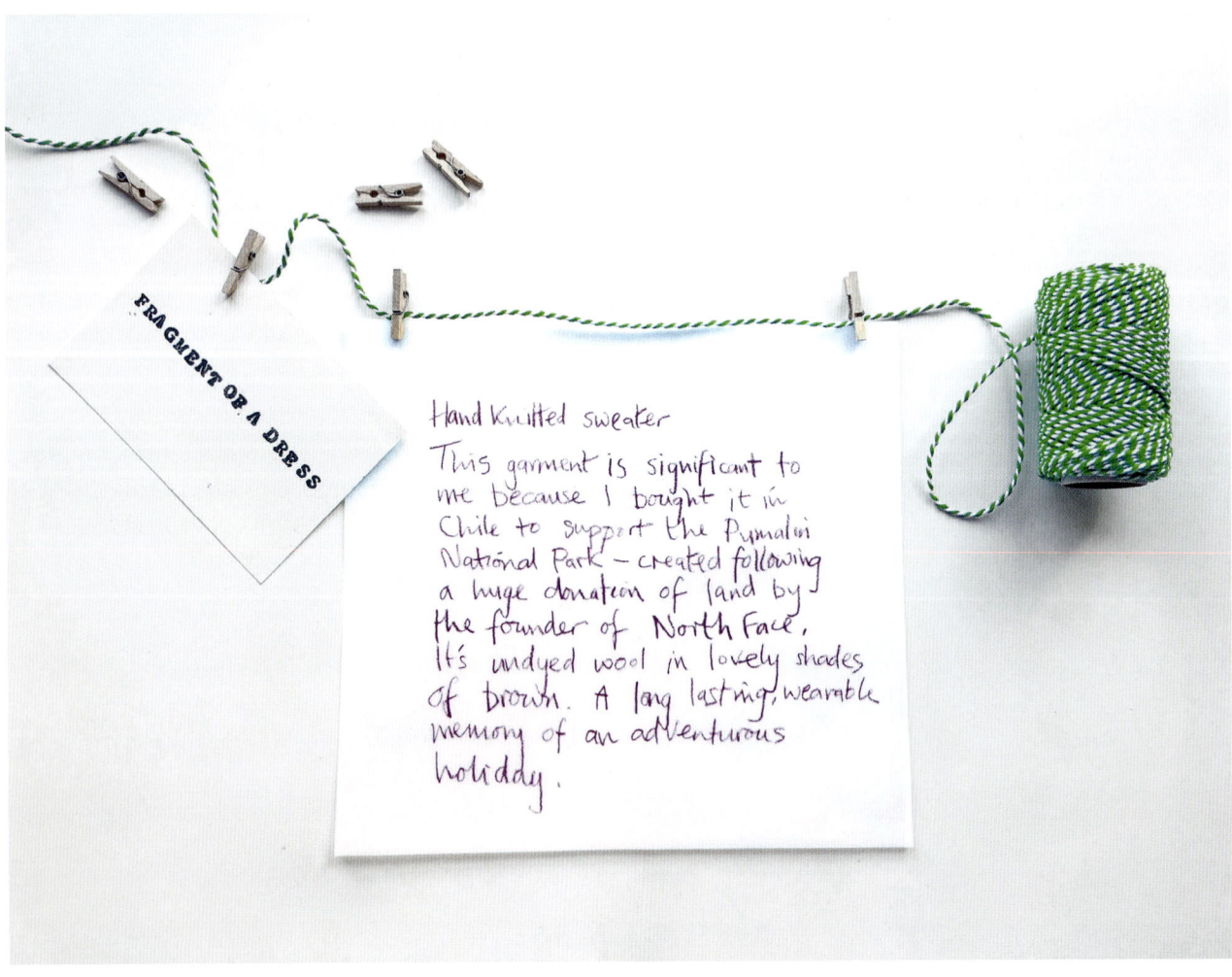

NEXT STEPS

The ability to create something original in response to something old often requires a creative leap, by looking at things in a new way. Throughout the remainder of this chapter, we are moving beyond the initial observation stage to start to see how we might bring together our historical textile sources with other collected imagery, words and visual ideas, to create an individual response.

Making connections

Initially, I like to spread out what I have already gathered: preliminary sketches and drawings, tracings, photographs, written notes, collected images and supplementary material (it can be helpful to make photocopies of pages from a sketchbook). I find that seeing everything together at once helps me to notice visual connections and that themes jump out at me.

Make a cup of tea, grab a notebook and stand back from your research. Consider the 'floodlight' and 'spotlight' modes (see page 16). You might like to start with a stream of consciousness, writing a list of words that come to mind, or use a spider diagram or 'mind map' to record your thoughts.

Looking at your gathered research, think about descriptive words, for example:

- Textures or material qualities (*creased, fuzzy, faded, shimmering...*)
- Main colours (don't just think 'blue', think *inky / jewel-like / rich / sugary...*)
- Decorative features, patterns or styles (*grids, stripes, swirls, floral, embellished, graphic, stencilled, typography, minimal...*)
- Structures (*looping, pleated, rigid, creased, padded, gathered, interlaced, scaffolding...*)

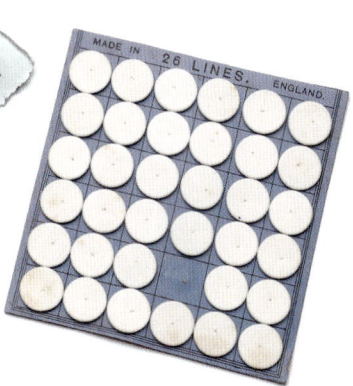

LEFT *Collected imagery, fabric scraps and objects.*

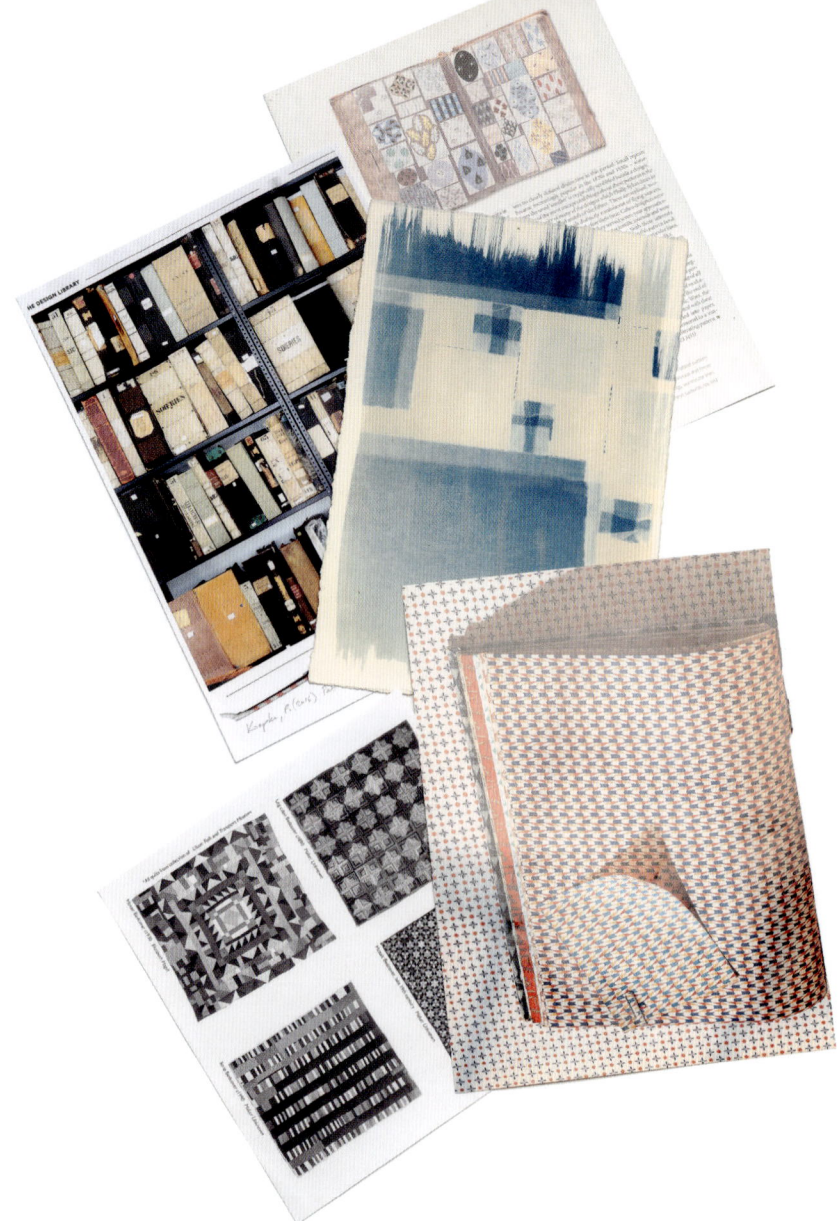

Using these initial thoughts alongside your research material, start to expand out to think of further connected things. What does it remind you of? Here are a few ideas to get you started:

- Things with a similar 'look' in terms of colour, pattern, texture, form (e.g. patchwork quilts remind me of paintings by Paul Klee, pavements and stained glass windows).
- Things with the same message or theme (e.g. designs with birds, suffragette memorabilia).
- Similar materials, textures or structures.
- Things made around the same time or place (e.g. 1920s Art Deco jewellery or architecture).
- Objects associated with your research (e.g. swimwear might link with sunglasses).

These are just a few ideas to use as jumping off points. With experience, making visual associations becomes intuitive and almost automatic. The more you put this into practice, the easier it will become.

Collecting

Once you have expanded your list of words and ideas, highlight those that interest you most. These can be used as the basis for gathering additional visual material. I like to make collections of images, objects, materials or phrases. Be led by what interests you and what feels 'right'.

Personal items from your own past can also be a rich area of research, either through actual objects or from memory – the recollection of the wallpaper in your grandmother's spare room, for example, or an old embroidered handkerchief... Found objects and collected materials can add depth and a more personal connection, and they can also help us to consider those materials we might use for making.

A sketchbook or visual journal is the classic way to collate your imagery, and many people like this format, but it can limit the way we 'read' things together. Mood boards or visual mind maps can be used to display things on the wall with immediate impact, while simple three-dimensional displays can be made on shelves or tables, or even suspended from the ceiling. By displaying things together, we can make interesting links and explore unexpected juxtapositions. I particularly like to be able to edit and rearrange things, which helps with the development of my ideas.

BELOW *The starting point for this group of images was a collection of hand-painted weave designs from the Bradford College Textile Archive.*

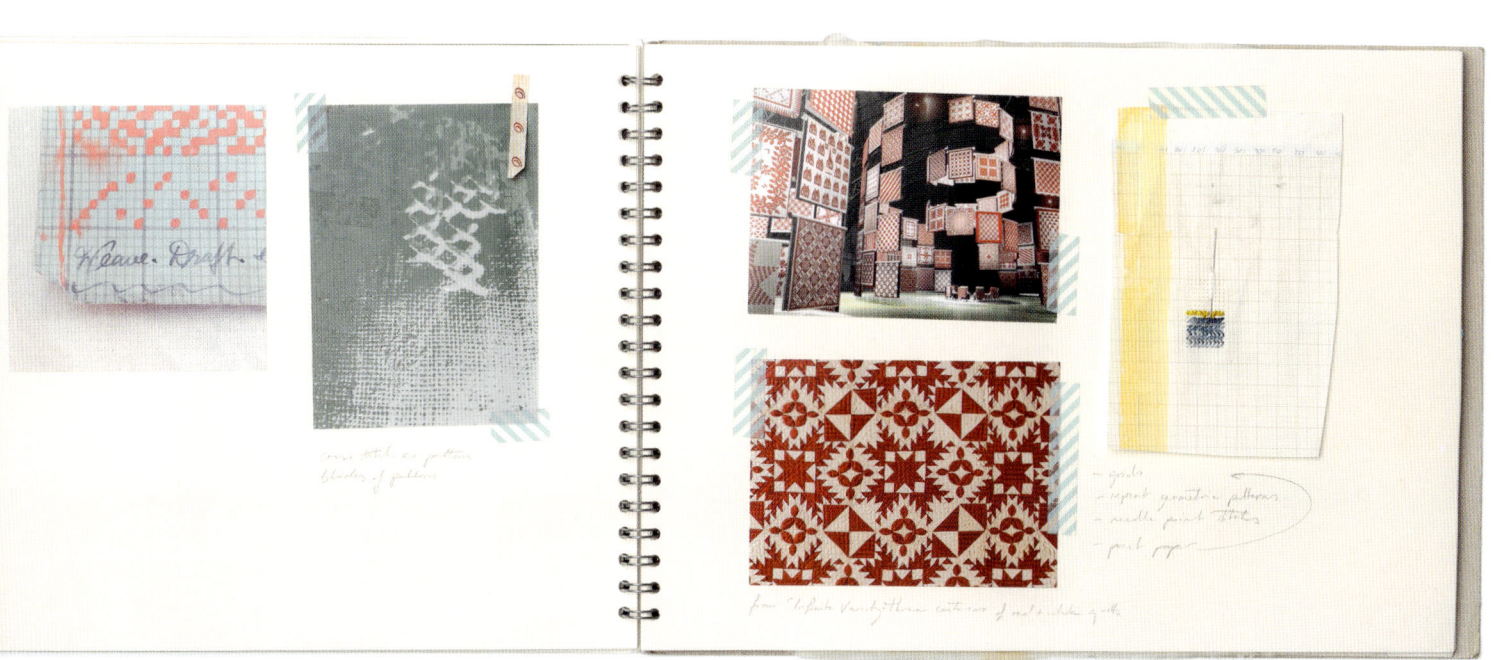

Mood boards

A mood board (or story board) is a place to gather together your visual ideas, so that you can see at a glance your main themes in terms of colour, texture, pattern and concept. It helps us to notice common themes, to connect parallel ideas, or to see where something doesn't fit with everything else. Sometimes I make a mood board in response to a specific brief or project; other times it might start off vague, capturing my current obsessions and interests, looking for patterns or threads that will coalesce into a story. Think of this as an ongoing collection of ideas that is constantly evolving, rather than a fixed idea. A mood board isn't about finished design ideas, but more about communicating the visual essence or story of your project.

BELOW *My studio noticeboard acts as an informal mood board.*

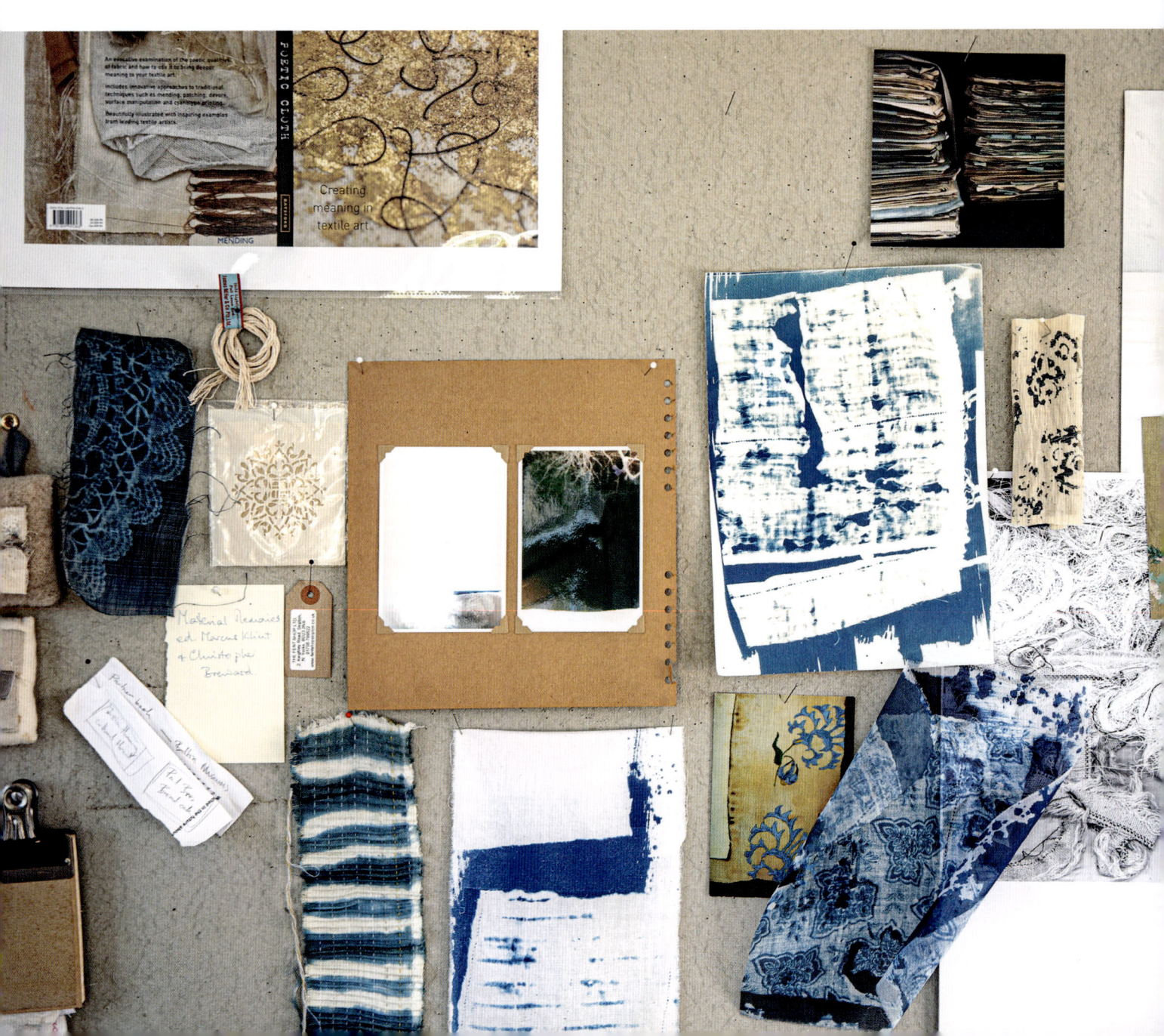

Mood boards can be physical or digital. The advantages of a digital mood board are that it is easy to share and collaborate online, it's low-cost and avoids consuming paper, and if you have the digital know-how, it's easy to rescale, recolour and tinker with your images. However, I find that I really crave the tactile qualities of physical materials.

A mood board could be any size you like, providing it is large enough to include your images. I like to use the large pinboard that covers a wall in my studio as an ever-evolving mood board. A sheet of white or grey mount board (used for picture framing) is a traditional choice, while a small cork noticeboard is a good reusable option.

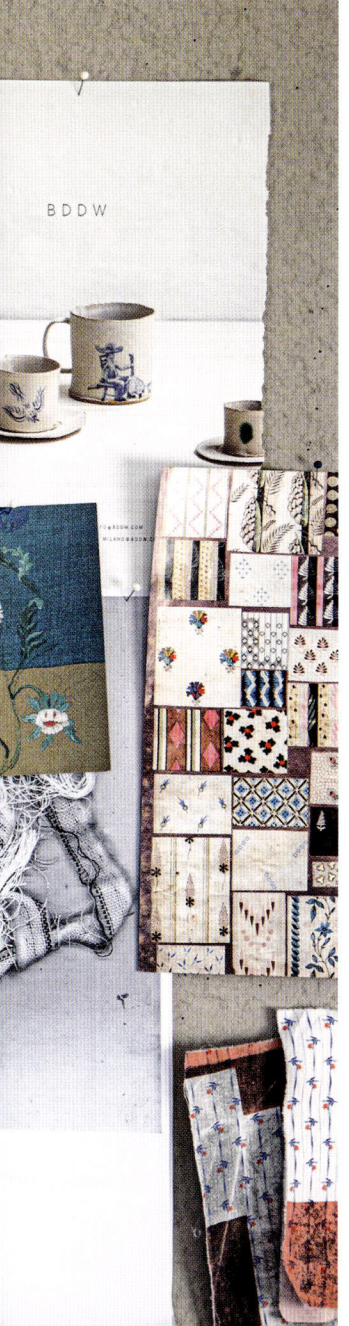

GETTING STARTED

I love browsing books and sifting through boxes of artist postcards and images. It's part of my thinking process, helping me to explore possibilities and gradually settle on ideas. I start by collecting a larger amount of visual material and then edit it down.

Gather photographs, cuttings from magazines, photocopies from books, threads, fabrics, other materials or real objects that help to tell your story. Think about colours, textures, patterns and forms that link with the 'feel' or story of your project. If there is a strong idea or narrative underpinning the project, it's also useful to look for a few key images that help to set the scene. These might be actual images linked to a specific place or time, such as a wedding or the interior of the Biba store, or they could be more abstract in nature, for example themes around childhood, war or renewal.

Once you have gathered your initial imagery, you may need to edit:

- Is there any repetition or any images that 'say' the same thing? Choose the best one.
- Is anything too dominant? Should it be a smaller image or removed altogether?
- Look for visual themes and similarities – i.e. things that look like they belong together.
- Take away anything that jars.
- What is missing? Add it.

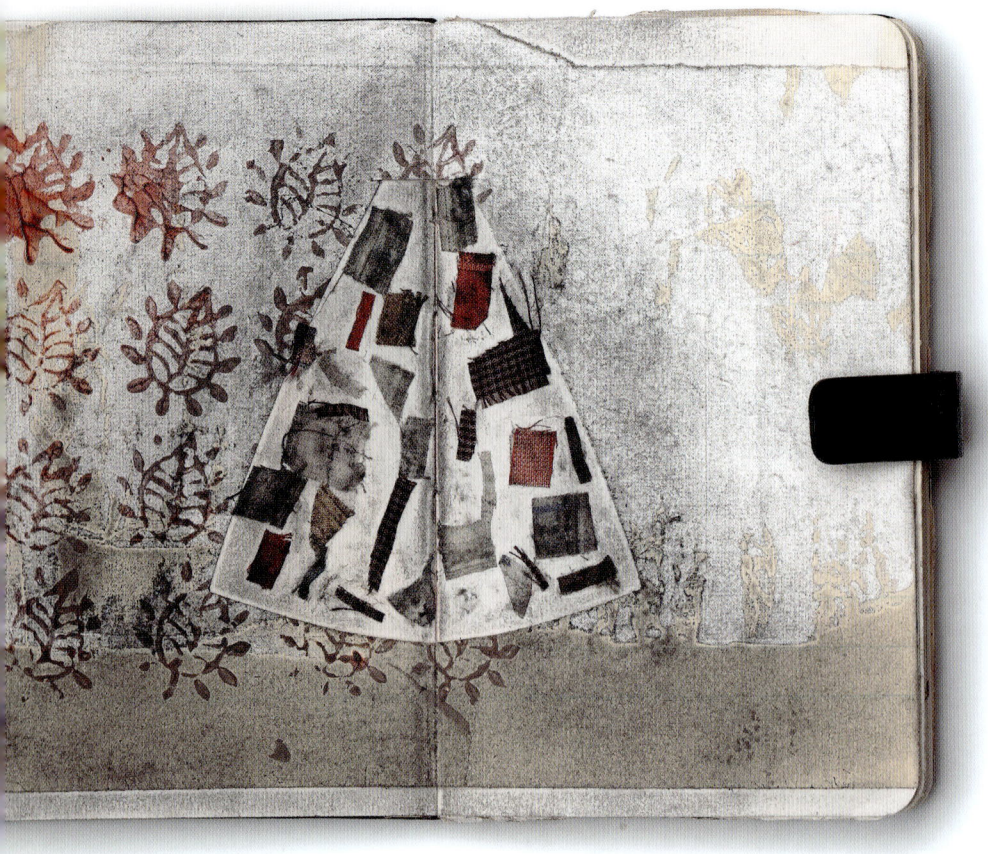

REVIEWING AND USING

Once you have created an initial mood board, it's a good idea to leave it alone and come back to it with fresh eyes. Allow it to surprise you; what themes emerge? Don't forget that your board can change as your ideas evolve and develop.

Creating a mood board can be a great way to begin a project, but it can also be useful as a way of checking in with your overarching project ideas as your work develops. I mostly make informal pinboards for my own reference and inspiration, but they can also be useful to communicate your ideas to other people, for example as a collaboration tool or to pitch an idea to a stakeholder.

Alongside my mood board, I also use a small pocket-sized notebook, and this travels with me wherever I go to collect all my notes, both visual and written. Some people prefer to use sketchbooks. There is no single right way of working; it's just about finding a good approach that works for you.

ABOVE *Pocket-sized notebooks are useful for making quick notes and capturing immediate visual ideas.*

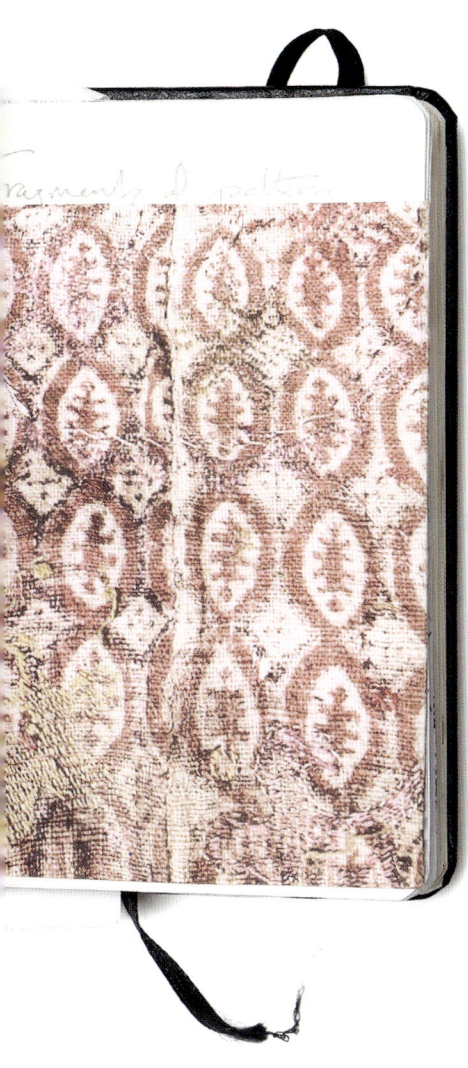

PATTERN AND PLAY

Having made some initial observational studies, gathered source material and made connections between different visual material, you may think – *what next?* You may be tempted to launch into creating a resolved textile piece at this stage, but sometimes it can be useful to step back and do some further creative 'play' first. By creating a wider range of responses rather than simply jumping to the first solution you think of, you will generate more possibilities and options to choose from. This allows you greater freedom to try things, to take more risks, to use your imagination and, therefore, to bring more individuality to the project.

So how might you go about being expressive, developing visual ideas and creating more possibilities? Sometimes this is about making choices and being more selective. By focusing on specific elements, you can then be more playful with these. If the garment or textile item is very complex, you might choose to focus on particular parts or visual characteristics (colour, texture, shape, patterns, symbols, rhythms and arrangements).

It is your choice how much detail to include in your artwork and how accurate, representational or abstract you want it to be. On the following pages are some prompts and techniques to consider when developing your visual ideas.

TRACING, MAPPING, DEFINING

Lay tracing paper over one of your previous drawings, blueprints or a photo of your object, and trace...

- Key shapes – focus on just the bits that are important to you.
- Edges – use your pen or pencil to follow the edge contours of the object, just as a line.
- Pattern or motif – trace a motif, move the paper and re-draw it, repeating and building up pattern.
- Stitch marks – trace only marks of stitching, from hems, seams, etc., to create a stitch map.

Try using different drawing media for different effects: fine-liner pen, white gel pen, marker pens, oil pastel, Indian ink...

BELOW *The border design of an embroidered Indian shawl was first traced with paint markers on tracing paper. An individual motif was then selected, repeated, scanned and repositioned. The possibilities are endless!*

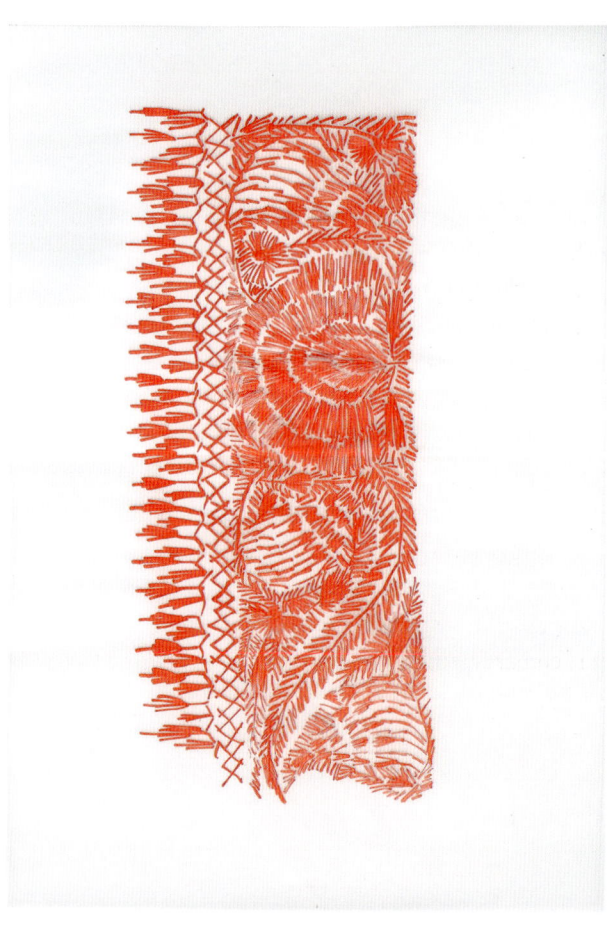

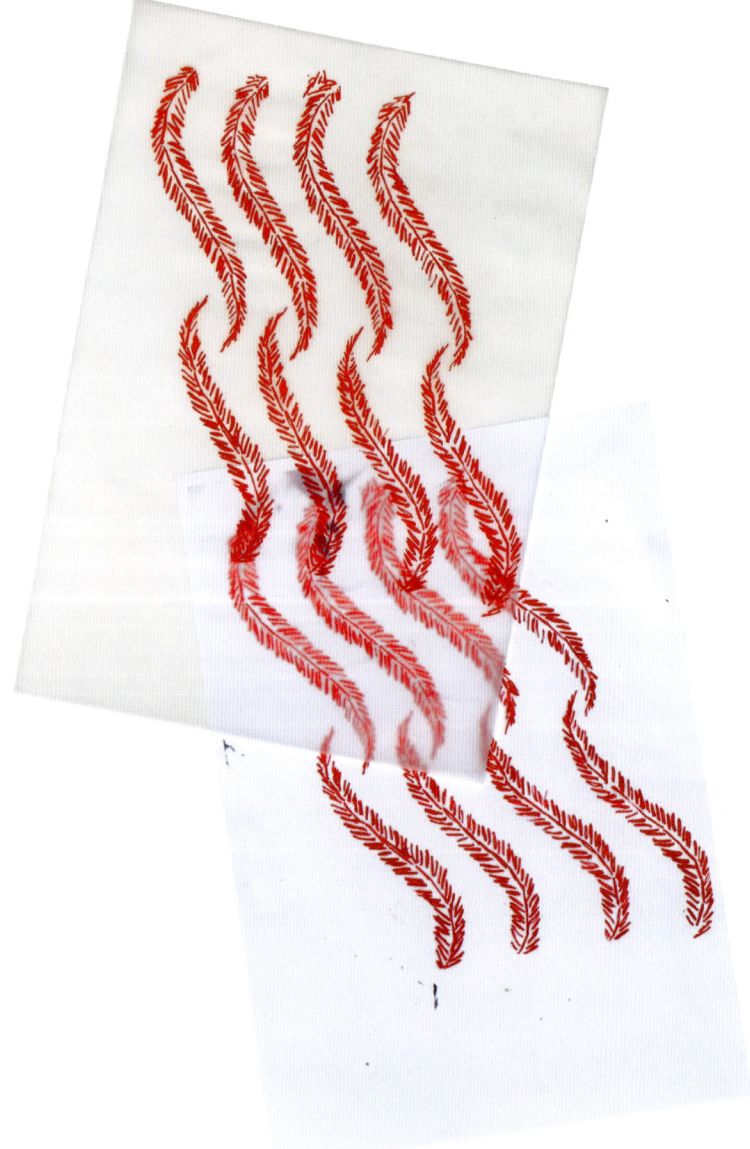

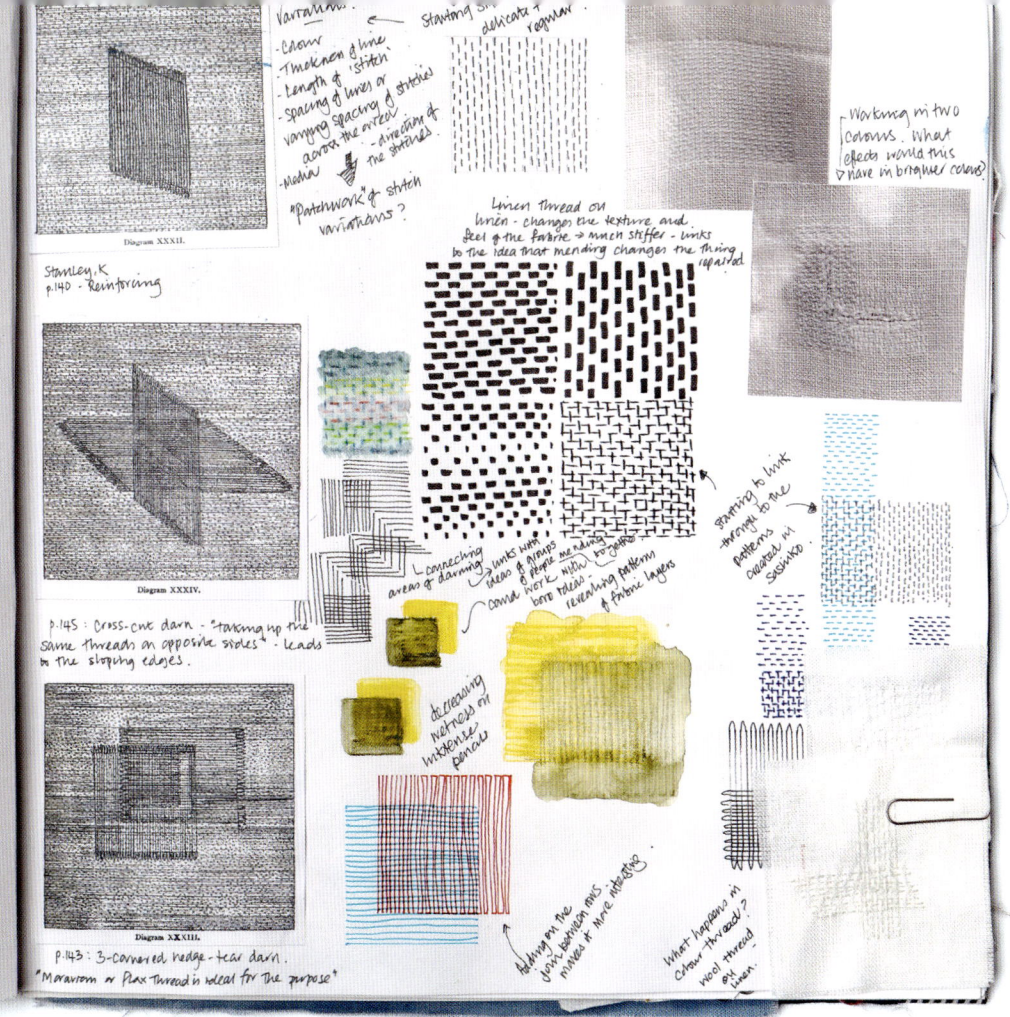

UNPICKING, CUTTING AWAY, TAKING APART

Imagine if you were to unravel areas of the textile piece: how would it come apart? What shapes would be left if you deconstructed it? Try cutting away sections of your drawings (photocopy them first), or slice them into strips.

How much can you remove, while still retaining its most important or fundamental qualities? For example, when does a paisley pattern stop being paisley?

Imagine how your object is constructed; follow the journey of a thread as a continuous line drawing.

Look at the spaces between threads or pattern motifs (the negative spaces). Use black ink and a paintbrush to paint the spaces, without first drawing the outlines.

Make a 'drawing' with scissors using coloured paper, again without drawing the lines. Don't over-think it, just freestyle it!

Cut out pattern motifs or garment shapes from coloured paper and rearrange them on a background. Photograph or scan different pattern layouts.

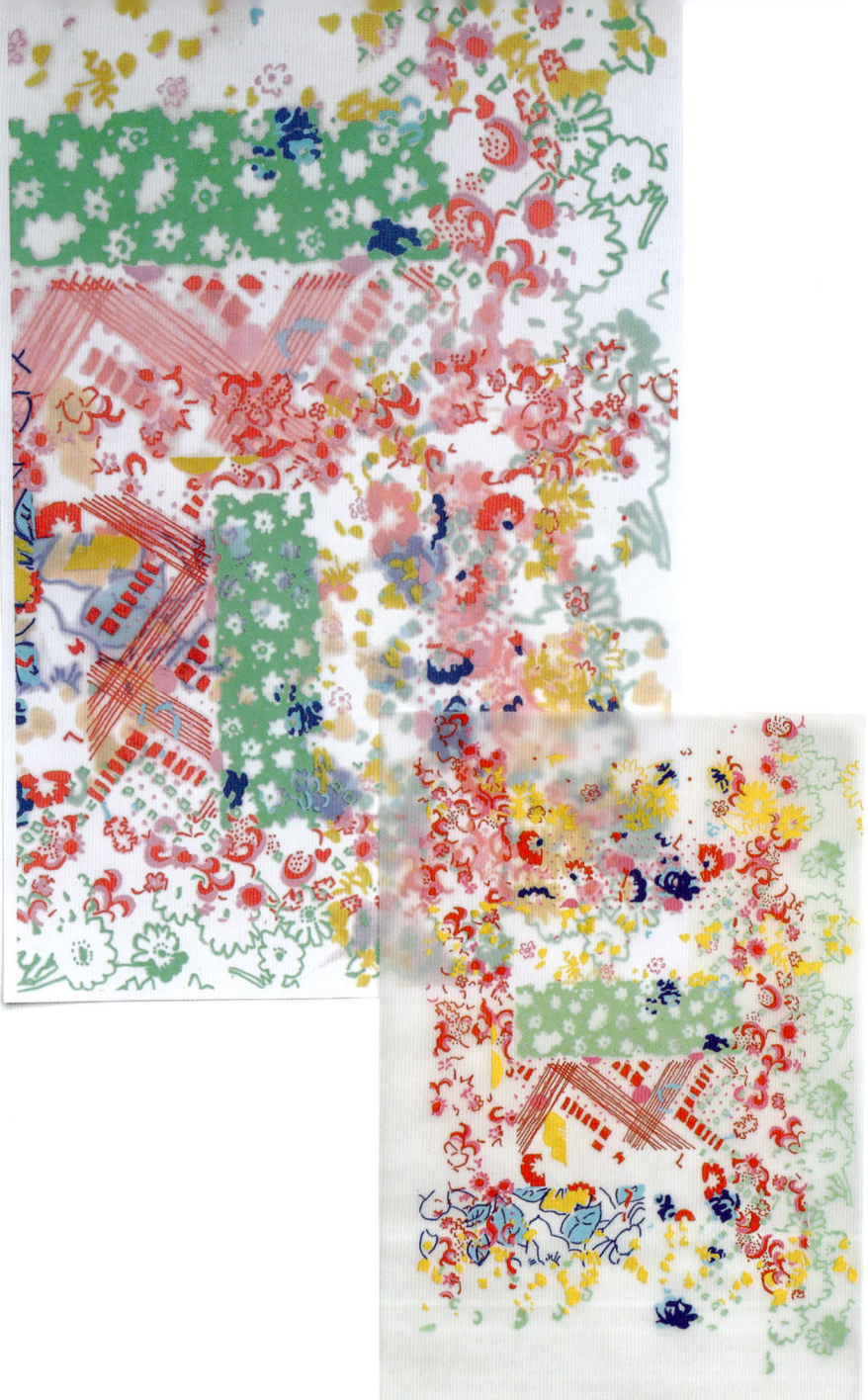

LEFT *I started out picking a single colour from a pattern to trace with a paint marker on tracing paper. I continued, tracing different colours and patterns, moving the paper when I ran out of space and sometimes overlapping patterns. To further emphasise the busy patterns I photocopied, layered and enlarged the image.*

HIGHLIGHTING, AMPLIFYING, EXAGGERATING

Working from existing drawings, scans or photos, use a digital scanner or photocopier to enhance certain qualities. Even a very basic photocopier can quickly create interesting effects:

- Enlarge – go big! Enhance areas of detail.
- Reduce – shrink; make mini versions; make multiples; repeat!
- Play with contrast; invert or reduce to black and white to highlight tonal qualities.
- Play with different effects to enhance colour and texture.
- If you don't mind losing some detail, try scanning and re-scanning your copies to really exaggerate.

MIXING, COMBINING, JOINING

Combine any of the previous techniques with supplementary imagery from your secondary research, such as old photos, details from period paintings, or found materials and objects. Scan or photocopy imagery to give you a supply of images to cut out and collage.

Try multiple layers of tracings, or use a scanner or photocopier to combine different motifs, shapes or elements together. It is often more economical to work with loose 'bits' rather than creating each idea from scratch and sticking down each time.

Stitch, staple, weave or bind together different images or components. Consider how you might combine them to tell a story.

Let your imagination run wild; fill in the gaps, doodle or build a story around your imagery.

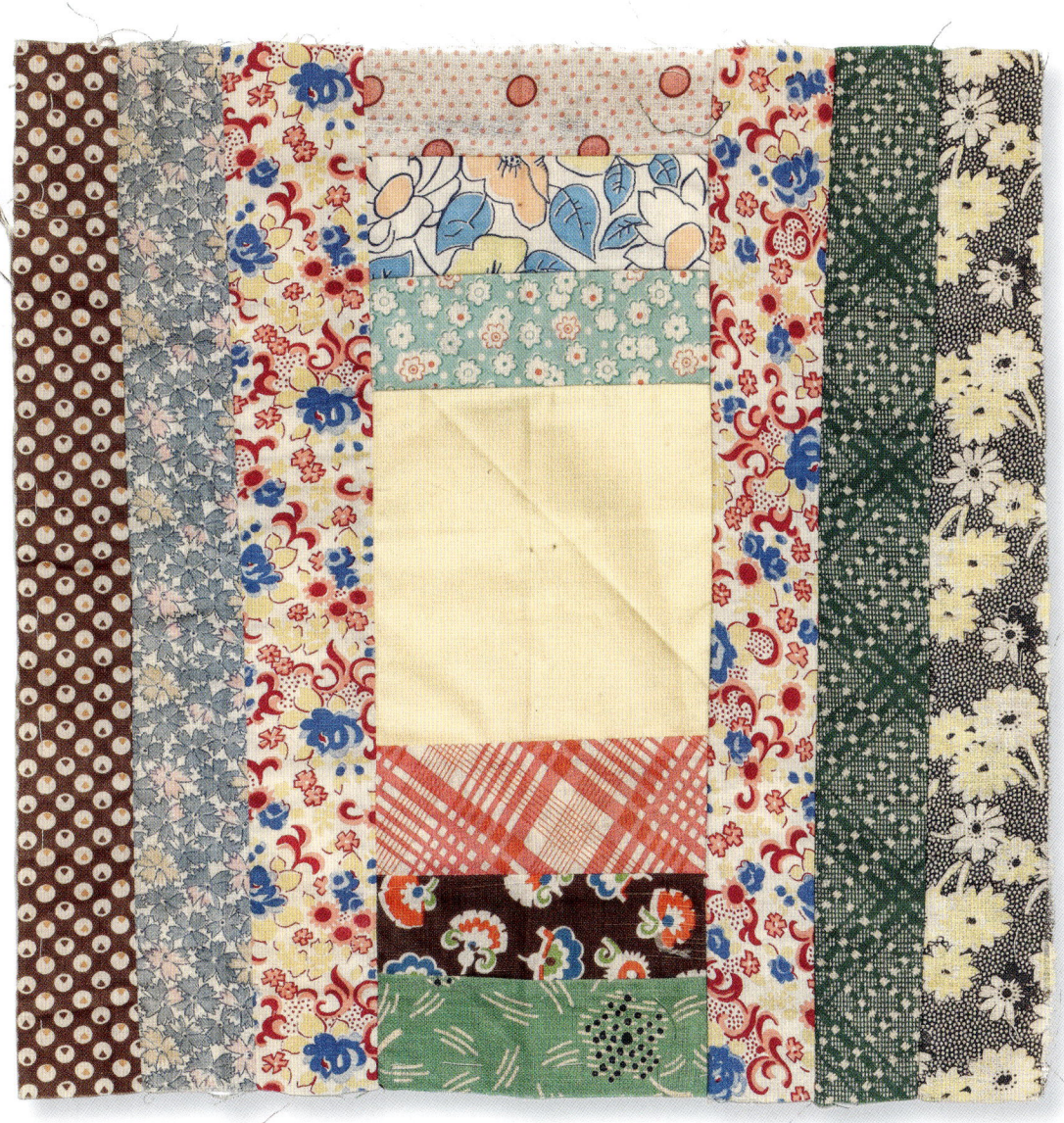

Stitched drawings

Once you have developed a range of possible design ideas, there are many different ways of transferring these onto cloth for stitching. Fabric markers, carbon paper and transfer pencils are all effective; however, a favourite method I like to use is 'prick and pounce'. This is a very old technique (pricked designs can be found in *The Needles Excellency*, c.1634) and, although it is a little time consuming, I find it a really mindful approach to stitch design.

BELOW *This stitch drawing is based on a sketch of the quilted panel opposite. I drew without looking at my paper, aiming to capture the essence of the floral patterns in a looser style.*

OPPOSITE, LEFT *This damaged section of a vintage quilt offers inspiration from the floral prints and pattern arrangement.*

OPPOSITE, RIGHT *Close up of a pricked drawing.*

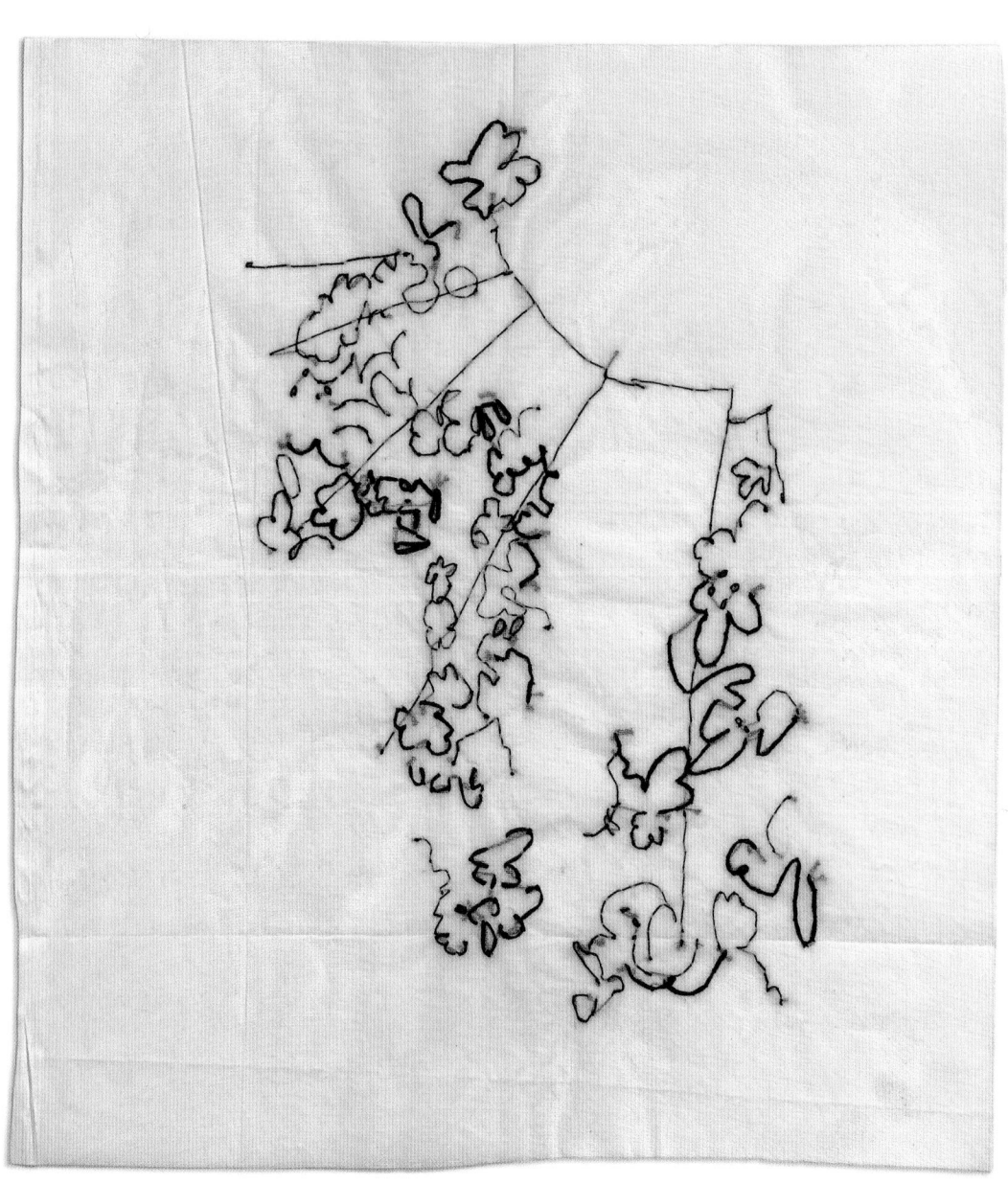

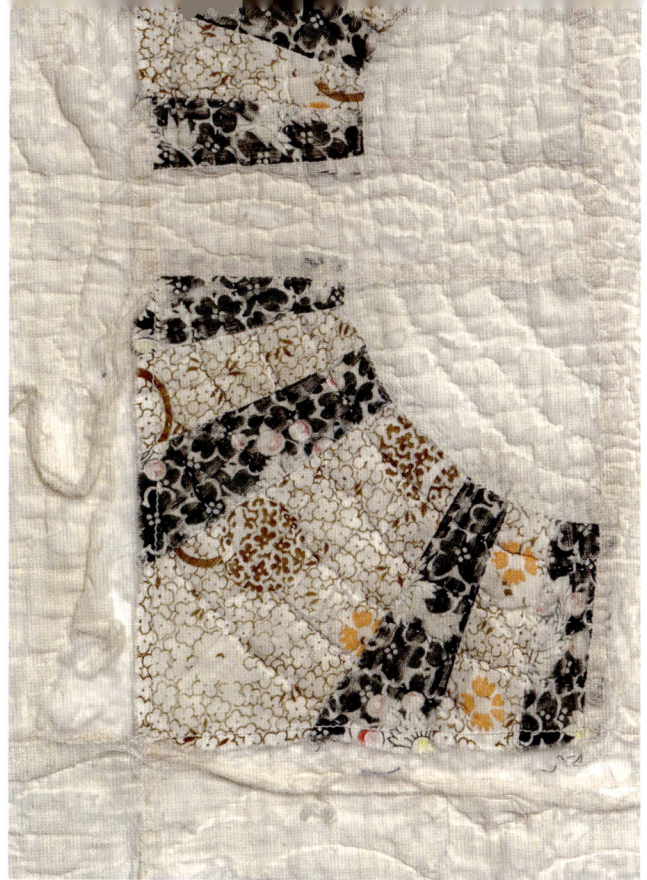

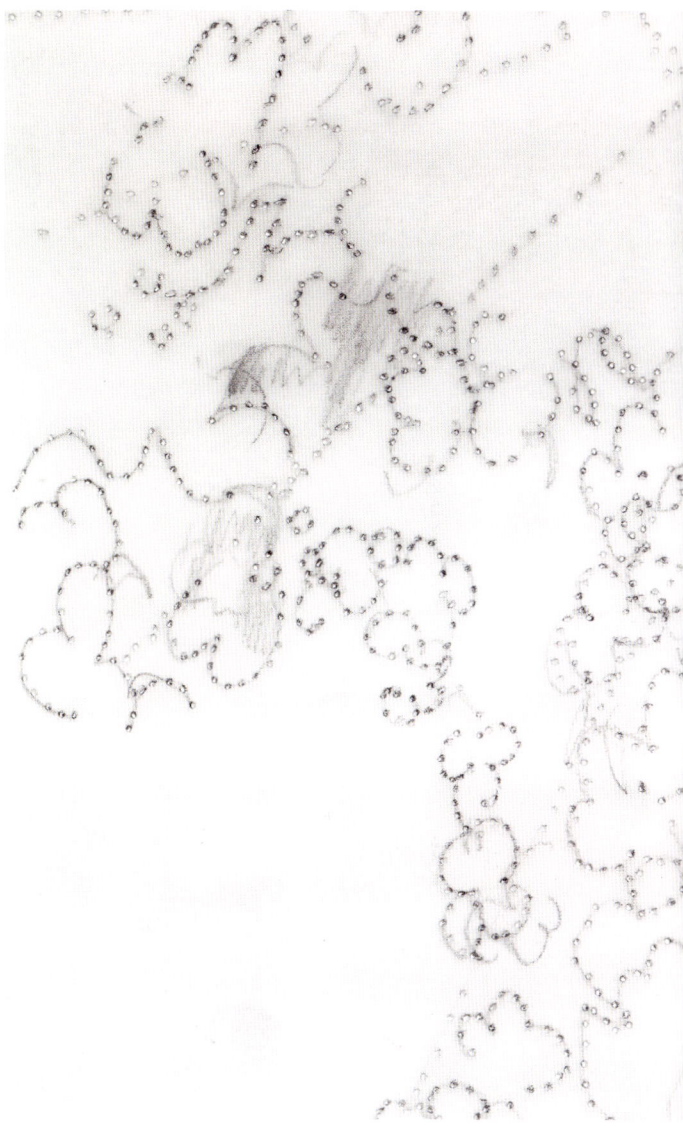

YOU WILL NEED

- Heavyweight tracing paper or velum
- Washi tape or low-tack masking tape
- Fine propelling pencil
- Piece of felt or old towel
- Grey board (i.e. the back of sketch pads), cork sheet or cutting mat
- Large-headed pin or a pricking tool
- Fabric for your final design (fairly smooth, fine-grained textiles work best)
- Embroidery frame (optional)
- Pounce powder (choose a colour that will show up on your fabric)
- Pouncing pad (a piece of duster or felt tied into a little pad will work fine)

PRICK AND POUNCE METHOD

1. Place the tracing paper over your drawing or image and hold the layers together with tape. Carefully trace your design in pencil, ensuring you faithfully capture any important details. Alternatively, you could make drawings directly onto tracing paper, or print a digital design on velum paper using a desktop printer.

2. Remove the tracing and place it onto a firm but yielding surface, such as a piece of grey board with a layer of felt or towelling on top.

3. Use the pin or pricking tool to prick around all of the lines on your tracing, ensuring you get as much detail as possible. The holes should be close together, but be careful not to prick too closely or the paper will tear.

4. Stretch your fabric taut, either in an embroidery frame or pinned out on a board. Position the pricked design on the fabric and pin or tape in place.

5. Gently dip your pounce pad into the pounce powder then tap on the edge of the container to remove any excess. Rub the pounce pad along the lines of your tracing, firmly pushing the pounce powder through the holes. I find that a slight twisting action helps.

6. Once you have gone over the whole design in this way, carefully lift off the tracing and blow away the excess powder, leaving a dotty outline of your design on the fabric.

7. Carefully join up the lines of your design using a fine propelling pencil.

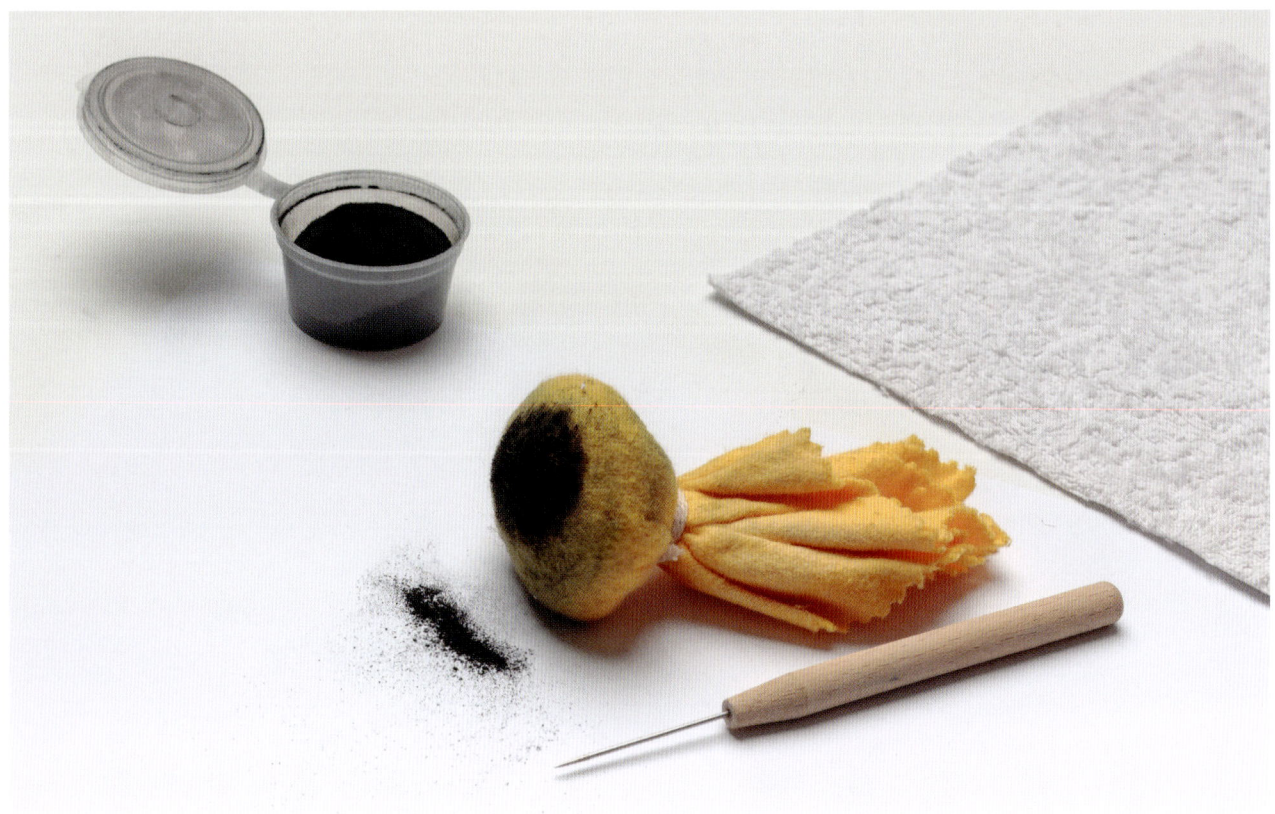

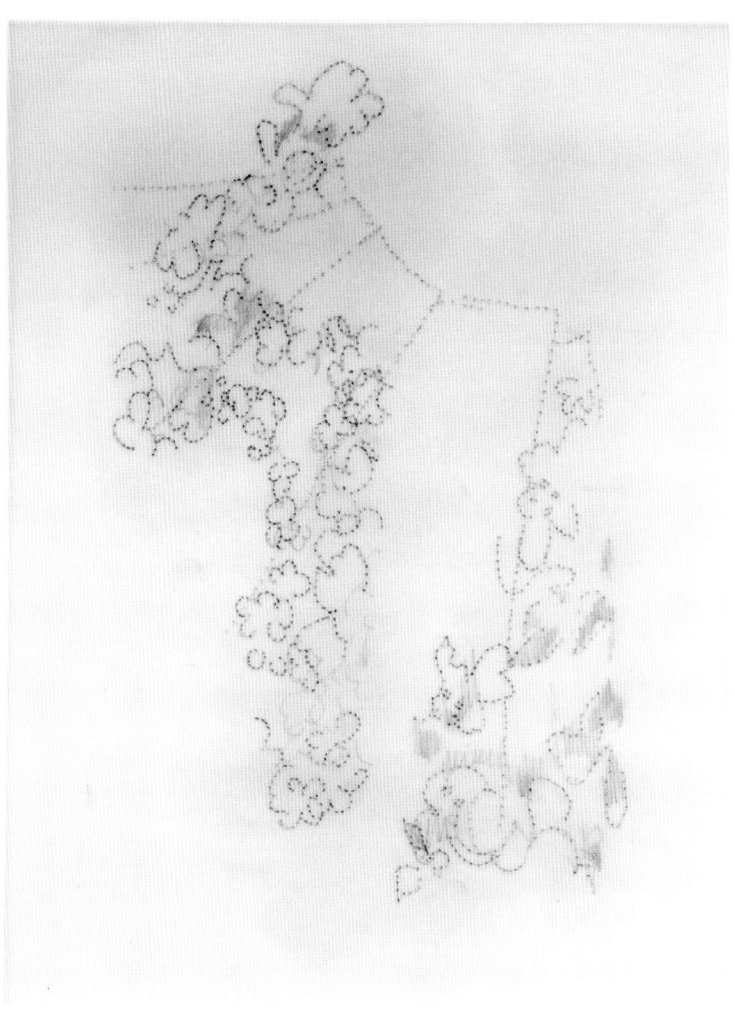

OPPOSITE *Pounce powder and tools.*

LEFT *This drawing was made directly on tracing paper and then carefully pricked, before the design was pounced onto fabric.*

BELOW *This stitch drawing combines running stitch, backstitch and a freestyle fly/open chain stitch. Using different thicknesses of threads adds variety.*

You are now free to stitch your transferred design in any way you like. I often choose a fairly freestyle approach, working with a combination of simple stitches to suit my design – couching, backstitch, running stitch, French knots, satin stitch, etc. You might like to combine this technique with other textile processes, on cyanotype prints (see pages 34–43) or digitally printed fabrics (see pages 83–85), for example, or with appliqué.

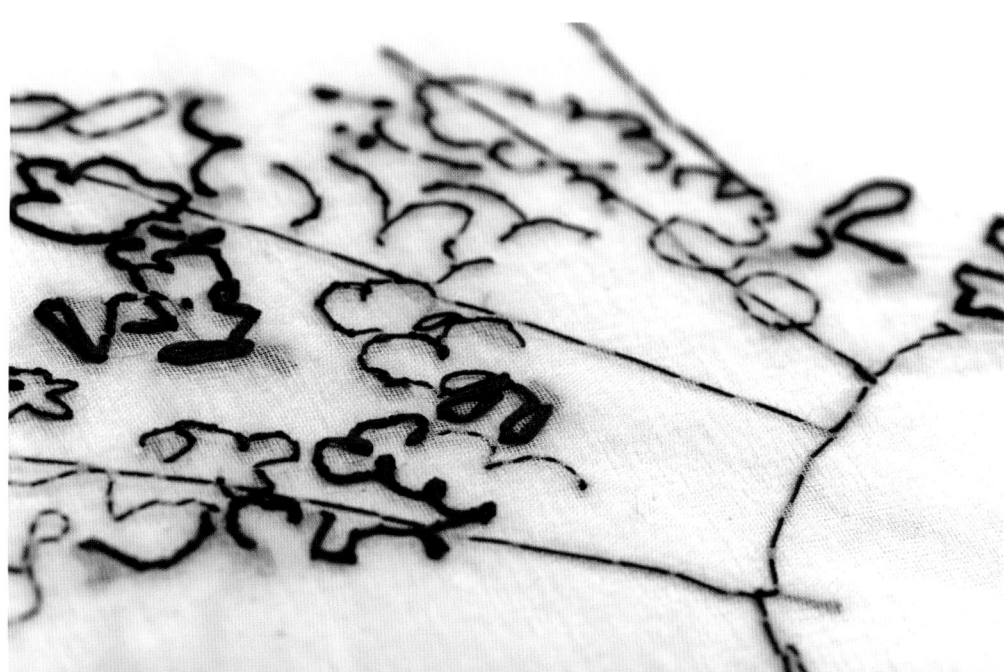

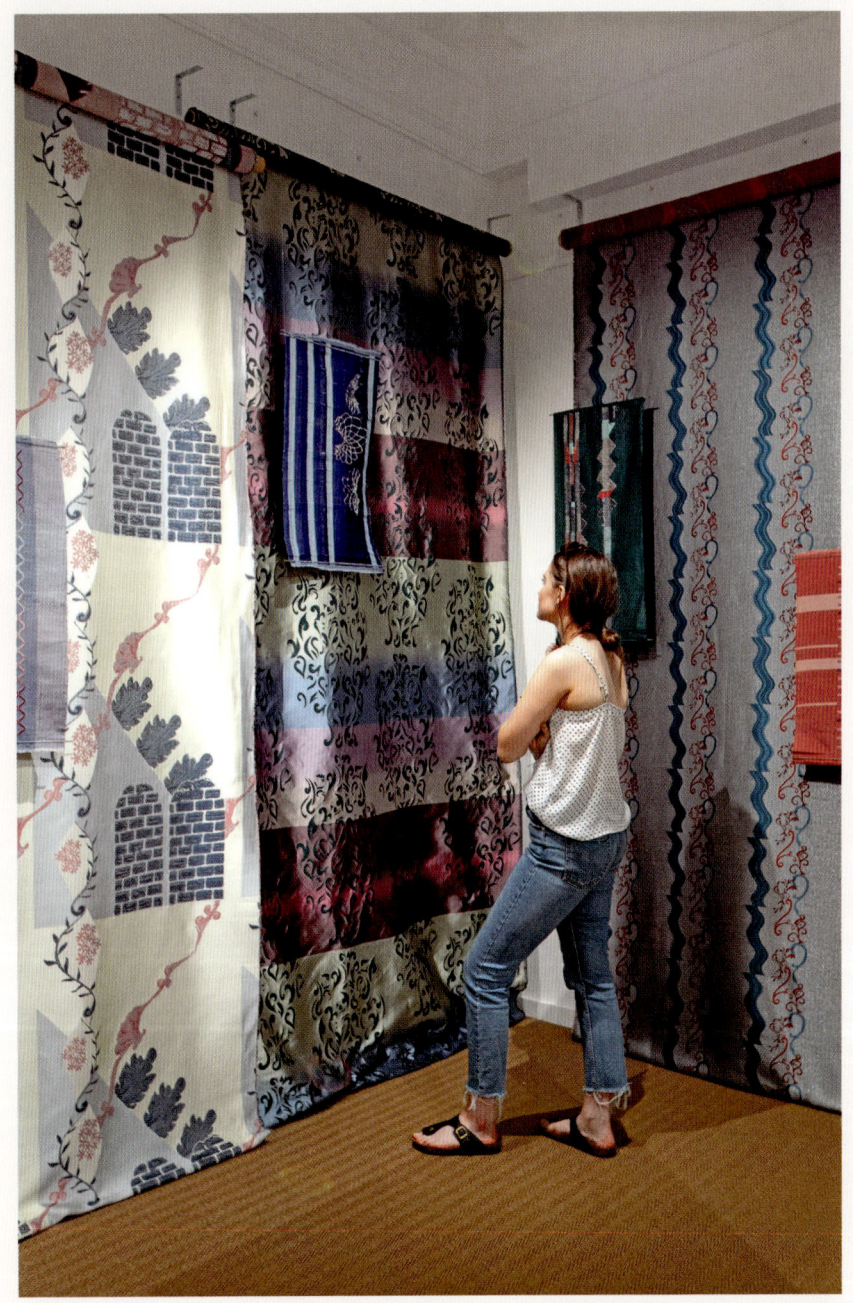

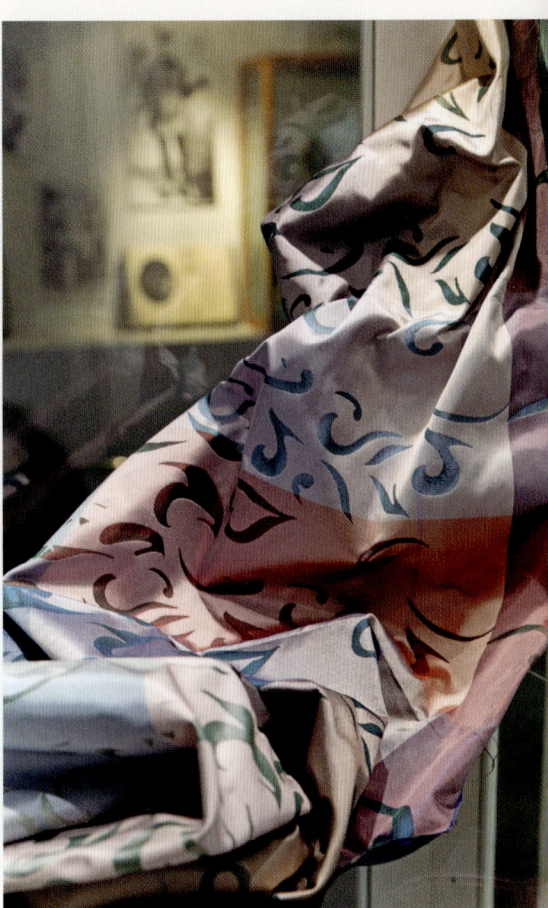

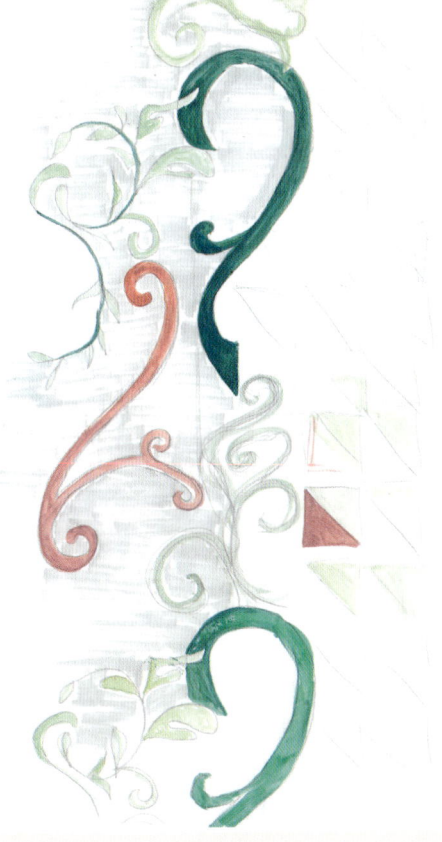

HANNAH ROBSON

Bizarre and curious silks

Reimagined patterns and imagery can inspire textile art with a range of media and techniques. Hannah Robson is a weaver based in West Yorkshire. She was commissioned to develop a project celebrating the legacy of the Huguenot silk weavers, Calvinist Protestants who fled religious persecution in France. She studied historical fabrics in the Warner Textile Archive and the company archives of David Walters Fabrics, as well as the objects and stories in the Huguenot Museum and French Hospital Collection. Researching Spitalfields silk weavers, she was inspired by the work of James Leman, whose name is now synonymous with the so-called 'bizarre' style of the early 18th century. Bizarre style is characterised by unusual combinations of motif, e.g. architectural details with Chinoiserie motifs, or florals with geometric forms. Hannah brought together her own unusual compositions, combining motifs and shapes found within the museum collection with floral elements from silk designs of the period. Her colour choices were inspired by the richness and strong, contrasting hues from her historical research.

Hannah worked with David Walters Fabrics to develop three jacquard fabrics informed by her research. She also created a series of handwoven pieces, inspired by historical weaving techniques.

OPPOSITE, LEFT
Bizarre & Curious Silks *(2019) by Hannah Robson. Jacquard and handwoven silk.*

OPPOSITE, ABOVE RIGHT *Jacquard woven silks by Hannah Robson.*

OPPOSITE, BELOW RIGHT *Initial museum sketches exploring 'bizarre' combinations of motif and pattern.*

IMITATION AND ORIGINALITY

Throughout the book so far, we have observed, documented and gathered imagery, creating a mini archive of visual source material. Whether brought together with a purpose or accumulated organically, the things we surround ourselves with inspire and feed our practice, often without us even realising it. Our 'original' creative work is the summation of a lifetime of sensory experiences, whether we know it or not. These influences, memories, images and objects combine to inform our own personal style. But where does inspiration end and imitation begin?

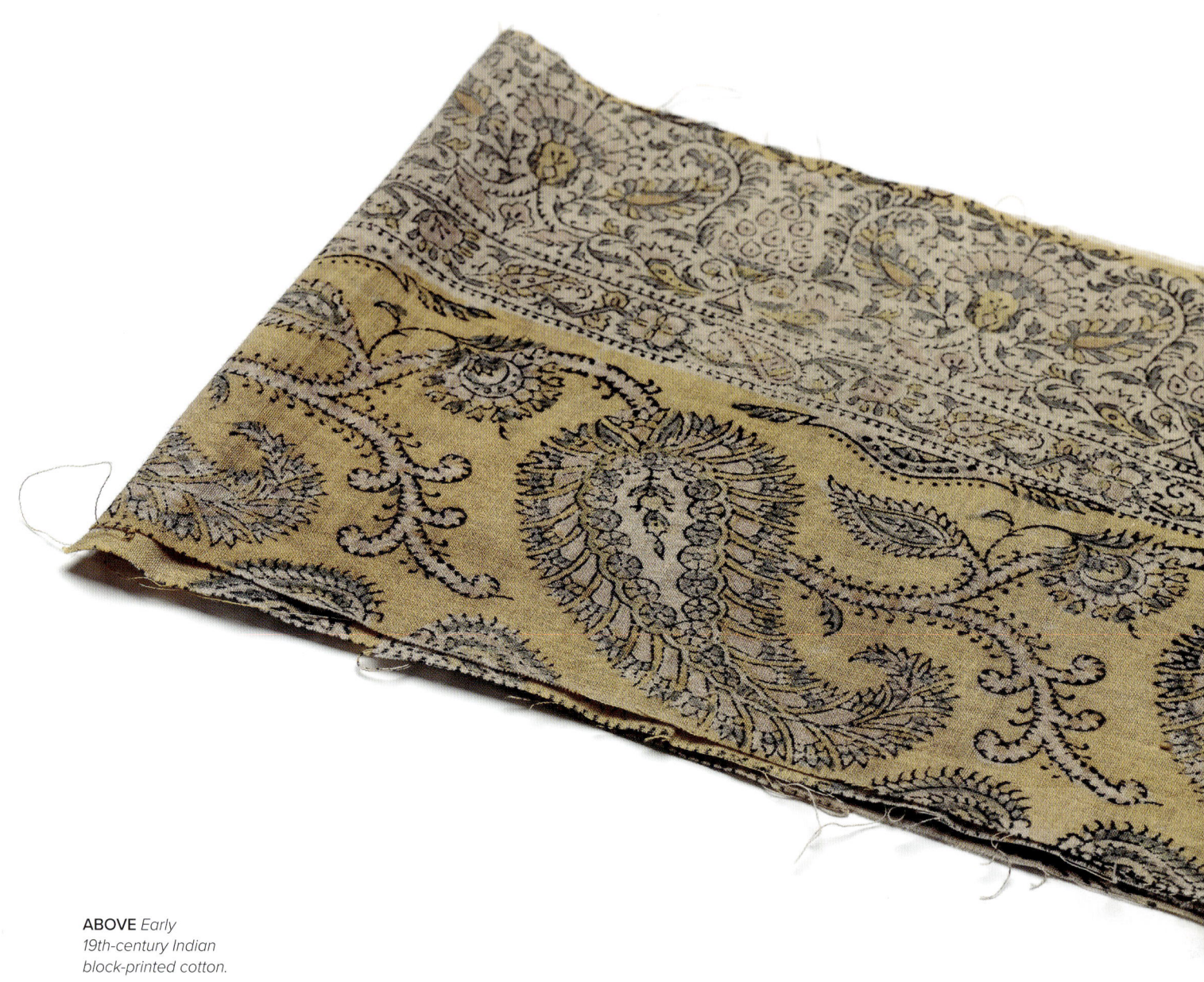

ABOVE *Early 19th-century Indian block-printed cotton.*

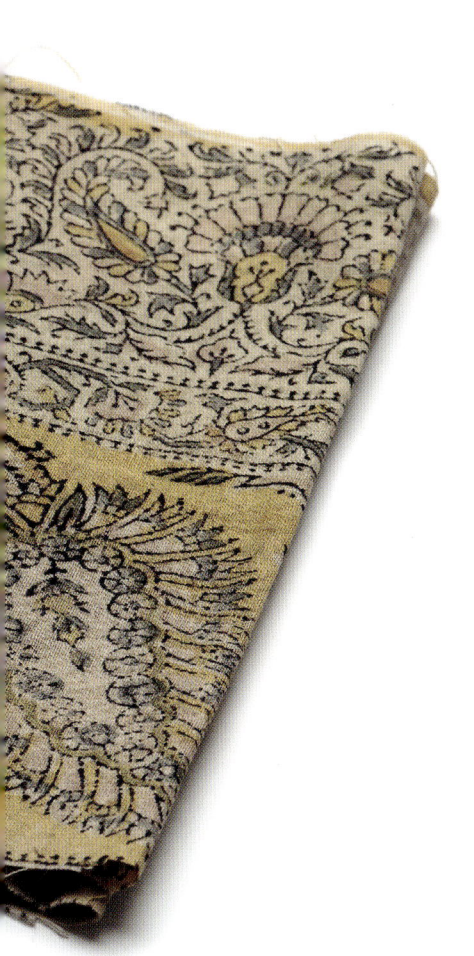

Textiles' tangled past

The history of textiles is full of stories of imitation and ideas exchanged back and forth across different cultures and times. The movement of cultural ideas – techniques, technologies, materials and patterns – is pivotal to the history of textiles. It is a fascinating and tangled web.

Cross-cultural influences can be seen in many of the world's iconic textile patterns, and many are less straightforward than they seem. Take, for example, the origins of the paisley pattern. The iconic feathered, teardrop-shaped motif known as 'boteh' (meaning bush or thicket in Persian) can be traced back to Iran to at least the 16th century. Europeans probably first encountered the semi-stylised floral patterns on fine handwoven shawls brought back from Kashmir and made fashionable by the trendsetters of Paris around 1800. This prompted a high demand for the exquisite shawls that took many months to weave by hand, which in turn enticed manufacturers in Britain and France to produce cheaper imitations. One of the centres of shawl production was Paisley in Scotland, where industrialists vied with each other to create designs more quickly or cheaply, or to introduce innovative design ideas, thus driving technological advancements. British and European paisley patterns became bigger and more complex and, due to the lack of cultural awareness, the designs lost their original identity. In turn, British and French design agents took these designs to the Kashmir weavers to be copied. This crisscrossing of inspiration, cultural appropriation and exploitation makes it hard to know where 'paisley' truly belongs. It certainly has a complex and international lineage.

Similar stories of imitation and exploitation can be seen in the lineage of Indian printed cottons, or 'chintz', which were imitated and bastardised by British and European manufacturers for European tastes; or the industrialised copying of Indonesian batik fabrics that resulted in the evolution of Dutch wax or African wax fabric, as it is known today, manufactured in Europe and the UK to exploit African markets. Today we would refer to this as cultural appropriation: 'the adoption of an element of one culture by members of another culture on their own terms and for their own profit'[5]. Cultural appropriation reflects an imbalance of power, enabling people of a more dominant (wealthier, more privileged) culture to exploit the material culture of another.

Many museums and collections owe their very existence to the practice of 'mining from the past'. The world-famous Victoria and Albert Museum (formerly the South Kensington Museum) was founded on collections purchased from the Great Exhibition of 1851. This international exhibition showcased the industrial and cultural products of many nations and promoted British colonial power. It is, perhaps, less well known that a vast number of exhibits were purchased as educational resources for the first Design Schools (later to become Schools of Art). Creating direct copies from existing examples of 'good' design from around the world was an established teaching method at that time, and many of today's college and university textile collections can be attributed to their use as teaching aids. Frequently, the items that survive are those that were thought to be most visually appealing, collected for their potential as a design resource for the next generation of designers to trace and copy from.

IS IT OKAY TO COPY FROM THE PAST?

From a legal point of view, today these issues come under the heading of 'intellectual property'. In the UK, in broad terms, this means that a person's creative output – designs, inventions, literary and artistic work, etc. – automatically belongs to them unless signed over or given away freely to someone else. There is no need to label your work as 'copyright' – it is already yours! This also means that it is against the law to copy someone else's creative work without permission. However, this protection only lasts for a set length of time: for written or two-dimensional artistic work, such as textile patterns, it's 70 years after the creator's death; where the author or artist is unknown, it's 70 years from the end of the year in which it was created, published or exhibited (whichever is later).

RIGHT *A combination of European and Indian patterns can be seen in this 19th-century quilt fragment in 'Turkey red'.*

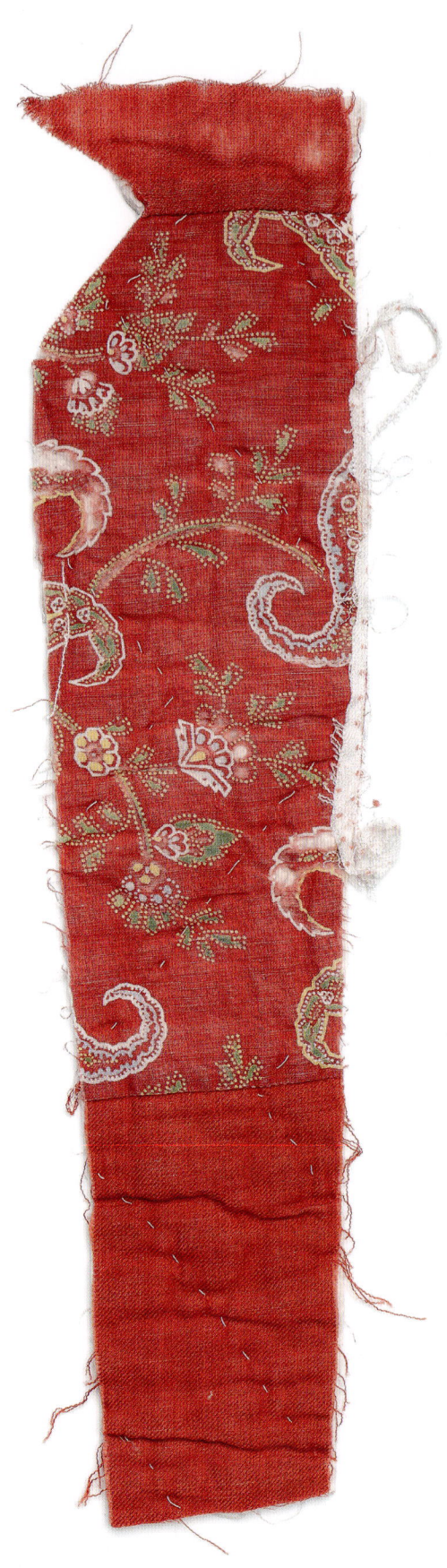

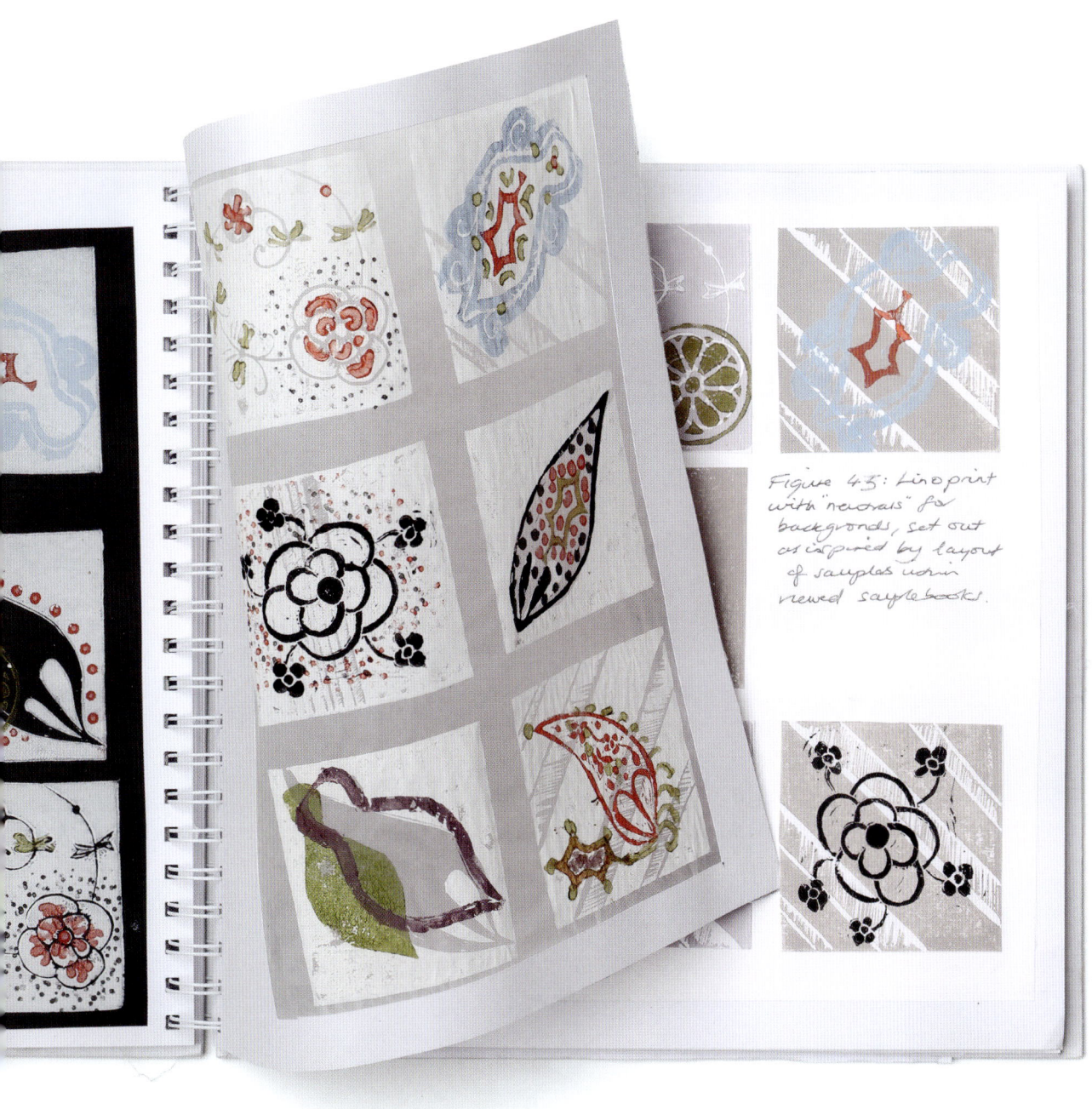

Figure 43: Lino print with "neutrals" for backgrounds, set out as inspired by layout of samples within viewed samplebooks.

From the point of view of using 'found' imagery or historic textile patterns in our own artwork, a lot of older designs will be beyond copyright and can legally be reproduced. However, before you reproduce a design, it is worth considering *why*? Are you hoping to create a replica of it? If so, what is the creative intention? Are you at risk of creating a fake or forgery?

Consider the word 'transcription', also a way of creating a copy: when we transcribe a letter or a piece of music, it goes through a secondary process that can subtly change it, even though the essential elements remain the same. By changing the materials, dimensions (2D to 3D or 3D to 2D), presentation or setting, we subtly alter the way an object is understood. Perhaps this is a way for artists to reference the past but challenge perceptions. We can also explore ways to combine new with old, to add layers or additional elements to tell a story.

BEING A CONSIDERATE TEXTILE ARTIST

These are sensitive issues for many, and rightly so. Generations of cultural appropriation and exploitation have left many communities feeling vulnerable and on their guard. So how can we explore historical sources in a respectful way?

BE MORE CURIOUS As we have seen, everything we experience influences us, everything in textiles is connected, so do your research. Before you 'take' inspiration from something, dig a little deeper; ask questions, read about its origins. What does it mean to the people who made or used it? Why is it here?

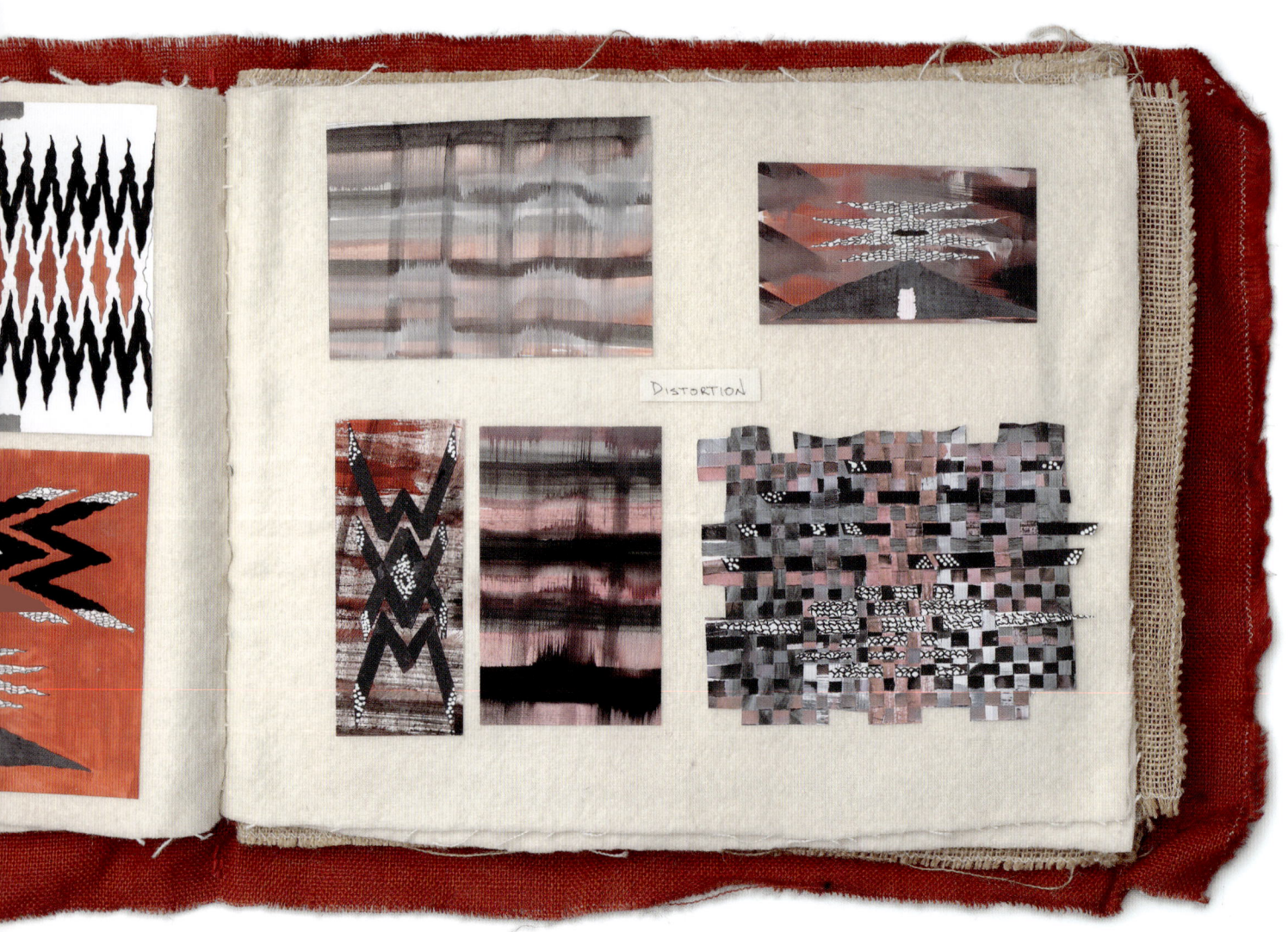

DISTORTION

ASK 'WHY?' Why does this object, pattern or costume interest you? What is it that you aim to achieve by studying it? Try to seek out authentic sources of information, such as oral histories or authors with direct cultural experience. Think about your own point of view and how this might influence your take on the subject. If you are researching it with a view to telling a story, are you the best person to do so, or is there someone else who could provide a more authentic point of view?

COLLECT WIDELY Look at a diverse range of sources (exhibitions, places, cultural objects, techniques, images, books, films), gather together the things that you love, and embrace a broad range of influences. Combining ideas from various sources to inform and develop your own individual response is a good way to be more authentic in your practice and avoid directly copying.

GIVE CREDIT WHERE IT'S DUE Acknowledging your sources is a positive thing, rather than an admission that you have 'pinched' someone else's ideas. In the academic world, it is a key principle that sources should be cited, whether that is the author of a book, the name of a designer, or the details of an item in a collection. This practice has several benefits, one being that by name checking and celebrating the originator, you show that you understand its origins and meanings; and by leaving these 'breadcrumbs', researchers (or creatives) following you can retrace your steps and look at the original context.

There are various ways to acknowledge your sources, depending on your work and how other people interact with it. Perhaps the easiest is to mention your research sources in the interpretive text that accompanies an exhibition. This might be in an artist statement, catalogue or exhibition label. In the digital world, a weblink or tag that directs your audience to further reading or source material can be a useful acknowledgement.

OPPOSITE *In her research journal, Karen Charlton explores the patterns woven into a Navaho rug. Through careful observation of the rug, she noticed subtle distortion of surface. Background reading helped her to investigate the origins of the motifs and possible links back to indigenous lands and natural phenomena.*

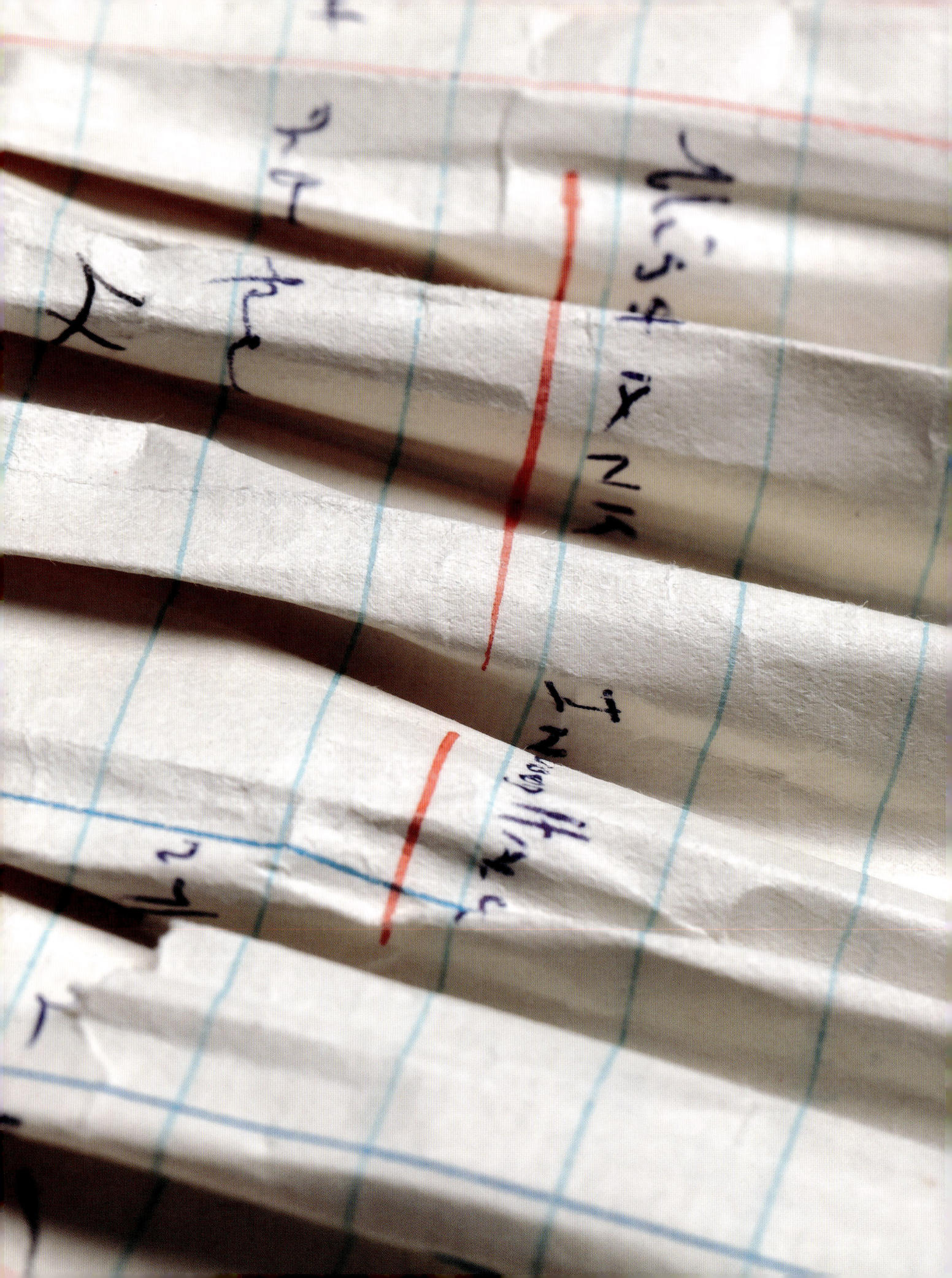

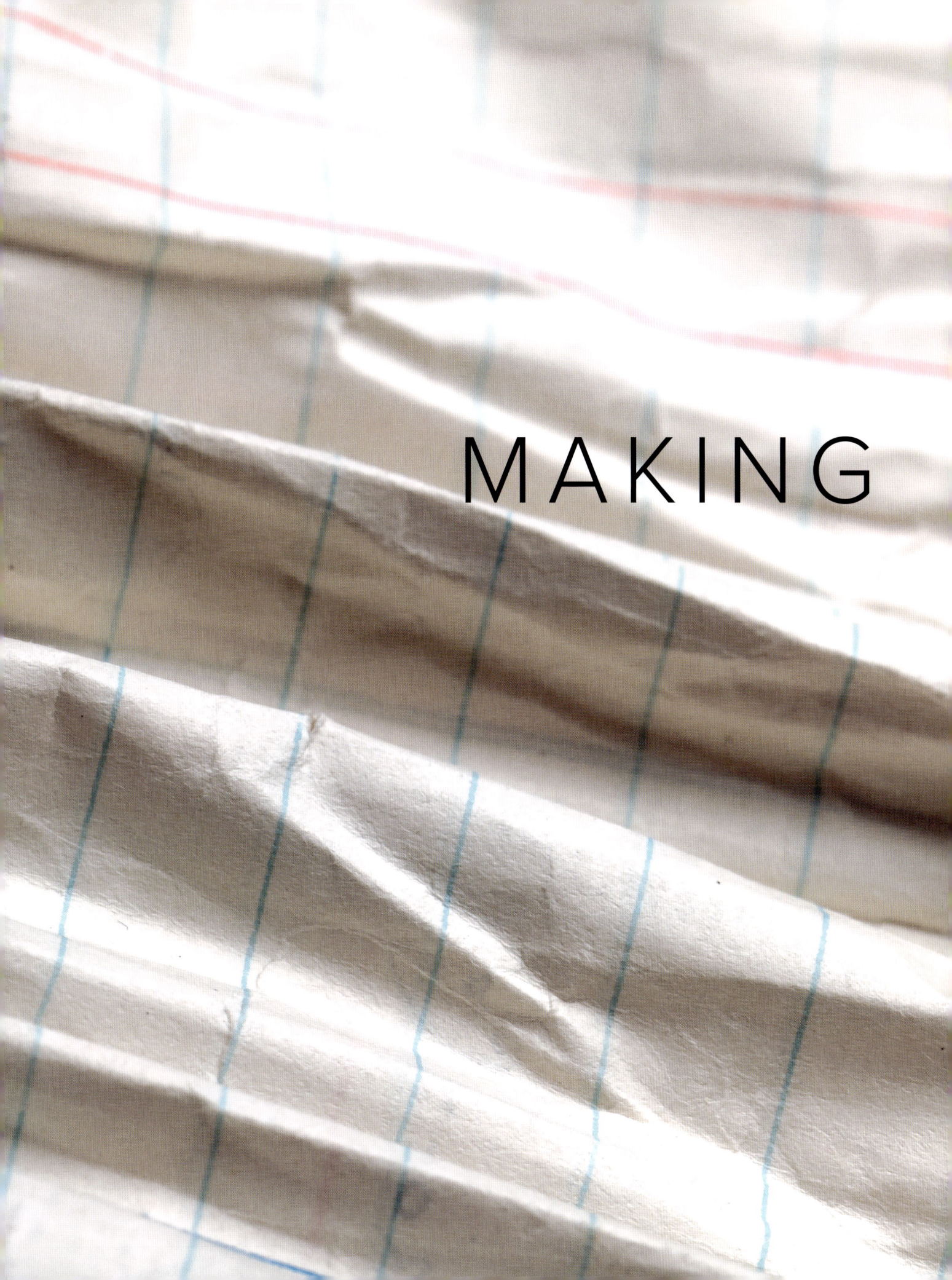

MAKING

MATERIALS

I love to use old textiles in my work. Age-worn cotton and linen sheets, vintage patchwork, snippets of printed silks and fancy woven fabrics all have their charm. The seductive qualities of vintage fabrics, sourced from second-hand shops or from your own scrap bag, make them both a visual treat and a sustainable option. Vintage fabrics can also lend an authentic quality to projects inspired by historical themes.

Old household textiles are often the most abundant: cotton and linen sheets, pillowcases, tablecloths and mats, from a time before duvets and wipe-clean surfaces. Old cotton and linen textiles are wonderful for dyeing and printing, but do check the fibre composition to ensure they are 100% natural fibre. Look out for embroidery, patches or old laundry markings, which can become interesting features in their own right.

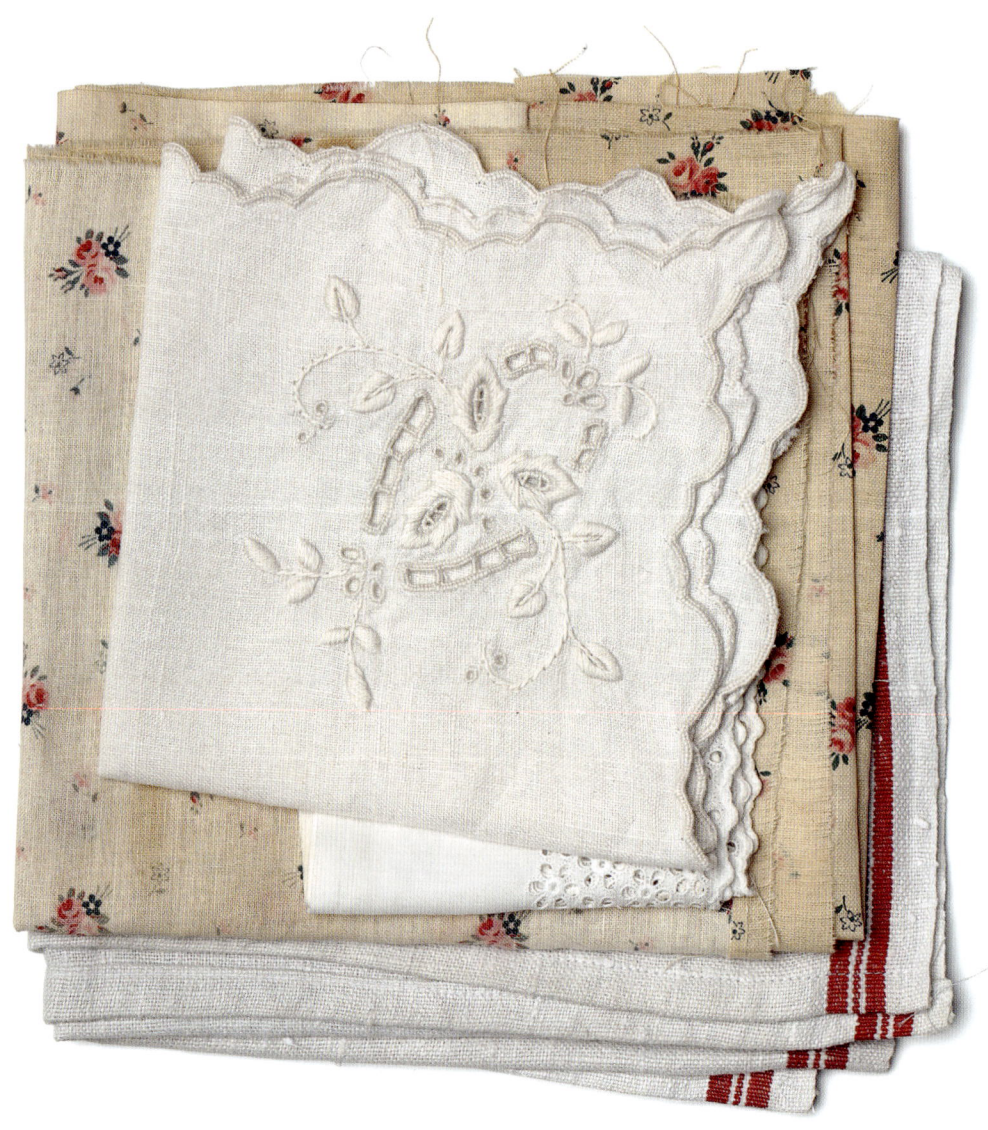

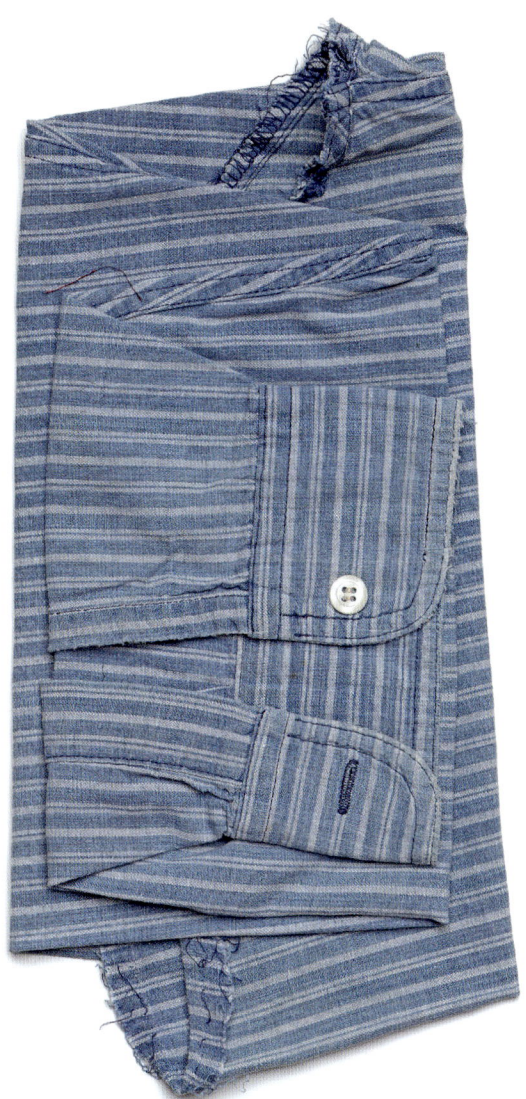

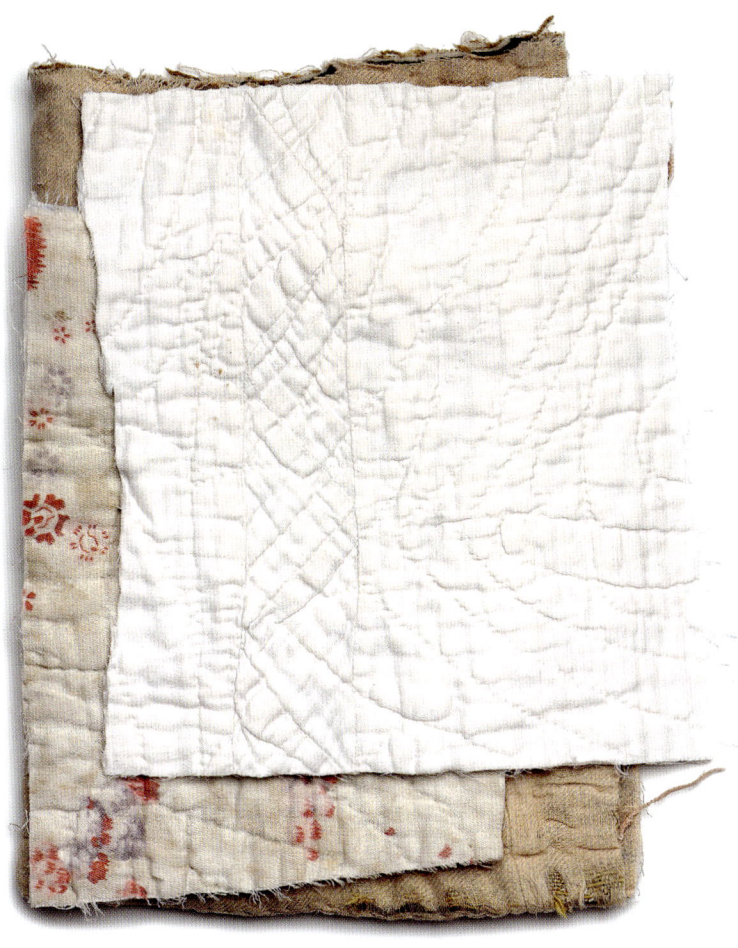

For coloured and patterned fabrics, look for vintage silk scarves, dress fabrics or old curtains, depending on the weight of fabric you require. If you struggle to find sufficient period textiles for your project, seek out similar colours or patterns in second-hand clothes. If carefully selected, pre-worn and washed fabrics, such as cotton shirts, denim or prints, can blend in well with older pieces.

To provide more substance to projects, heavier-weight textiles, such as old wool blankets, sacking or canvas, can become useful backings, and if these are an undyed natural fibre, they can easily be dyed to co-ordinate with a colour theme.

Alongside the textiles themselves, I collect vintage threads, trimmings and buttons. My thread boxes are idiosyncratic, full of unrepeatable, faded colours and unusual thread qualities – glacé cotton, art silk, linen carpet thread – and I love to have old cotton reels around my studio, as they are so tactile and often have beautiful labels.

OPPOSITE AND ABOVE
Woven linen towels, embroidered table linen, old cotton shirts and old quilt pieces.

Caring for old textiles

People often worry about how best to store old textiles to keep them from deteriorating, but there are a few simple things we can all do to care for our precious fabrics. While each item will have slightly different requirements, there are four main 'enemies' to consider.

LIGHT

Ultraviolet (UV) light causes fading in coloured textiles and can make fabric (especially silk) brittle over time. Avoid displaying precious textiles in direct sunlight and ideally store away from sunlight altogether. I display antique textiles in my hallway, which has no windows and only indirect sunlight.

DIRT

Stains can cause chemical reactions and also make your textiles more delicious to pests such as clothes moths (see Pests). Embedded dirt can damage fabrics if left uncleaned. Robust white cotton or linen fabrics can be carefully washed and air dried. Before laundering any coloured or printed items it is best to do a test, ideally in an inconspicuous area. Use damp cotton wool to dab the area and observe any colour transference. If in doubt, seek advice from a conservation professional.

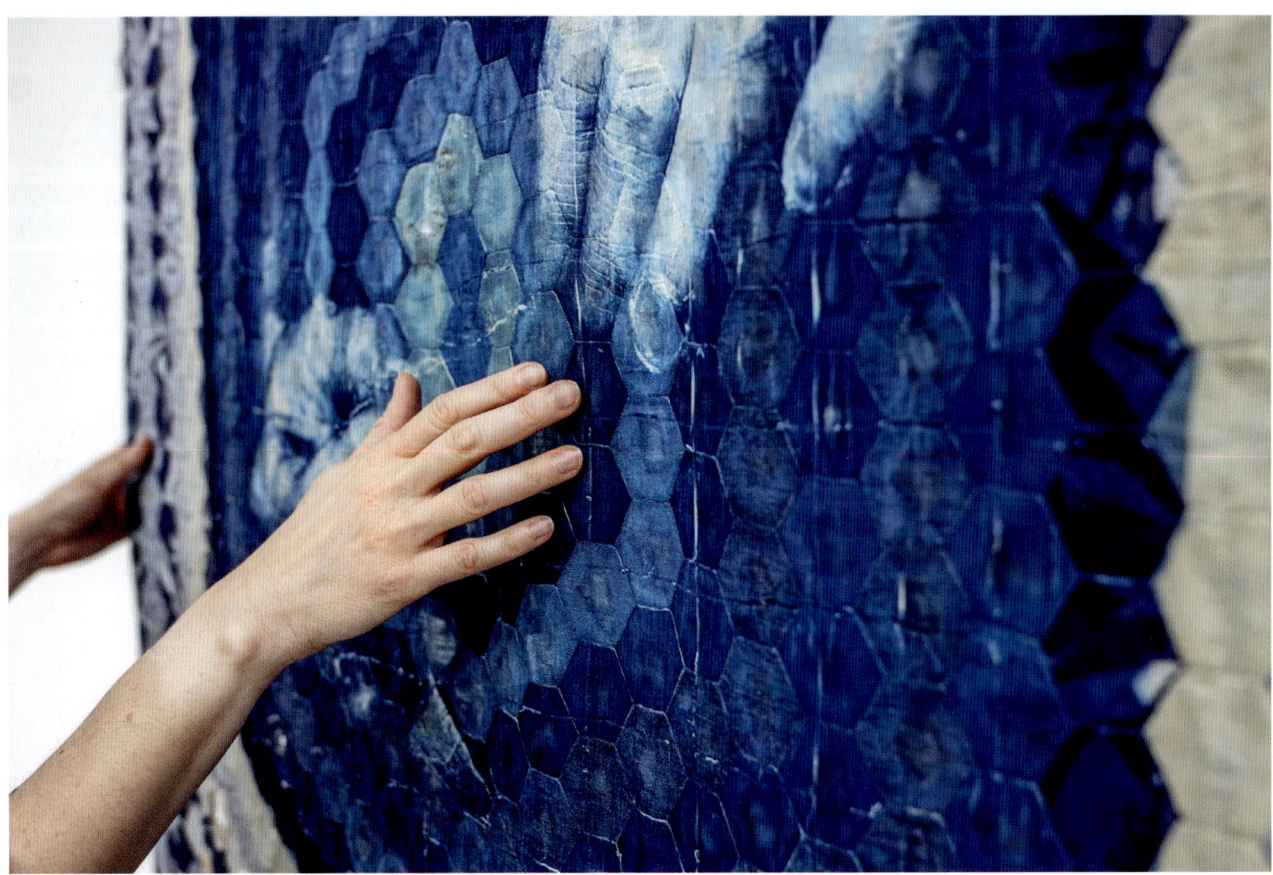

DAMP

Moist conditions can cause mould and mildew on textiles. Excess humidity can also act as a catalyst for chemical reactions with old dyes, causing textiles to break down. Weighted silks (those mordanted with iron or tin salts) are particularly susceptible to this. From a conservation point of view, 50–60% humidity is considered to be ideal for most textiles, with an ideal temperature of 13–14°C (56°F). Avoid wrapping textiles in plastic and keep them away from radiators. A steady temperature and good ventilation are preferable.

PESTS

When bringing old textiles into your home it is worth taking some basic precautions to avoid introducing pests. One of the most common issues I encounter is clothes moths, which find wool fibres particularly tasty. Freezing is the best measure and can be done successfully at home. I double or triple wrap the textile, first in tissue then in a polythene bag, and place it in my home freezer for two weeks. I then leave the textile wrapped up at room temperature for a week or two, then return it to the freezer for a further two weeks, to be absolutely sure of breaking the moths' lifecycle.

It is a good idea to check stored items regularly for signs of pests or damage, shaking clothes and vacuuming around the base of wardrobes and cupboards.

Storing old textiles

Most garments can be hung on a coat hanger (padded with acid-free tissue paper) and covered with a cotton (not polythene) garment bag, such as a Tyvek bag, which is open at the bottom. My most treasured textile items, however, are wrapped in layers of acid-free tissue paper and stored in archival storage boxes in a dry, dark place, such as a wardrobe.

While it is important to know about the risks and how they can be mitigated, you should consider a balance between preservation and practical application and how much you want to be able to view, handle or use old textiles. Nothing lasts forever and even heritage professionals talk about 'managing change'. If you have precious textile items in need of conservation or specialist storage, it is best to get advice from a professional (see page 124 for more details).

OPPOSITE Inheritance (2024) by Hannah Lamb, detail. Cyanotype on vintage patchwork.

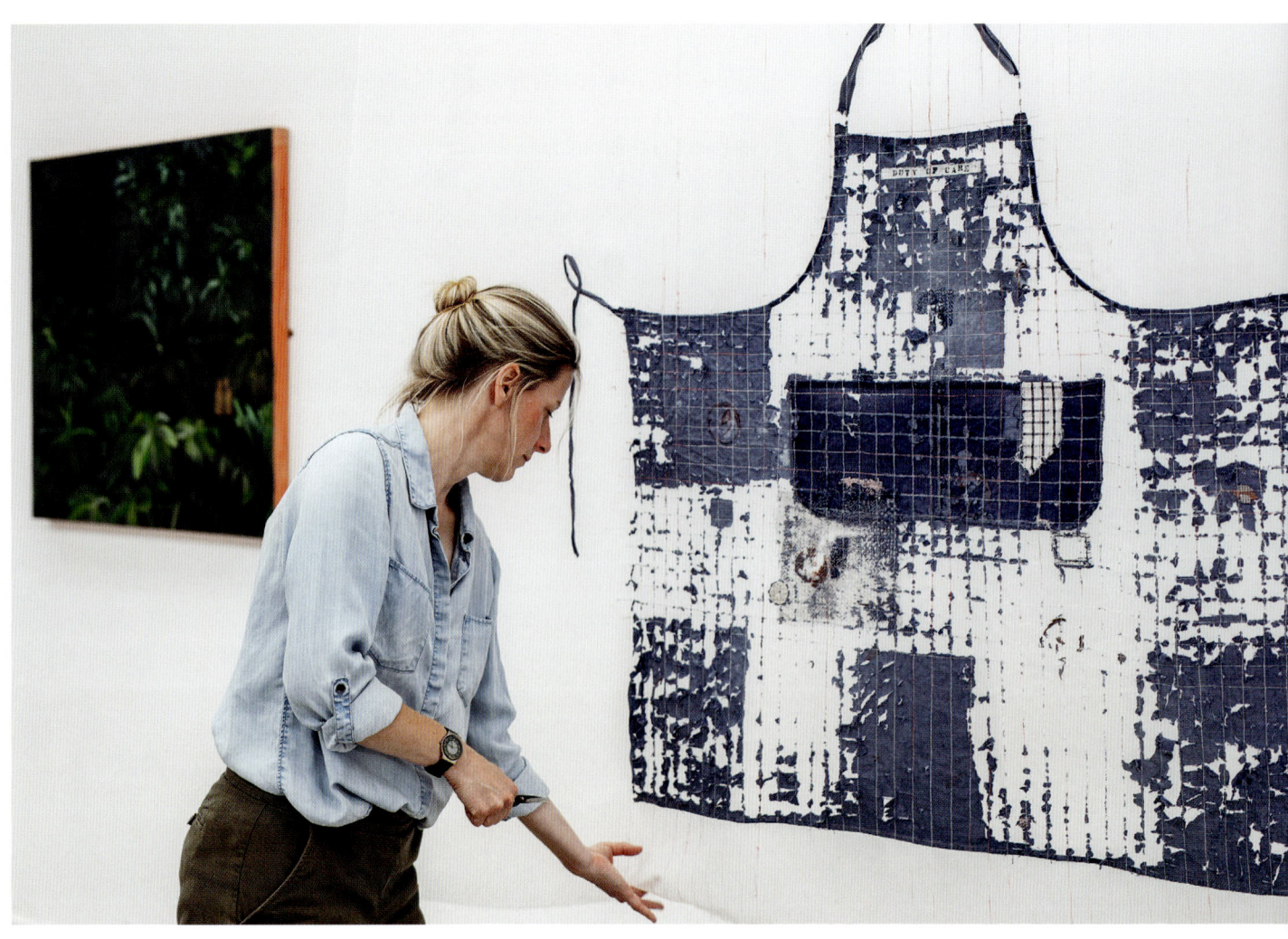

To cut or not to cut?

If you are lucky enough to have a collection of vintage textiles or costumes, you may be faced with some tricky decisions. If you have inherited some pieces, you may be thinking, 'What do I do with all this stuff?' You may feel conflicted about what to keep, what to reuse or repurpose, or whether items should be kept intact. Ultimately, they are yours, so it is your choice what you do with them. Below I have included a few questions that may help you to make some decisions:

What does the item mean to you? Does it have a family connection or hold good/bad memories for you?

What does it mean to other people? Is it a particularly rare or valuable piece? Does it have symbolic meaning for someone else? Are there other people you should ask before using or transforming it?

ABOVE Duty of Care II (2022) by Hannah Lamb. This vintage apron already had damaged areas and darning. Additional patches, hand and machine stitch were added before deconstructing with a devoré print process.

Would cutting into this textile remove its original meaning or significance? Or would it extend its life if you were to transform it into something more useful, beautiful or meaningful? Is it more sustainable to use up this fabric rather than buy new?

Where you have a plentiful supply of a particular material, you might consider keeping the best or most interesting pieces for your collection, using any that is damaged for your projects. If you are unsure, it's always best to give it some time, and if in doubt, don't cut!

Digital print alternatives

As we have seen, it isn't always appropriate to cut up and work directly with historical textiles. It could be important to preserve the original, or we might just have a tiny fragment to work from. When a material is particularly precious or scarce, I am sometimes reluctant to make a first cut or to try out something, for fear of messing it up. But if I have plenty of fabric, I am free to test ideas and explore different possibilities. This is where digital print can help, enabling us to recreate something that closely resembles the original.

Digital print has lots of wonderful qualities when it comes to reproducing historical textiles. Incredible detail can be reproduced and it's perfect for capturing subtle colour variations, such as age marks or delicate print and dye effects. Professional digital print retains the original handle of the cloth, unlike transfers, allowing you to stitch and work into the cloth after printing. Digital print can also be done on a really large scale. This might mean enlarging your imagery, or it could be that you repeat a small design across a much larger area, even an entire length, of fabric.

There are a number of online services available to the general public. These allow you to upload a photo or digital artwork, and to select the fabric and size of print, then the finished fabric is mailed directly to your door. The turnaround is usually quick and the quality of print is generally excellent. While it is possible to successfully feed fabric through a home inkjet printer, which can be useful for quick results and small pieces, the range of fabrics can be limited and the print may not be washable. I would always recommend outsourcing to a professional digital printer where the outcome needs to be long-lasting, wearable or washable (see Suppliers, page 124).

DEVELOPING DIGITAL ARTWORK

The quality of your finished digital print relies heavily on the quality of your original imagery. If you are working from a digital photograph that is blurry, distorted or out of focus, you can't easily put that detail back in. Even though photographs can be digitally retouched to change colour or erase blemishes, it is always much easier to start with the best-quality image you can get. I generally create digital images by using either a digital camera or a digital scanner:

Digital camera Whether using a digital camera or a smart phone, check your settings and aim for images to be a minimum of 300dpi. Pay attention to the photo you are taking to make sure the image you capture is at the correct angle, in focus and well lit. Wherever possible I try to take photos in natural daylight – a north-facing windowsill is ideal. Once you have taken a photo, check it for quality and colour.

Digital scanner Whether a separate desktop scanner or part of a home printer, a scanner is great for capturing flat objects such as fabrics, buttons, trimmings and even some garments. The only limitations are the dimensions of your scanner. Your source object should be scanned at a high resolution, usually at the same dots per inch (dpi) as your final print. However, I particularly like the effect of scanning objects at a high resolution and then enlarging for print. If you want to do this, you will need to scan at a higher resolution to ensure that the image retains its detail when enlarged. Below is a guide to some common sizes:

- **FROM A4 TO A2:**
  Scan your work/object at 600dpi for A2 artwork at 300dpi.

- **FROM A4 TO A1:**
  Scan your work/object at 850dpi for A1 artwork at 300dpi.

- **FROM A4 TO A0:**
  Scan your work/object at 1300dpi for A0 artwork at 300dpi.

ALTERING YOUR IMAGERY

Once you have your scans or digital photographs, you may wish to make some changes. How you go about doing this may depend on your skill with digital media. At a professional level, software such as Adobe Photoshop holds an infinite range of possibilities, with digital tools that can completely transform your imagery. Although exciting, the sheer scale of possibilities may surpass what you actually need for your project.

It's worth noting that many of the digital printing companies include basic editing tools within their online interface, meaning that you can upload your image, change its size, crop it, or collage different images together. This allows you to try out ideas and visualise them on your computer screen, saving time and money and avoiding waste. I would

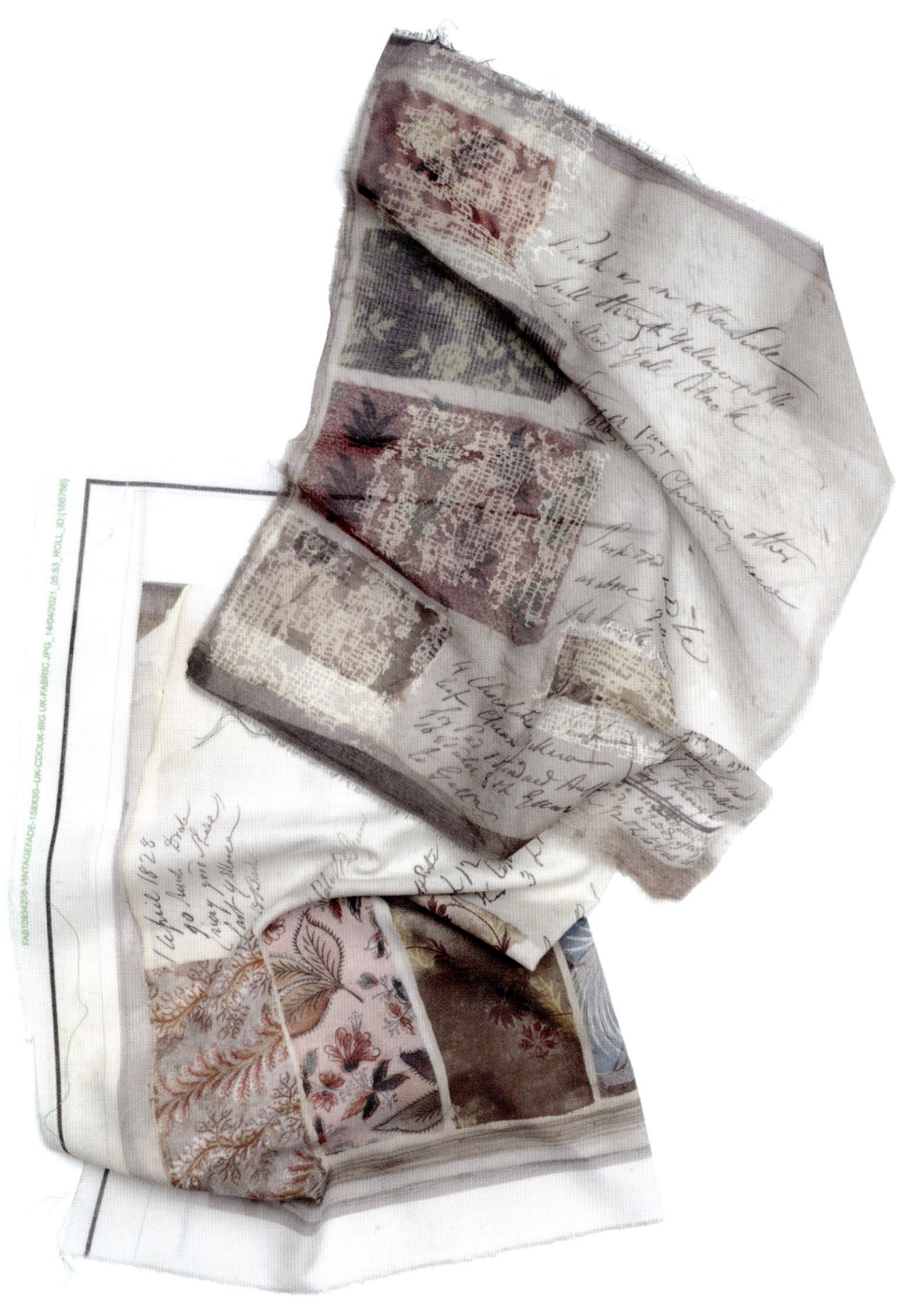

recommend that you play around with your imagery online first, then order a printed sample to see how it looks on your chosen fabric.

A NOTE ON FILE FORMATS

If you are uploading your digital artwork to an online print platform, it's likely that only certain kinds of image files will be accepted, so always check before creating your artwork. The most common digital file format for this purpose is JPEG (.jpg or .JPG). These compressed files take up less space and are quicker to upload or transfer. Because of the way they are compressed, some information (and quality) can be lost, so they are not always best for very large-scale or high-quality projects.

TEXT AND TEXTILES

Through the ages, text and textiles have gone hand in hand, whether boldly exclaiming their message or quietly whispering a name. Banners, ceremonial objects and religious textiles expressed ideas with bold lettering, or imbued the wearer with prayers or charms in sparkling gold and silver. These very public textiles were designed to communicate a clear message to an audience, testifying to the beliefs and ideals of the groups they represented. Similarly, sports kits also hold powerful significance for the wearers and their followers. Team and player names need to be easily identified from a distance, but the kits often hold some special magic off the pitch, as souvenirs capturing a moment in time.

On household linens, elaborate monograms were a signifier of status and family connection, while smaller versions might be seen on handkerchiefs marked with the owner's initials. Hand-stitched laundry marks, picked out in red, were used to identify personal and household items in communal laundries.

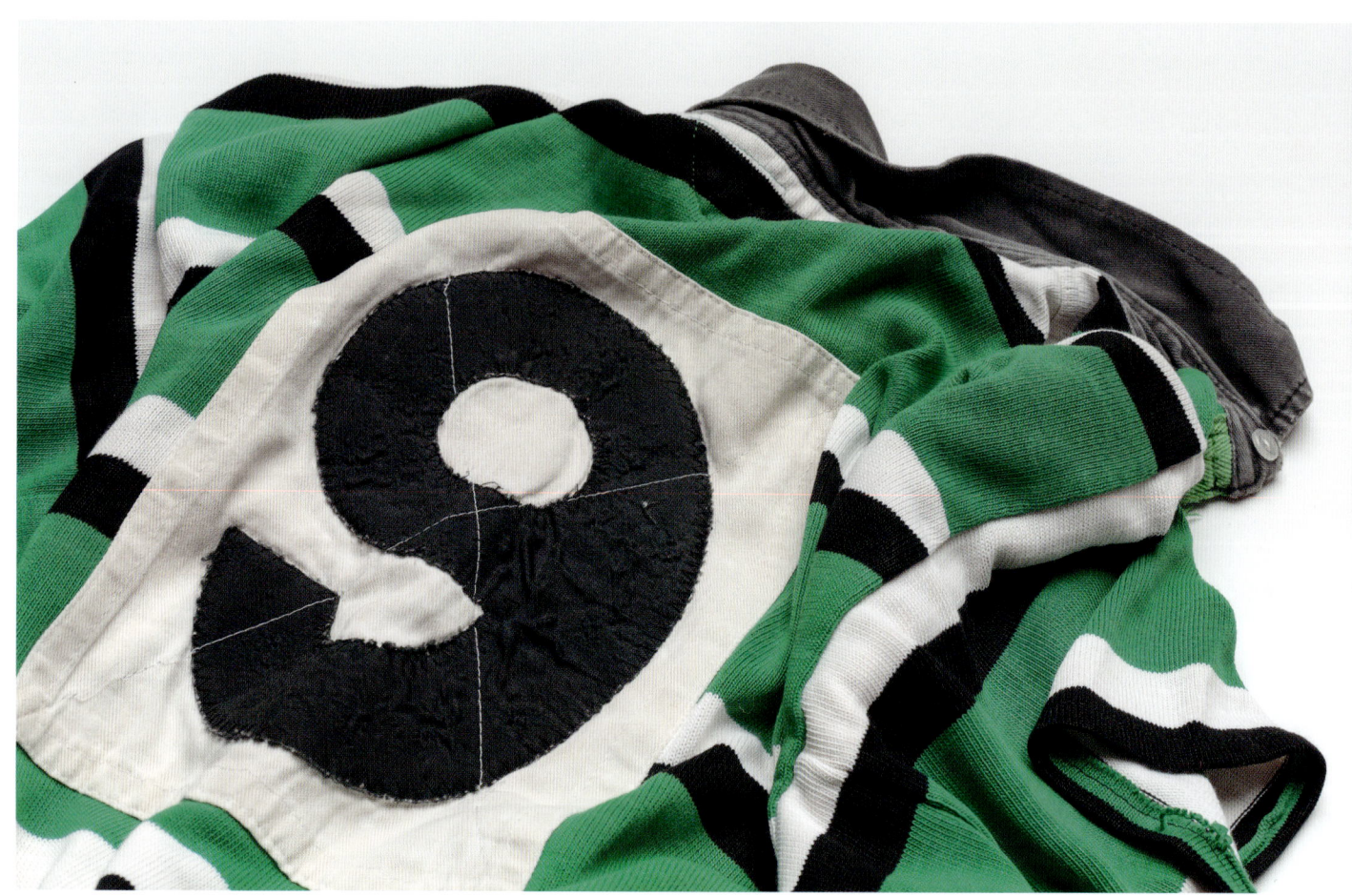

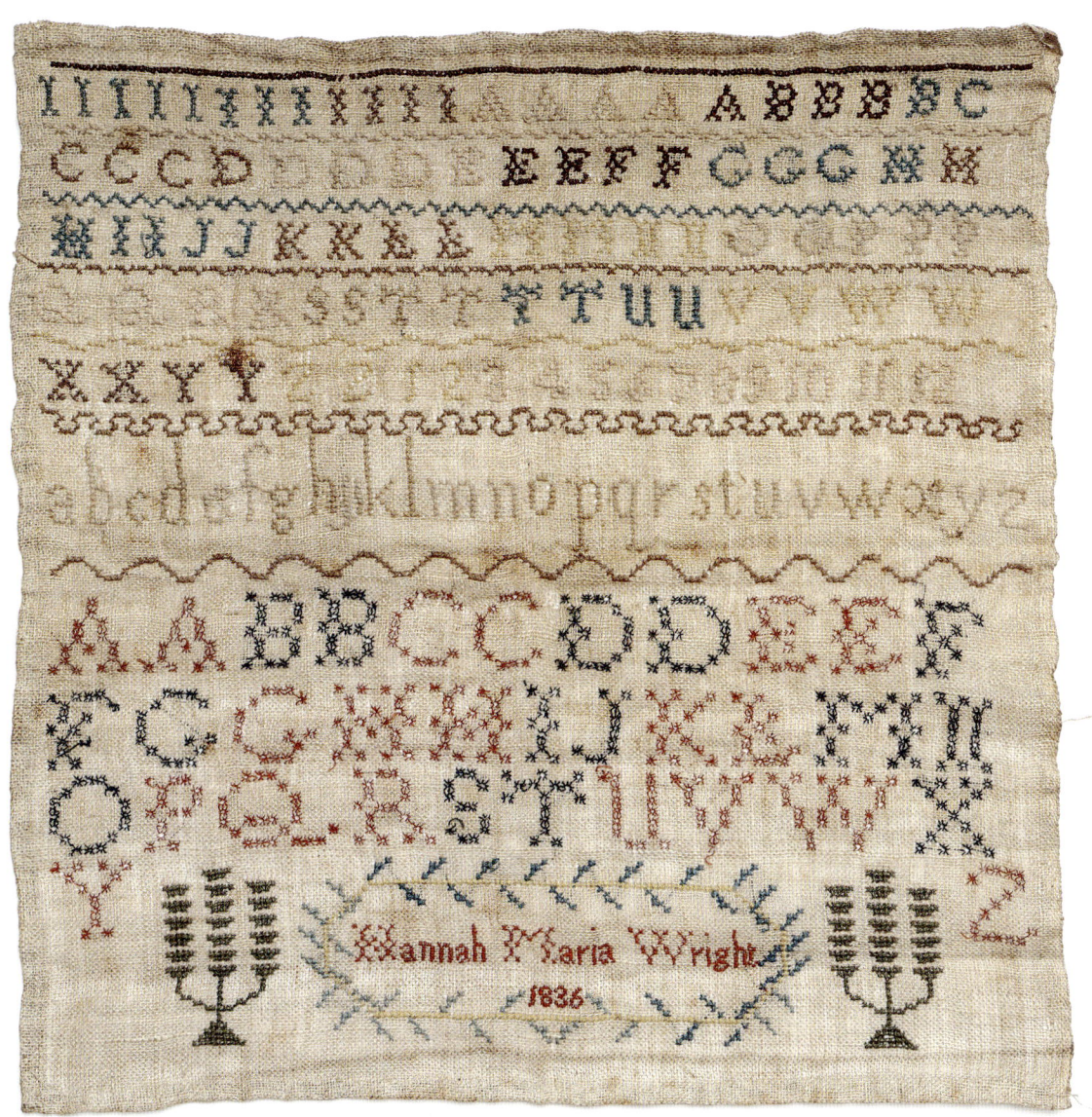

Another example of stitched text commonly seen in historical collections are needlework samplers. These were usually created as instructional or practice pieces, with the stitcher learning important skills for her future life. In my family, we have a sampler created by my four-times great aunt Hannah Wright. She would have been aged eight in 1836, and would have stitched this piece both as a way of learning her letters and practising the stitching that might help her gain a good position working as a servant in a wealthy household. The rows of carefully stitched alphabets were important practice for labelling the household linens and under-garments of a big household. Needlework samplers were also worked by more affluent women and girls, as a respectable pastime. Stitching samplers and other items demonstrated feminine accomplishment and piety. While stitched samplers had a purpose, they also provided a creative outlet for makers at a time when European societies imposed significant restrictions on women's lives. The fact that some samplers include the name of the needlewoman gives us a rare glimpse into women's lives that is seldom seen in historical written documents.

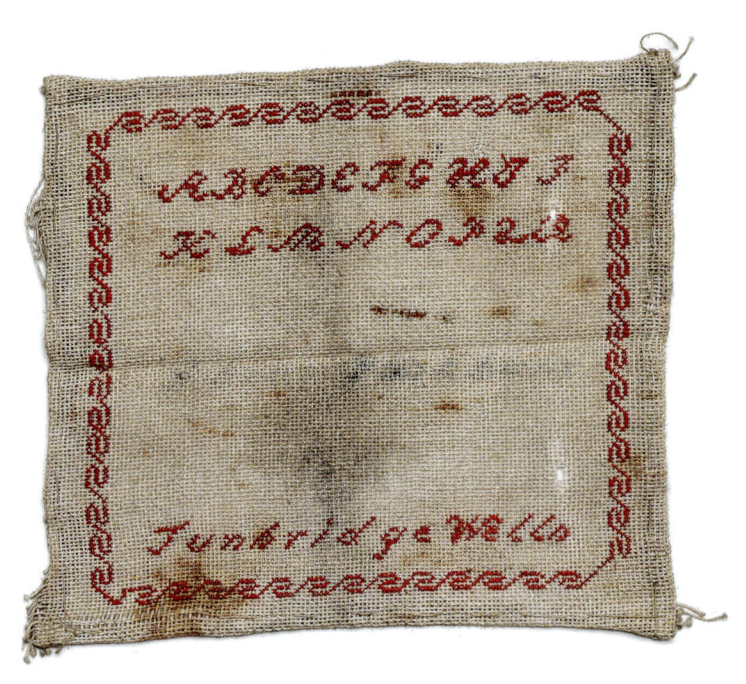

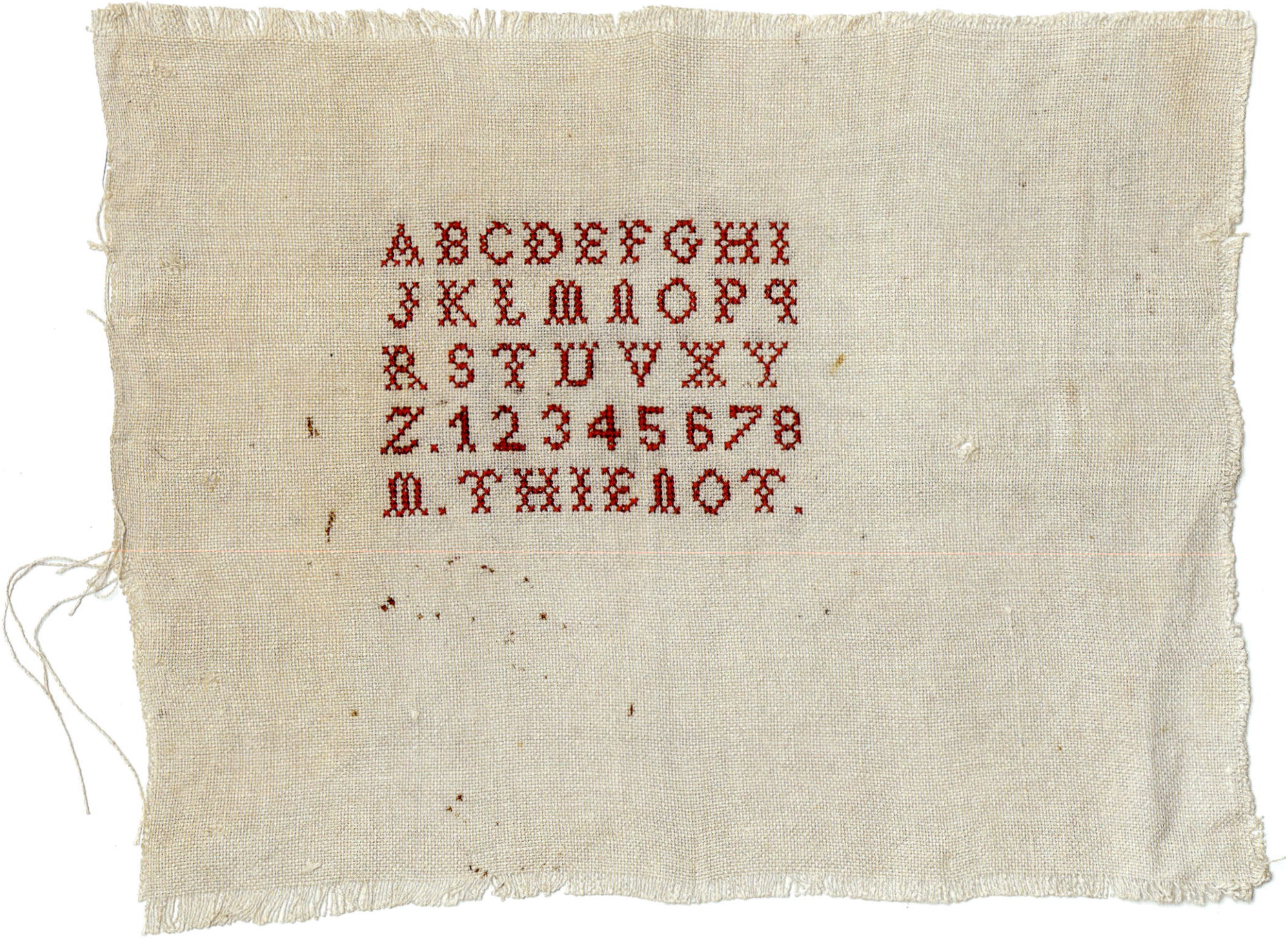

Why use text?

As modern-day textile artists, we can choose to echo traditional stitched lettering styles or create newer interpretations to suit our needs. We can incorporate text into our artwork for practical purposes (to label or sign a piece of work), to communicate a message, or perhaps to add another layer of meaning to a piece.

When planning a piece of work with text, it is important to consider what your message is and why it requires lettering. It's easy to fall into a trap of thinking we need to literally spell out our message or story, but this isn't always necessary. If you feel that text will significantly add to your piece, consider the style that will work best; will the text be the main feature of your artwork, or a more subtle or even slightly hidden part? Do you want the words to dominate, or would you prefer for the audience to have to work a bit harder to find the message or meaning?

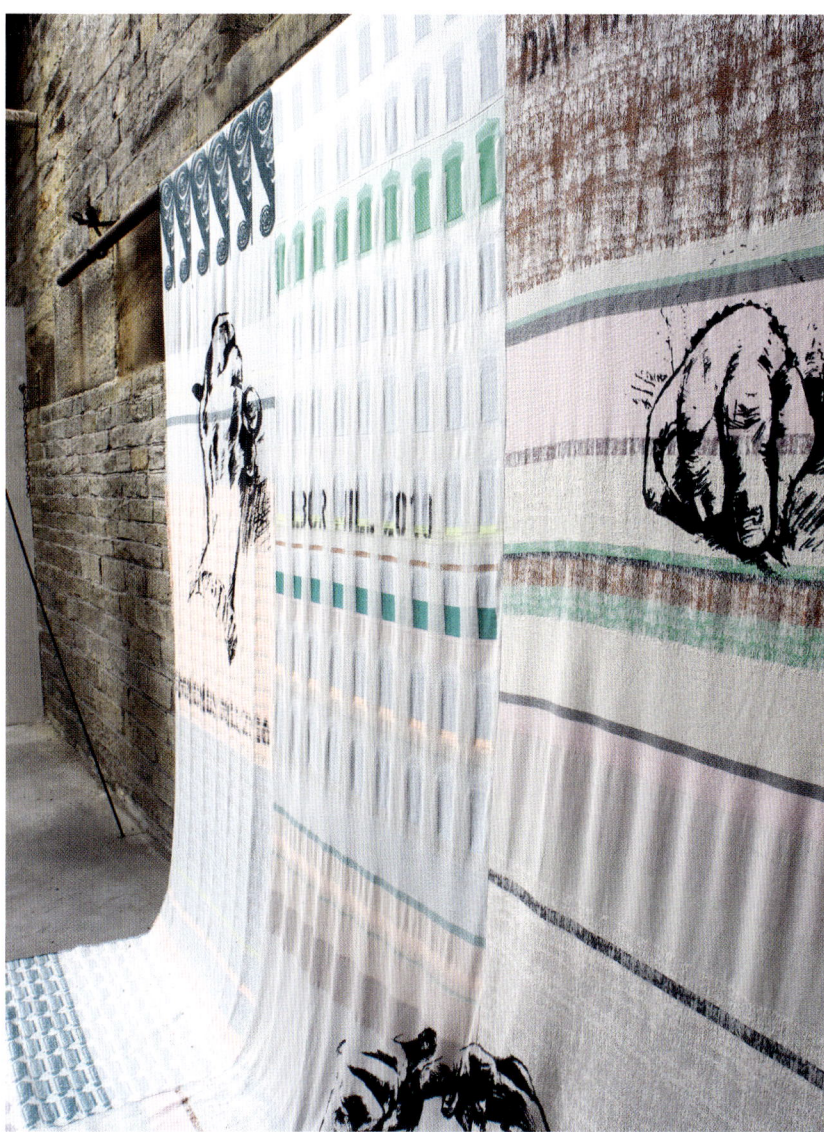

OPPOSITE, ABOVE
19th-century embroidered sampler on linen.

OPPOSITE, BELOW
An alphabet sampler of unknown origin.

RIGHT A Cloth for the Lost Mills *(2024) by Hannah Lamb and Hannah Robson. The names of 'lost mills' were stencilled onto the cloth.*

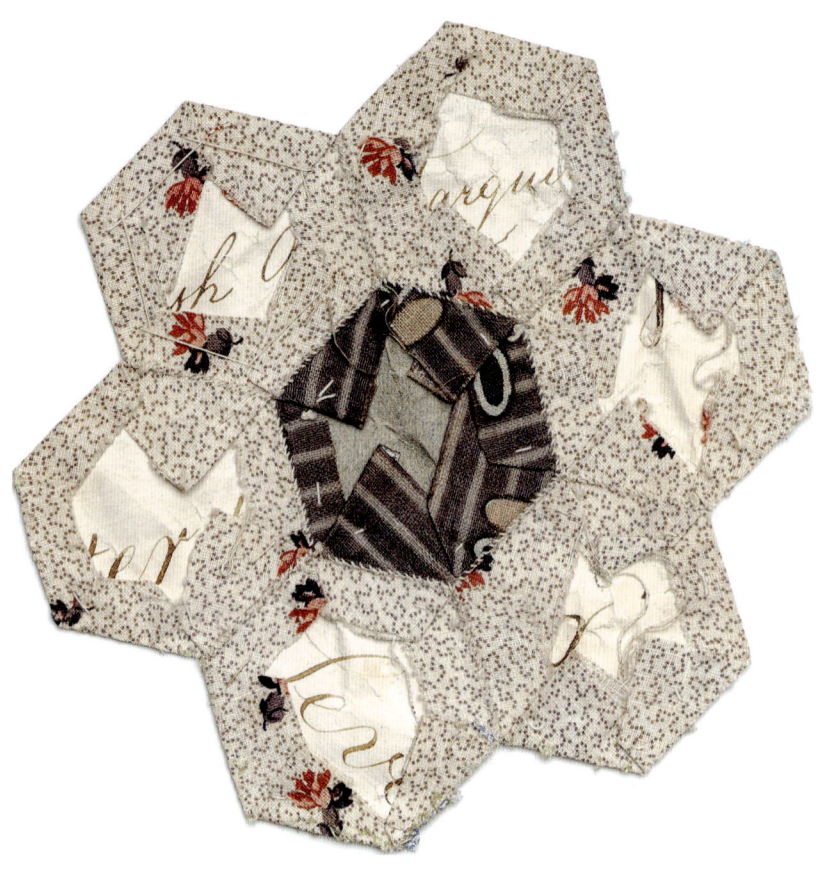

Text styles

'It's not what you say but the way you say it' is a phrase that is certainly true when it comes to using text in textile art. Different styles of text convey different meanings with a range of associations. Choosing an appropriate style will not only help you to communicate your message but to 'say' it in a way that suits your work.

CURSIVE SCRIPT This is a form of joined-up lettering commonly seen in handwriting, lending a personal touch to creative projects. Linear stitches lend themselves to looping letters; stem stitch, backstitch and variations on chain stitch all work well, while couching allows a continuous thread to be laid down on the surface of the fabric, much like an ink line on paper.

TYPED LETTERING This is composed of individual letters. The range of different typefaces (or fonts) is vast, from small fixed-width typewritten text and traditional lettering of printed documents, to bold poster or playbill type. Block lettering can be effectively translated to textiles using appliqué, stencilling or screen printing. On a smaller scale, cross stitch can be used on even-weave fabrics to create a traditional look, reminiscent of samplers and domestic needlework.

ABOVE *Just visible from the back of this patchwork block are the original paper templates, made from recycled handwritten letters or notes.*

OPPOSITE *If you can't get hold of vintage stencils like these, look for traditional or industrial fonts that feel in keeping with your project.*

Stencilling

I have a particular fondness for the stencilled industrial lettering seen on wool bales and jute sacks. Stencilling is a simple yet effective way to apply bold type onto fabric. I am fortunate to have some lovely vintage metal stencils, but thin plastic stencils are readily available from suppliers, or you could cut your own design from stencil card or mylar sheets.

Fabric to be stencilled should be ironed flat and pinned or taped in place on a suitable surface. Mark a temporary line for your text using tailor's chalk or a disappearing ink pen. Place the stencil so that the base of the letter is on the line. Use a suitable fabric paint or medium on a stencil brush or sponge to stipple through the stencil until you have the coverage you want, then carefully lift away the stencil to reveal the letter. If working with individual letters, it is best to wait for each one to dry before moving on to the next, to avoid smudging.

Alternatively, fabric spray paints can be used to stencil onto a variety of surfaces. When working with spray paints, you must take care to mask all areas that you don't want to paint.

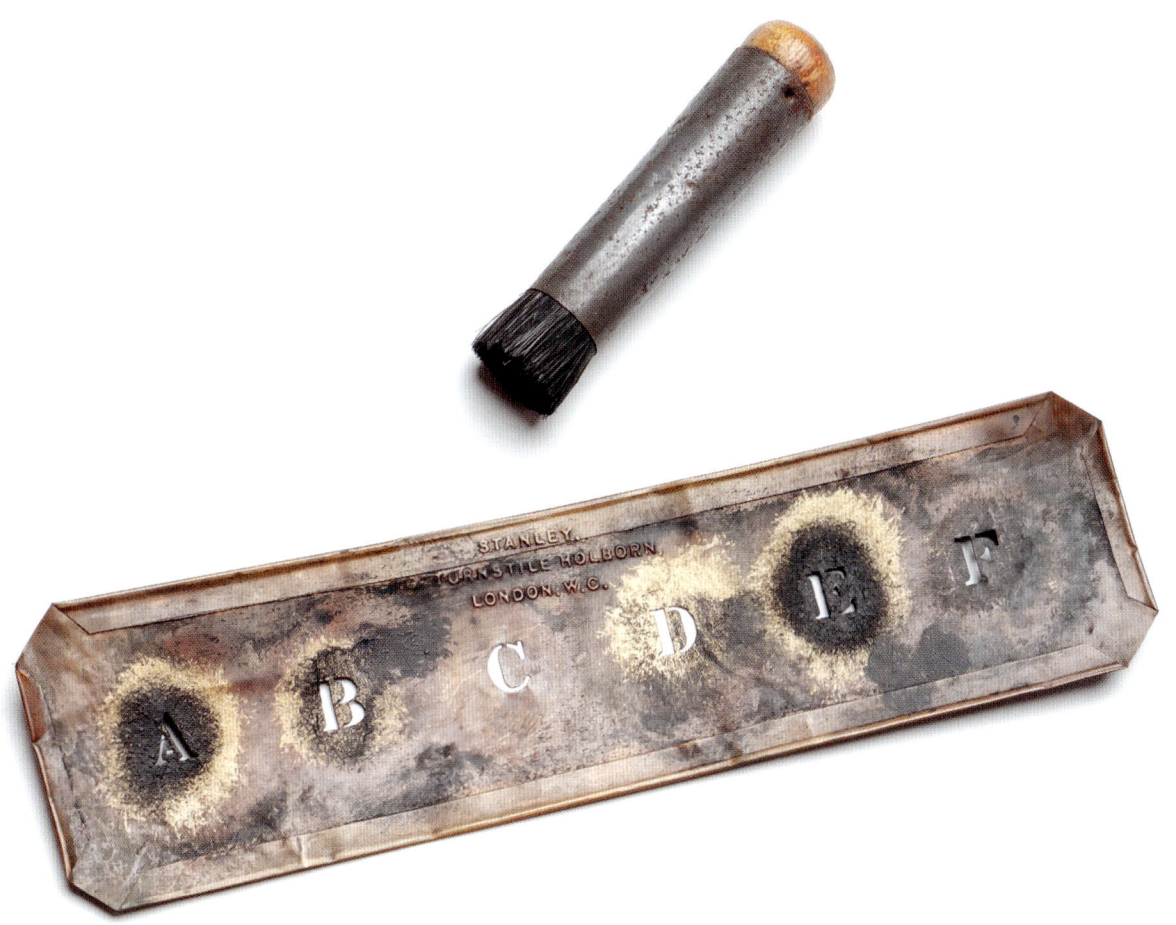

Translating from archival documents to textiles

During the course of historical research, you may come across interesting documents, letters or records offering first-hand information. Particularly important texts can be integrated into artworks, perhaps overlaid with other imagery, print or appliqué materials. This can be done with free-motion embroidery, which is particularly effective for translating handwriting. Trying to trace this kind of design onto fabric is tricky, so I prefer to use an alternative approach to translate the design into stitch.

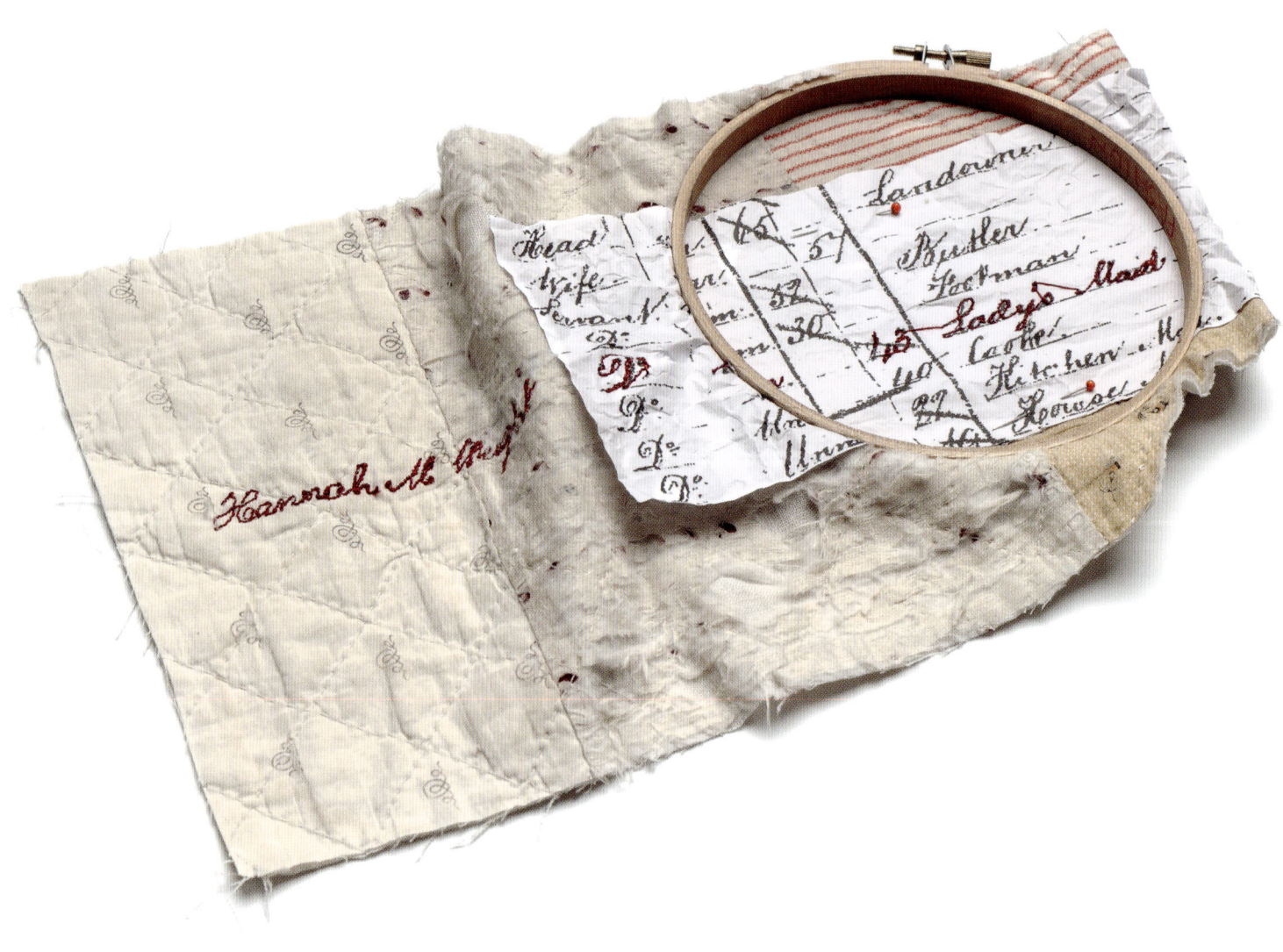

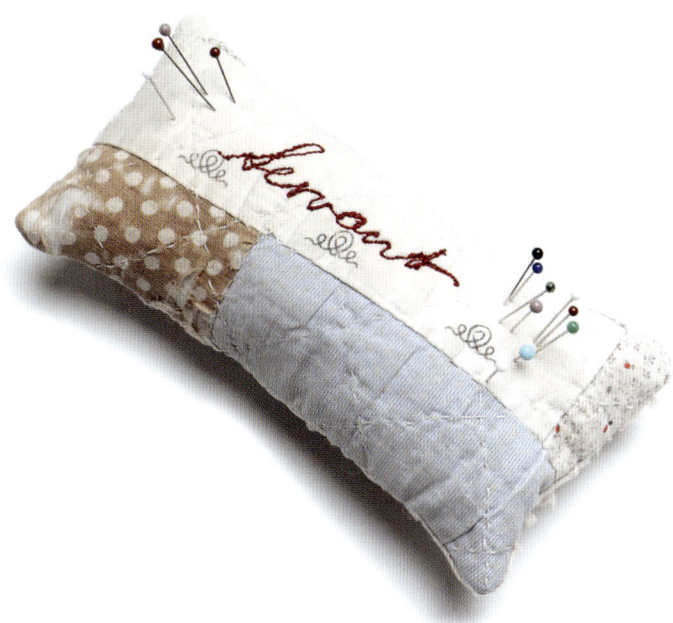

YOU WILL NEED

- Sewing machine with feed-dog lowered and darning/embroidery foot attached
- Embroidery hoop or frame
- Base fabric (big enough for your design, with space around so that you can move the embroidery hoop if needed)
- Machine sewing thread
- Photocopy or print of source handwriting scaled to your desired size

FREE-MOTION EMBROIDERY METHOD

1. Stretch your base fabric in an embroidery hoop or frame, making sure it is drum tight (if your fabric is very lightweight, you may need to use a stabiliser fabric). Pin the photocopy or print in place on top of the fabric.

2. Carefully lower the sewing machine needle into position at the start of your lettering. Bring both threads to the top of the fabric and hold them firmly (keeping your fingers away from the needle) while you do a few stitches on the spot to anchor them. Trim the ends of the threads close to the stitching.

3. You are now free to start stitching your text. Take your time to follow the lettering as carefully as you can, keeping the stitches small so that they follow the shape effectively and don't become spiky. It is helpful to look at the way the letter shapes have been created and, where possible, follow this as a continuous line.

4. When you come to any breaks in the letters or words, stop the machine, lift your needle and move to the next part without cutting the thread. This saves time, and the loose jump stitches can easily be trimmed at the end.

5. Once you have finished stitching, first trim any jump stitches or loose threads before tearing away the paper. Any very tiny pieces of paper may require more careful picking with a pin or sharp tweezers to remove, although some people like to leave parts of the paper design in place.

OPPOSITE *Machine stitching a line from the 1871 census, when my ancestor Hannah Wright was working as a Lady's Maid. To make it easier to stitch, the record was enlarged on the photocopier.*

ABOVE *In the 1881 census, Hannah Wright's occupation was listed simply as 'Servant'.*

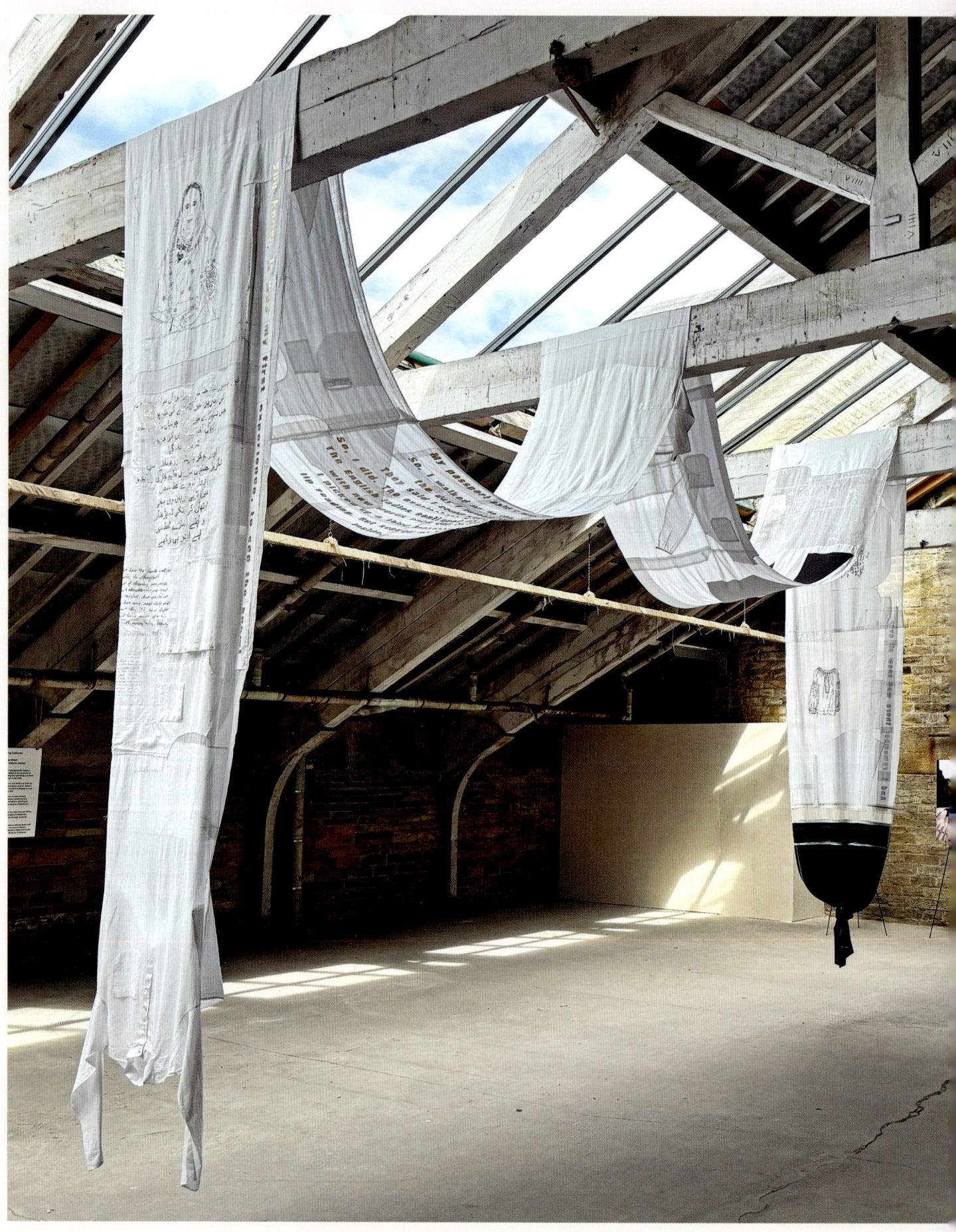

ALISON WELSH

Layering Cultures

Alison is a textile artist with a background in fashion design. *Layering Cultures* is a large-scale textile installation based on the accounts of Bradford mill workers, including the testimonies of those who migrated to the UK to work in the textile mills. The work is Alison's response to oral testimony from the Lost Mills and Ghost Mansions project by Bradford-based arts organisation, 509 Arts.

Hand and machine stitching were used to form a bolt of cloth that embodies Bradford's industrial legacy and the personal memories and life experiences of its diverse communities. Sections from Alison's father's memoirs (he worked at Listers Mill in the 1960s and 1970s) were hand stitched and set alongside quotes from migrant workers. Layers of transparent cloth, drawings, a poem by Nabeela Ahmed, and an embroidered blouse were collaged together and combined with timeworn historical garments to represent a range of memories from Bradford's diverse cultures. Text is integral to this piece of work as a way of conveying the original, authentic voices of Bradford's textile workers. The outcome was a complex mix of narratives and images, bringing together a broad range of very personal experiences.

OPPOSITE Layering Cultures *(2024) by Alison Welsh, commissioned by 509 Arts.*

RIGHT Layering Cultures *(2024) by Alison Welsh. Detail showing embroidered memories from former mill workers.*

STRUCTURE /
DECONSTRUCTED

So far the focus has been on observing details, patterns and surface textures, but the three-dimensional structure of historical textiles, sometimes constructed from many complex parts, is also fascinating. From tiny details of pleats and pin tucks, to elaborate underpinnings with internal supports, historical costumes can provide clues about the times they were made in, as well as the individuals who wore them. They hint at the cultural norms of a period as well as technological changes in manufacture and materials. Many historical pieces show signs of alteration or mending, lending another layer to their story. From a creative point of view, structural pieces encourage textile artists to think about sculptural forms and construction methods, providing further inspiration.

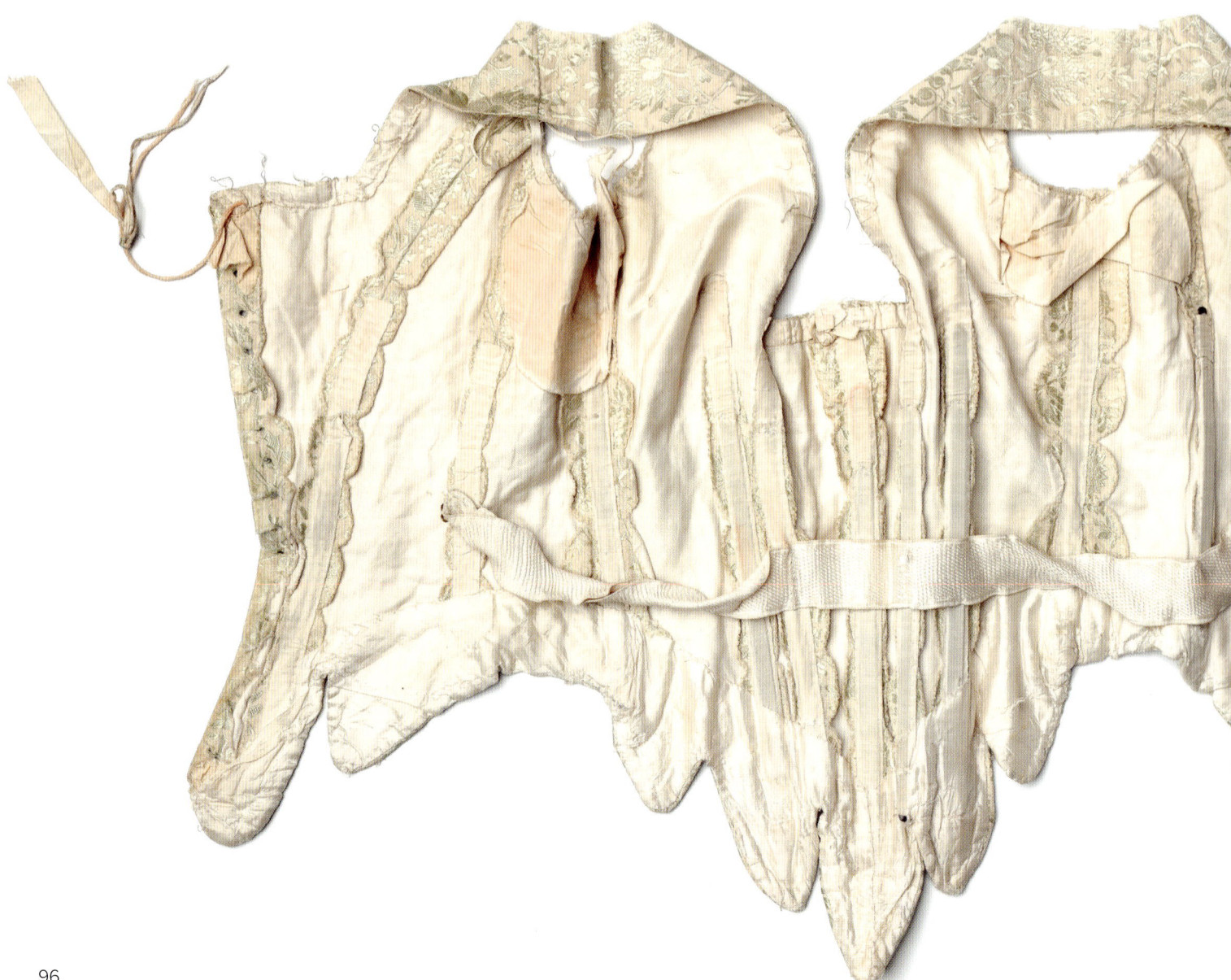

Alteration and mending

When researching historical textiles and costume, it can be tempting to try to pin an item down to a single date of manufacture; however, many garments may have led multiple lives. In past times, when materials were scarce or expensive, it was much more common to make alterations and repairs, or to remake a garment into something entirely different. We can learn a great deal from tracing these changes, understanding how a piece may have evolved over time and questioning why.

Returning to 'slow seeing' (see page 25), meticulous observation is often needed to spot the clues of a previous life. Careful examination of seams and hems can give us some helpful hints: a hem let down as a child grows, or seams unpicked and let out to accommodate a changing body shape due to pregnancy or weight gain – look out for lines of pricked holes where stitching has been unpicked or evidence of creases from old hems. A section of subtly different material, perhaps a different weight of linen in a shirt, could suggest that areas have been replaced due to wear. Garments were sometimes dramatically remodelled to suit changes in fashion or repurposed into items with an entirely different use. Patterned fabrics that don't match as you might expect or seams in unexpected places could suggest that smaller pieces have been patched together from another item.

Repairs, too, can tell us about the life of an item, although often these are very well hidden, with the darns or patches made as inconspicuous as possible to avoid drawing attention to the thrifty mend. Take your time to study the surface of the fabric looking for tiny darns or reinforcing stitches, as these can blend in almost seamlessly. Carefully sewn patches can also hide in plain sight. If possible, hold an item up to the light or shine a light behind the cloth, to show any denser areas of stitching or additional layers of fabric. Making a rubbing is also a useful technique for capturing an imprint of joins and repairs (see page 31).

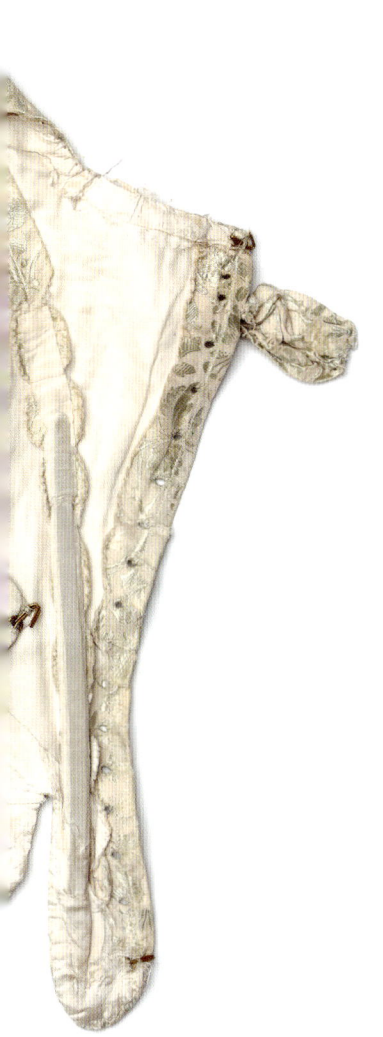

OPPOSITE *The interior of this bodice reveals a complex construction of shaped panels with boning providing structure.*

Conversation pieces

'Cloth holds an imprint that contains the trace of another human being'[6], says artist Debra Roberts. In 2010 Debra embarked on a project to research the hidden histories within fragments of 18th-century fabric. Without a personal connection to the material and no background history, her only option was to learn to 'read the cloth', to see what could be revealed. She meticulously noted stitch marks and folds as well as traces of threads from unpicking and alteration, each a reminder of everyday life and personal histories. Creating a 'literal tracing of how the fragments had been altered over time', Debra chose to map all of the evidence onto a drawing. She explains how 'mapping the surface of the fabric presented a visual record of the history, as a means to navigate the unknown terrain'.

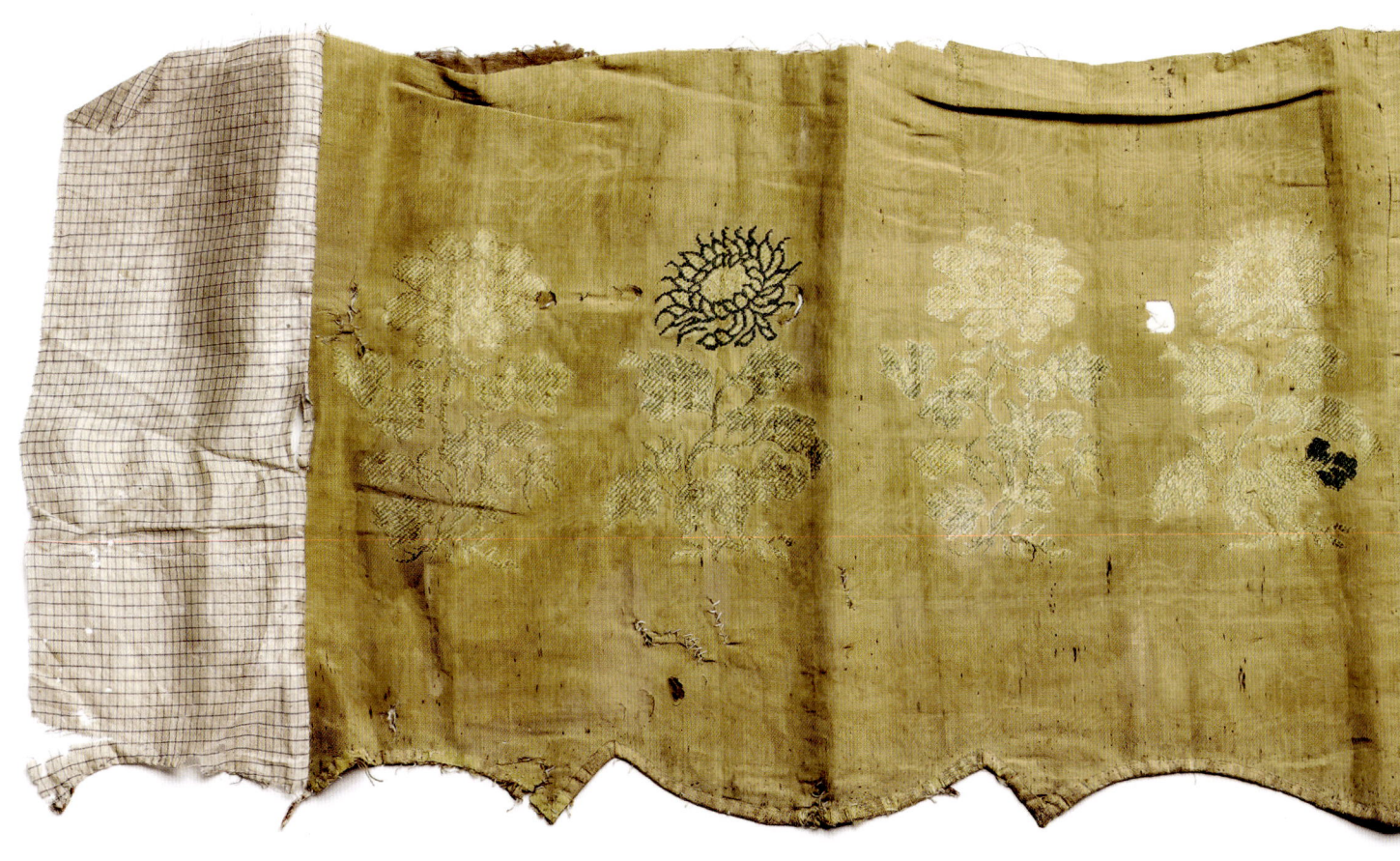

BELOW, LEFT
18th-century handwoven silk panel. This piece appears to have been part of a pelmet or bed hanging, but may have had multiple 'lives' through alteration and repair.

BELOW, RIGHT
Experimental swags in brown packaging paper by Wendy Cooper.

By comparing this textile 'map' with examples of garments from the period, Debra was able to ascertain that the fragments had been part of a dress and consider how that dress may have looked. Creating a partial reconstruction helped her to imagine the person who wore the dress and gave her a deeper understanding of its construction.

I love that Debra chose to 'map' the evidence found in her historical textiles. All of the stitch marks, creases and previous unpicking reveal the way the material has been manipulated over time. These markings could be interpreted as symbols on a map, alluding to the changing surface of the ground fabric. By flipping this idea, it can also be interesting to unpick garments (not precious ones!) and use the pieces as backgrounds to work onto. A sleeve, collar or shirt front could make an interesting 'canvas' on which to tell a story.

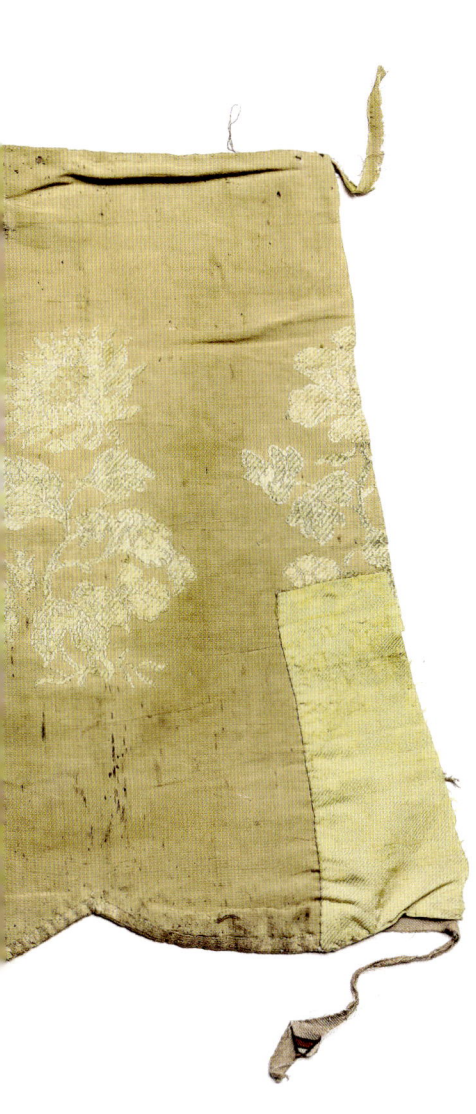

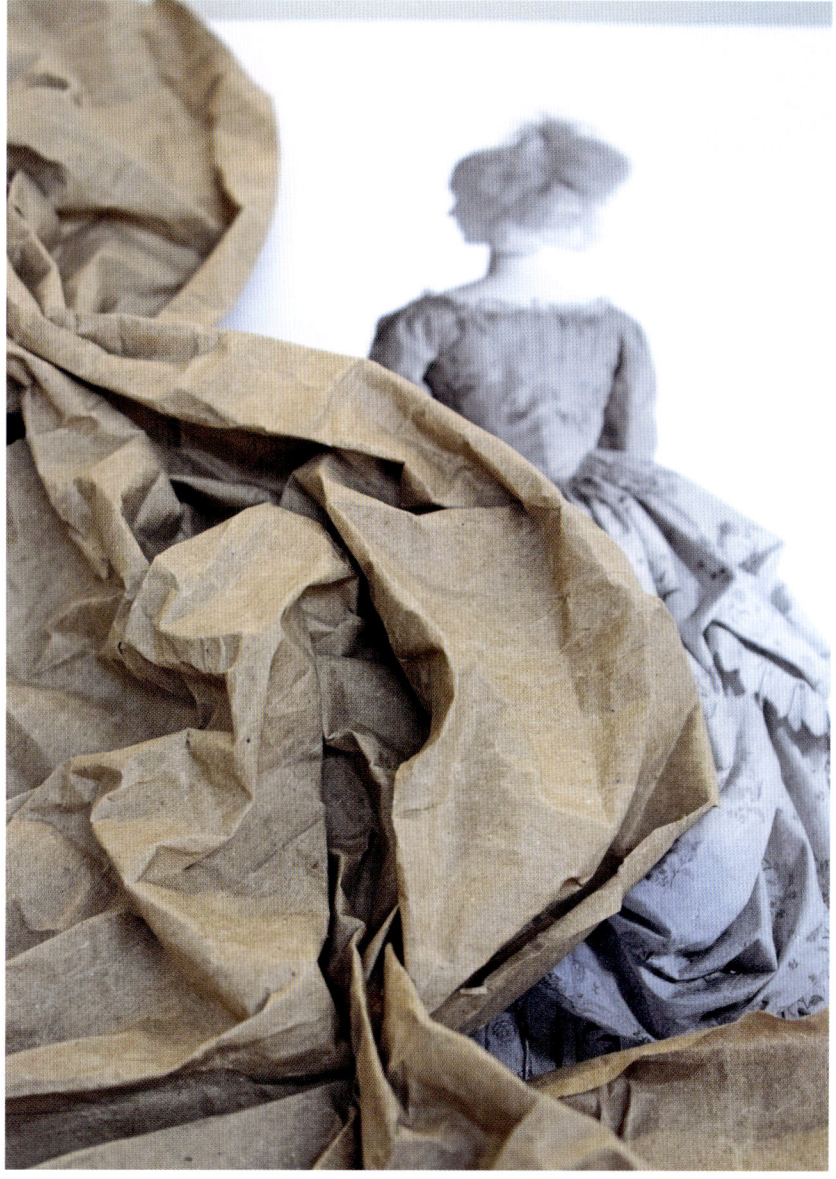

99

Structure

I have always been fascinated by the structures underpinning historical fashion. Throughout history, elaborate constructions have been worn beneath clothing to alter silhouettes and accentuate body shape. Wires, boning, hoops and padding were used to emphasise different parts of the body; at times controlling or restricting, in other instances creating more volume. Sometimes these elements are hidden on the inside of garments, but they can also be pieces in their own right; corsets that squeeze and control, hooped crinoline cages, paneers, ruffs or highly structured collars. Some costume pieces include structural elements on the outside as decoration. Pleating, gathers and flounces can all be used to create and control fullness or volume, with the choice of fabric making a huge difference to the overall effect. On a softer, surface level, corded and quilted garments provide structure, substance and warmth.

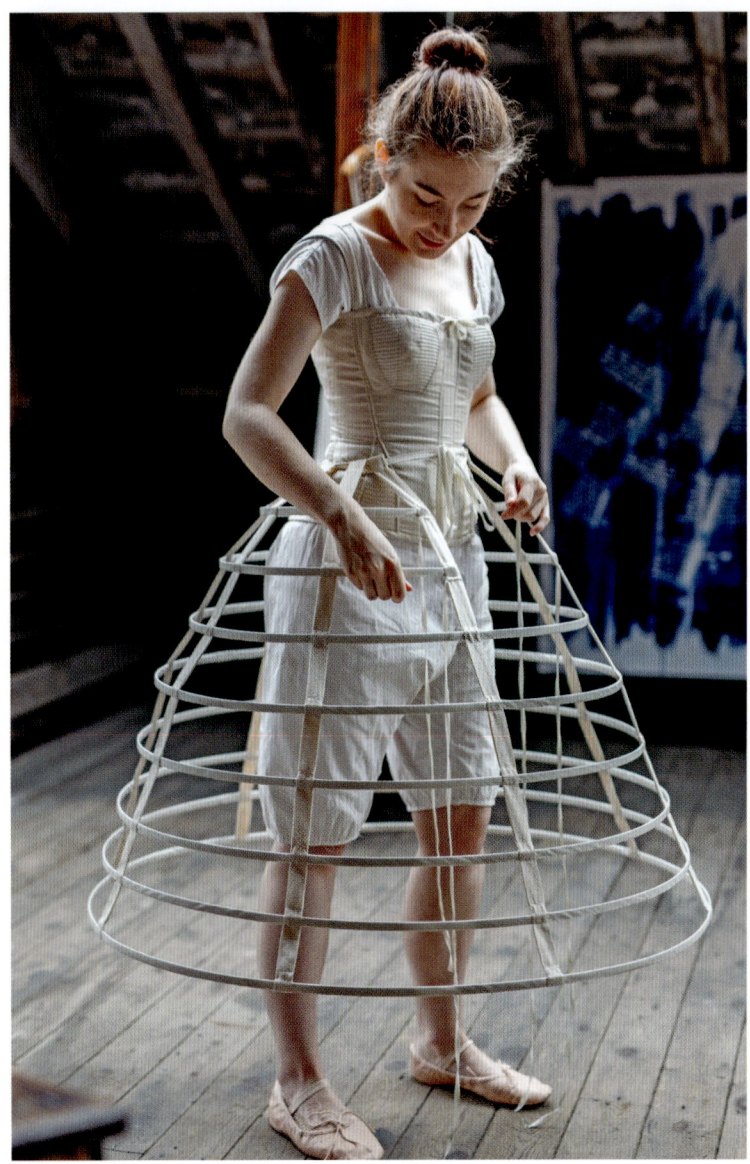

LEFT *Getting dressed in a corset and steel crinoline cage.*

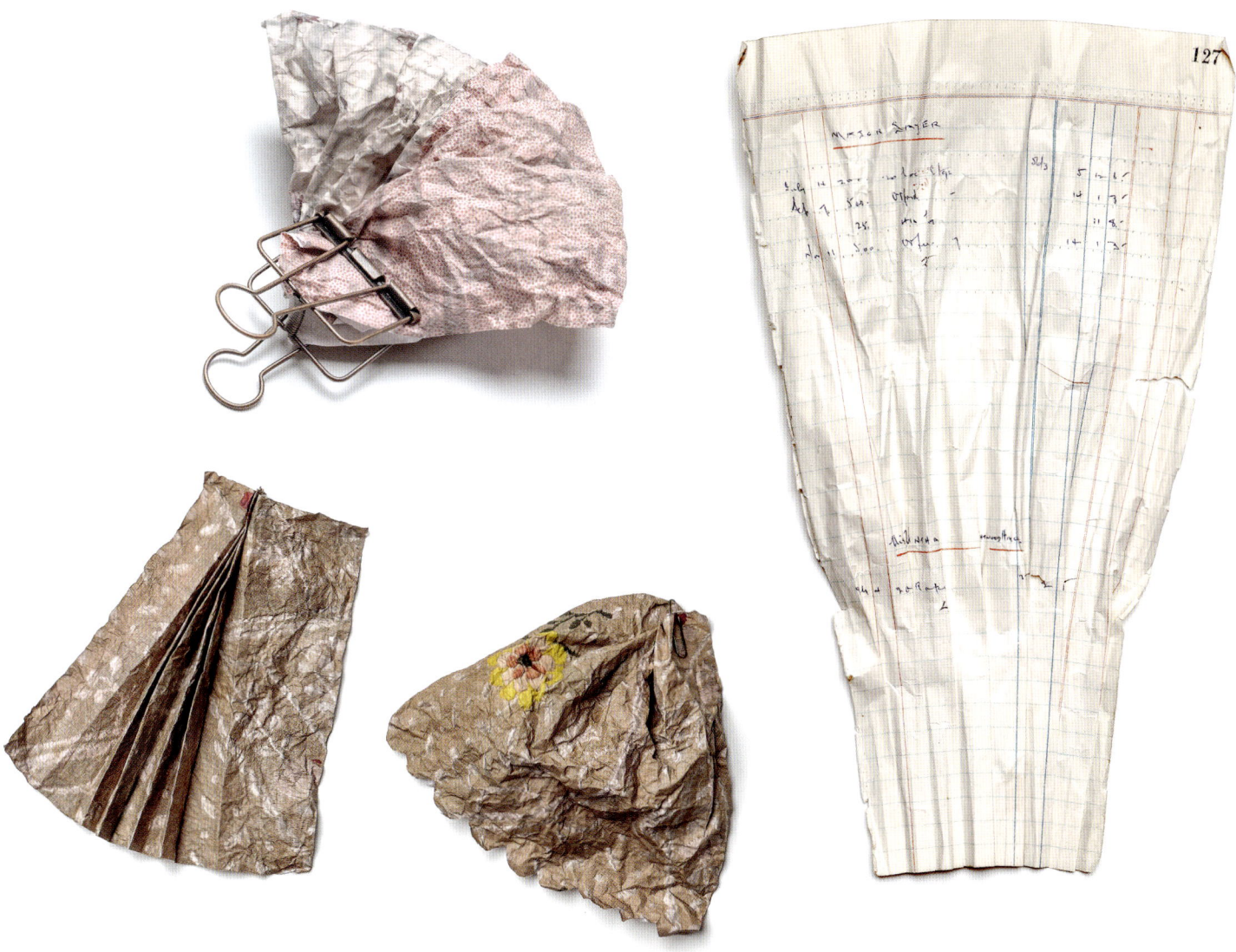

PAPER STRUCTURES

All of these structural effects can provide inspiration for three-dimensional textile art. While sketching can be useful in observing construction, using paper manipulation techniques to create small 3D studies can spark further ideas.

Collect a range of different papers, such as tissue paper, wrapping paper, napkins, crepe paper, newspaper, brown parcel paper, paper straws, recycled envelopes, cardboard cartons or boxes. All of these have different material properties in terms of stiffness, softness, drape, bulk, etc. Looking back at your initial research, word prompts or mood board, think about the different structural and surface qualities that interest you.

Try manipulating your paper by cutting, folding, creasing or weaving. If the paper tears too easily, or you want to create a softer handle, scrunching can be used to create a lovely soft, fabric-like paper. Start off with a piece of paper and scrunch it tightly into a ball in your hand, making sure not to tear it. Now open it out, then scrunch it again, and keep repeating until the paper is soft and pliable.

ABOVE, LEFT *Using enlarged photocopies of an 18th-century woven silk, the standard office paper was first scrunched to soften it and then manipulated with pleats and gathers to create a range of different effects.*

ABOVE, RIGHT
Old ledger pages transformed into pleated structures by Päivi Raine.

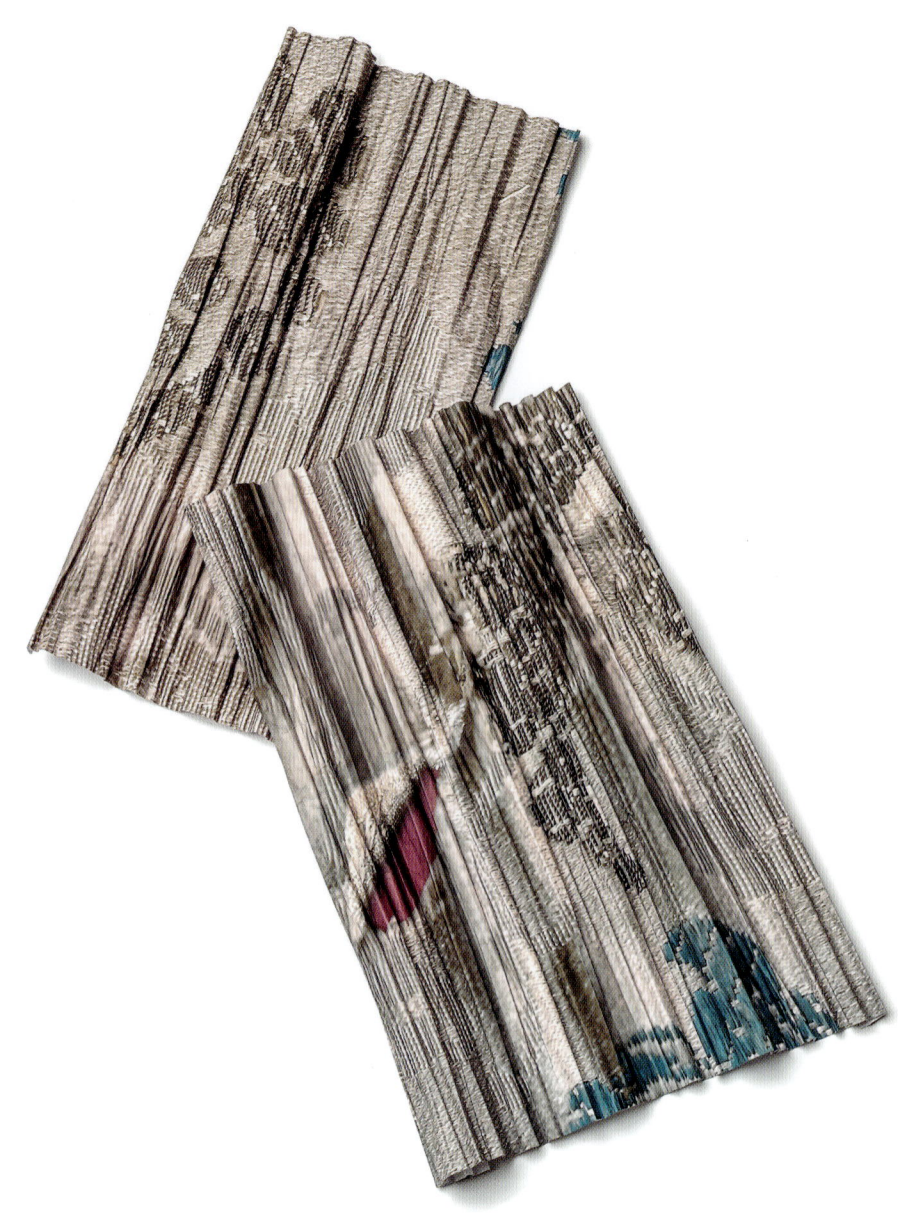

To create paper with creases or crinkles in just one direction, roll it into a tube that fits in your hand. Now make a fist around the tube and squeeze it, pulling the tube through your fist to crush it along its length. Open it out and you should see creases running along the length of the paper; if you want more creases, repeat. If you want to further distort the surface of this creased paper (or bought crepe paper), squeeze it between thumb and finger, stretching cross-wise across the grain; this can create a rib-like effect when done in the middle of the paper, and on the edge, it will flare out.

Although it might seem counterintuitive, many papers can be successfully stitched by hand or machine. If you have access to a sewing machine, this can be an easy way to introduce gathers, darts and ruffles. Make sure you set a long stitch length and handle the paper with care to reduce the risk of tearing. Alternatively, you could experiment with running the paper through the machine without any thread, to create lacy pin pricks over its surface.

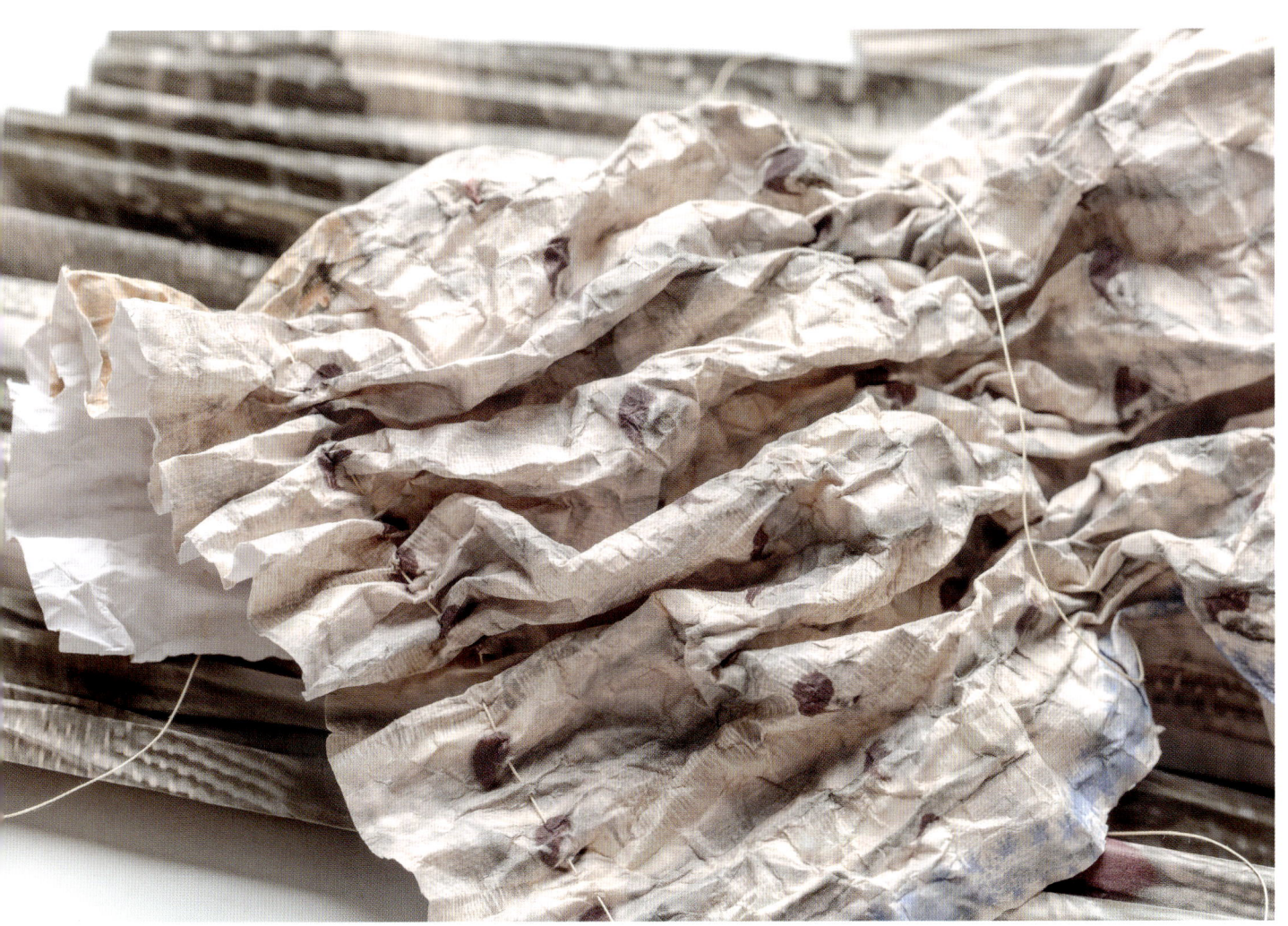

It is a good idea to try these paper manipulation techniques as quick experiments. If something doesn't work out, move on to explore a different combination of paper and process. If you find something that seems interesting, see how far you can take it; repeating, exaggerating, emphasising and rescaling elements. There may be opportunities to combine structural ideas with colour, pattern and imagery. Any design you can put on paper can be used as the basis for a 3D piece. Alternatively, you could try staining your paper pieces after construction, using leftover dyes, food colouring or even tea. Experiment with how you apply the colour, by dipping, painting, sponging or spattering.

Once you have created a set of three-dimensional samples, sit back and review them. When I am developing ideas, whether in 2D or 3D, I sometimes like to sketch my samples. This allows me thinking time to observe; to ponder what works, what I like and what I want to take further. It can be useful to move between quick testing and slow looking, and I find that the change in pace helps to shift my thinking and make creative developments. Small paper samples can become ideas for larger sculptural work, garments or resolved pieces in their own right.

ABOVE *Printed papers were first scrunched to soften them, then hand stitched with strong linen thread to gather.*

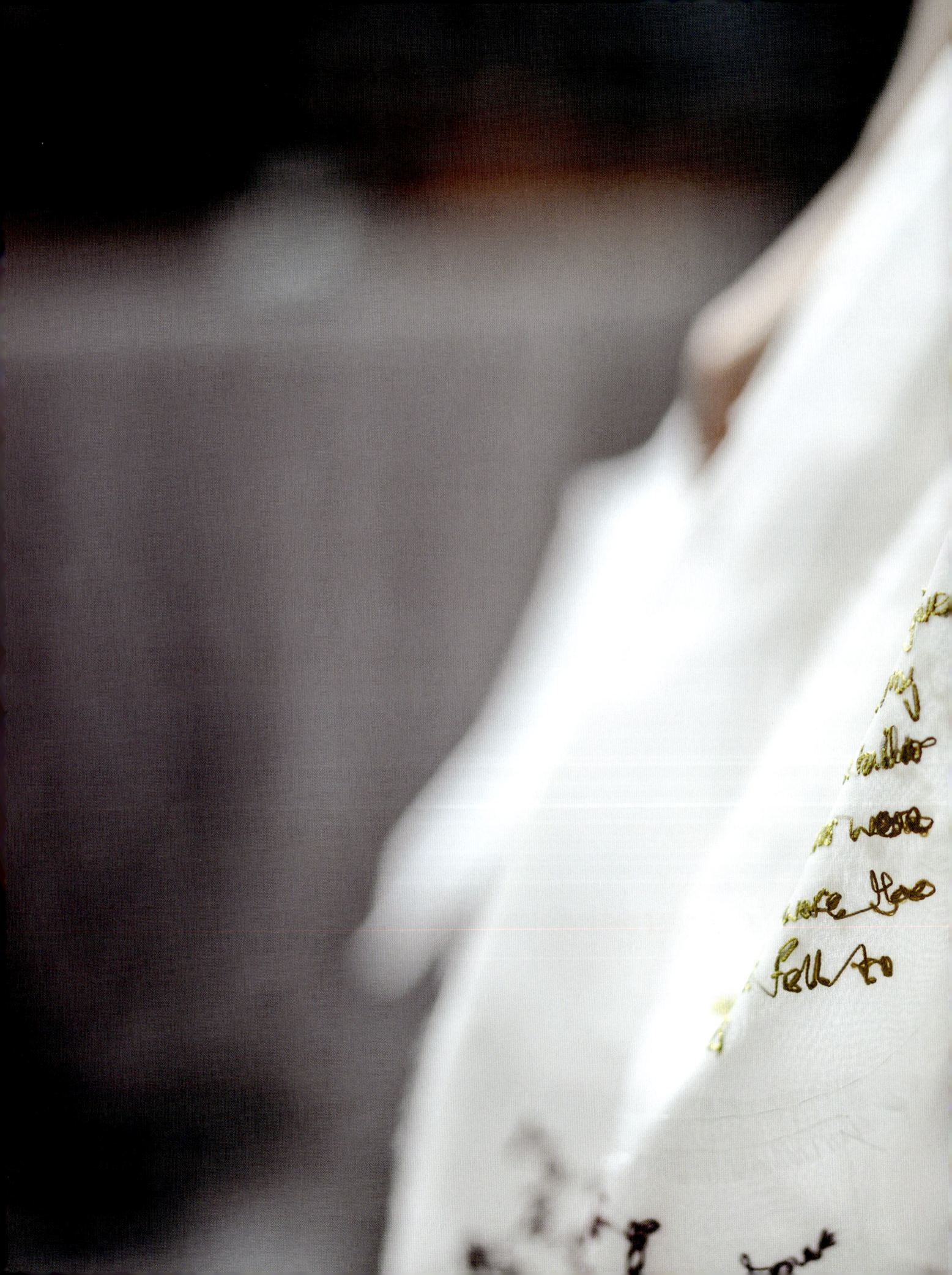

GATHERING

HERITAGE AND PLACE

I am fortunate to live on the outskirts of Bradford, West Yorkshire, an area steeped in textile heritage. The heyday of textile manufacturing in the region is long gone, but a small number of highly specialist companies remain. Such was the scale of the local textile industry that remnants can be seen all around, if you know how to read the landscape. Textile heritage is in the canals and railways that brought raw materials and coal to the mills and took finished cloth away; it's in the remaining mill buildings, some now repurposed as galleries, apartments and offices, while the fate of others sits precariously in the balance, their vast skeletons of stone and steel waiting for someone to breathe new life into them, or for a spark to turn them to cinders. Surrounded by such riches of textile heritage, I find it plays a huge part in my creative outlook, seeping into my work and the way I think.

A 'sense of place' is a term often used to describe areas of natural beauty but it can be applied to any environment that has special qualities or unique significance for an individual. It identifies the particular atmosphere of a place, its essence or 'genius loci', and how this makes a person feel. For me the vast empty mills and former industrial spaces around Bradford are evocative and magical, but to someone else the same spaces might be dingy and dirty, or a reminder of hard times. Our experience of place is shaped by our individual perceptions and prior experiences.

As artists, the unique response we have to heritage locations gives us great scope to create exciting and engaging work. Inspiration can be found directly from the physical environment, its form, textures or decorative features; by researching a site's history; or by using our imagination to explore intangible histories and invisible lives connected with a place. We can create art about a place or in a place, and sometimes both. However we choose to engage with place, it is important for us to experience it first-hand: to sense it, move through it and to get to know it.

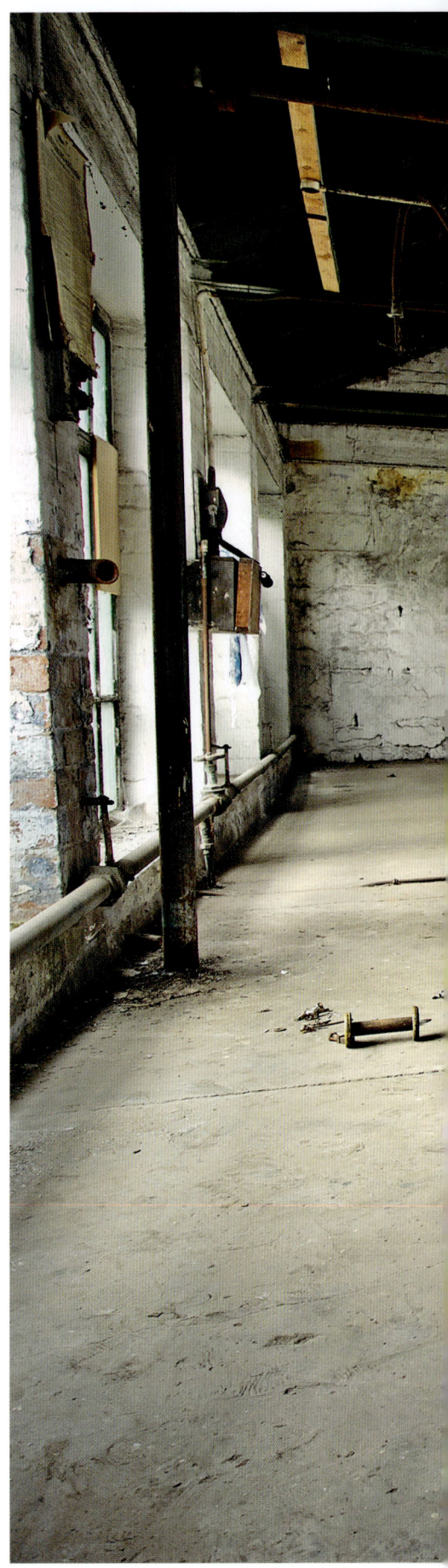

RIGHT [De]Constructed Cloth *(2019) by Hannah Lamb. Shown here in the old mechanics workshop at Sunny Bank Mill.*

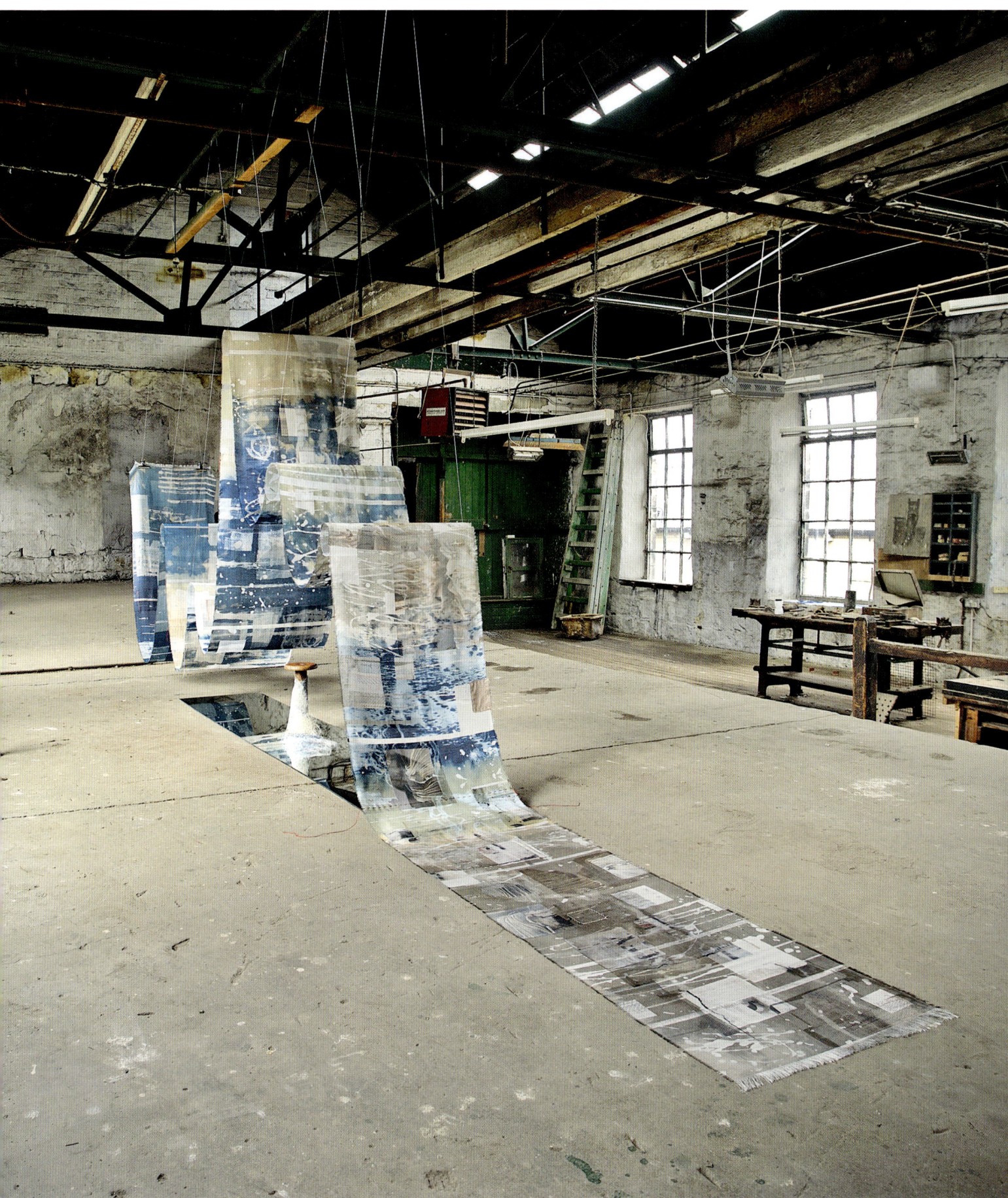

Site-sensitive work

'Site specific' is a term used to describe artwork created specifically for and connected to a particular site. This is sometimes confused with the term 'art installation'. While these two terms can overlap, it does not automatically follow that an installation will be site specific if it doesn't have a specific relationship to the site. Site-specific works can be created from any media and in any format, but they always have a strong connection to the site they are placed in. In many ways, I prefer the term 'site sensitive'[7], which suggests a deeper understanding of and respect for a site.

While site-specific art can be situated in any kind of environment, I am particularly interested in artworks responding to heritage locations. Historic buildings vary hugely; from grand stately homes, castles and places of worship to humble cottages; from vast industrial sites to single-room museums. Each individual site has its own stories and specific cultural context.

BELOW *These artworks installed in the roof space at Salts Mill make effective use of existing features in the building to hang the textile work. Easels were used to display large-scale photography.*

Layering Cultures (2024) by Alison Welsh (foreground) and A Cloth for the Lost Mills (2024) by Hannah Lamb and Hannah Robson (background), with photos by Carolyn Mendelsohn.

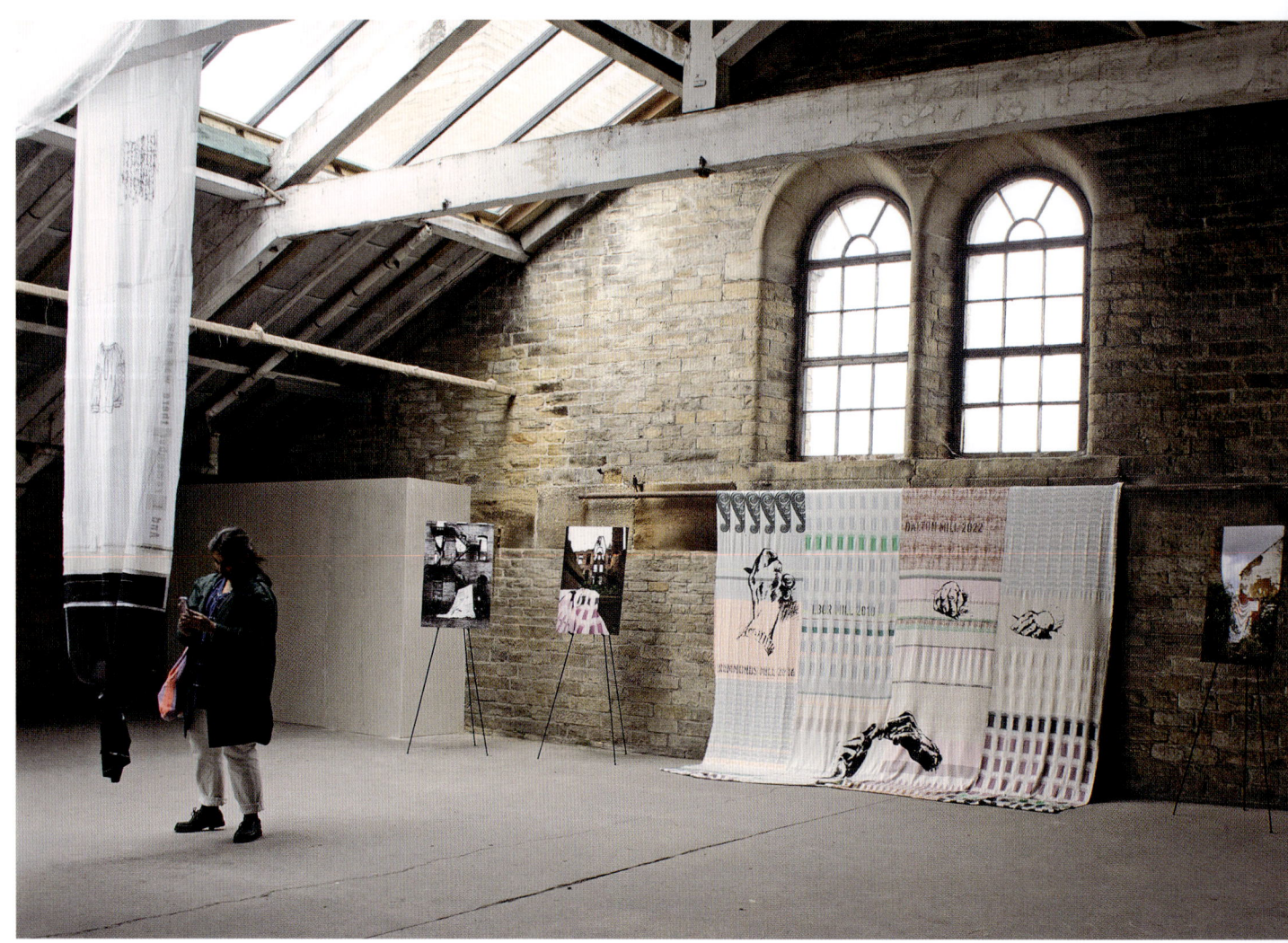

In recent years, there has been a growth in heritage organisations developing links with artists to reanimate historic buildings and bring new ways of understanding their collections. Artistic responses can make history more engaging and accessible, or encourage more dynamic audience interactions. As an artist, the chance to respond to unusual locations and spaces can be invigorating. It may present opportunities to make work on a bigger scale or for unusual settings. It could be a chance to reach different audiences or engage in collaborative or community-focused practice.

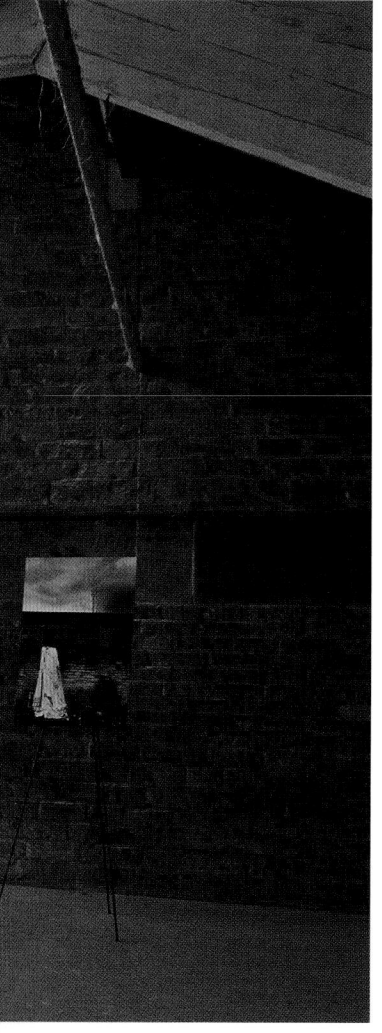

PRACTICALITIES OF WORKING IN HERITAGE SPACES

Before starting a project in a historic location, it's a good idea to do some basic research about the place, including access to it and any organisations involved. Depending on the condition of the site, there may be safety issues to consider. Do you need to wear a hard hat? Are floors safe? Are there any 'out of bounds' areas? Before undertaking a site visit, review any conservation restrictions. Do you need to leave bags and coats somewhere? Will you be allowed to take photos? Consider also what you hope to learn and prepare accordingly.

MEASUREMENTS Do you need measurements of display spaces or specific details for installing work? Pack a suitable tape measure. Make a sketch or plan of the space and add your measurements to it.

PHOTOS What purpose will these serve? Are they for general creative inspiration, for choosing colour palettes, or to provide technical details about the space?

DISPLAY OPPORTUNITIES Look for suitable places to hang or fix work, or spaces that might frame or contain the work (e.g. niches, apertures, openings). Can work be placed within existing exhibition displays?

TECHNICAL DETAILS Check access to power, if needed, and what the lighting is like.

ENVIRONMENTAL CONDITIONS Is there anything that might have an impact on your work, such as damp, dirt, light, heat or visitor interactions?

As well as these key practical considerations, it's also important to be present in the space and soak up the atmosphere. Try to spend some quality time observing and noticing the details. How does daylight illuminate the space? What are the views from the window? Are there any distinctive textures, colours, scents or sounds? Consider your overall impression of the space and make some notes. If you have time, you might also like to make some quick sketches of elements of interest.

PLANNING AND DISPLAYING SITE-SPECIFIC WORK

When making work for display in a heritage location, there are some particular considerations uncommon in traditional gallery settings and, to avoid frustrating compromises later, it's important to have these in mind as you develop ideas. Consider how your project can enhance and work with the space, perhaps highlighting interesting features or ensuring important architectural details remain visible. For example, in a room with a beautiful window looking out onto a garden, it might be a shame to put up blackout blinds to show a video projection.

- Is there power/artificial lighting? Too much/not enough daylight?
- How will visitors access the space and move around the work? How do you want them to engage with/touch the work (or not)?
- Is there a particular height that is best for viewing work?
- Can you attach things to the fabric of the building (walls, ceiling, floor)? If so, is there a maximum weight or particular kind of fixing allowed?

When working in heritage buildings there are often restrictions on attaching artwork to the walls, floors and ceilings, so alternative solutions may need to be found. When planning *Fragment of a Dress* for display at the Brontë Parsonage Museum (see page 117), for example, I knew I couldn't attach anything to the fabric of the Grade I listed building. So I decided to create a piece that could be displayed on a freestanding mannequin, sourcing one that was in keeping with the setting. Sometimes, however, existing elements in the building, such as joists or beams, can be used to drape or suspend work from.

You may also find you can show work within permanent exhibition spaces, in display cabinets or even within room settings. Artwork presented in this way can create dynamic and interesting displays that become part of a narrative, but this needs careful planning and discussion with the curators.

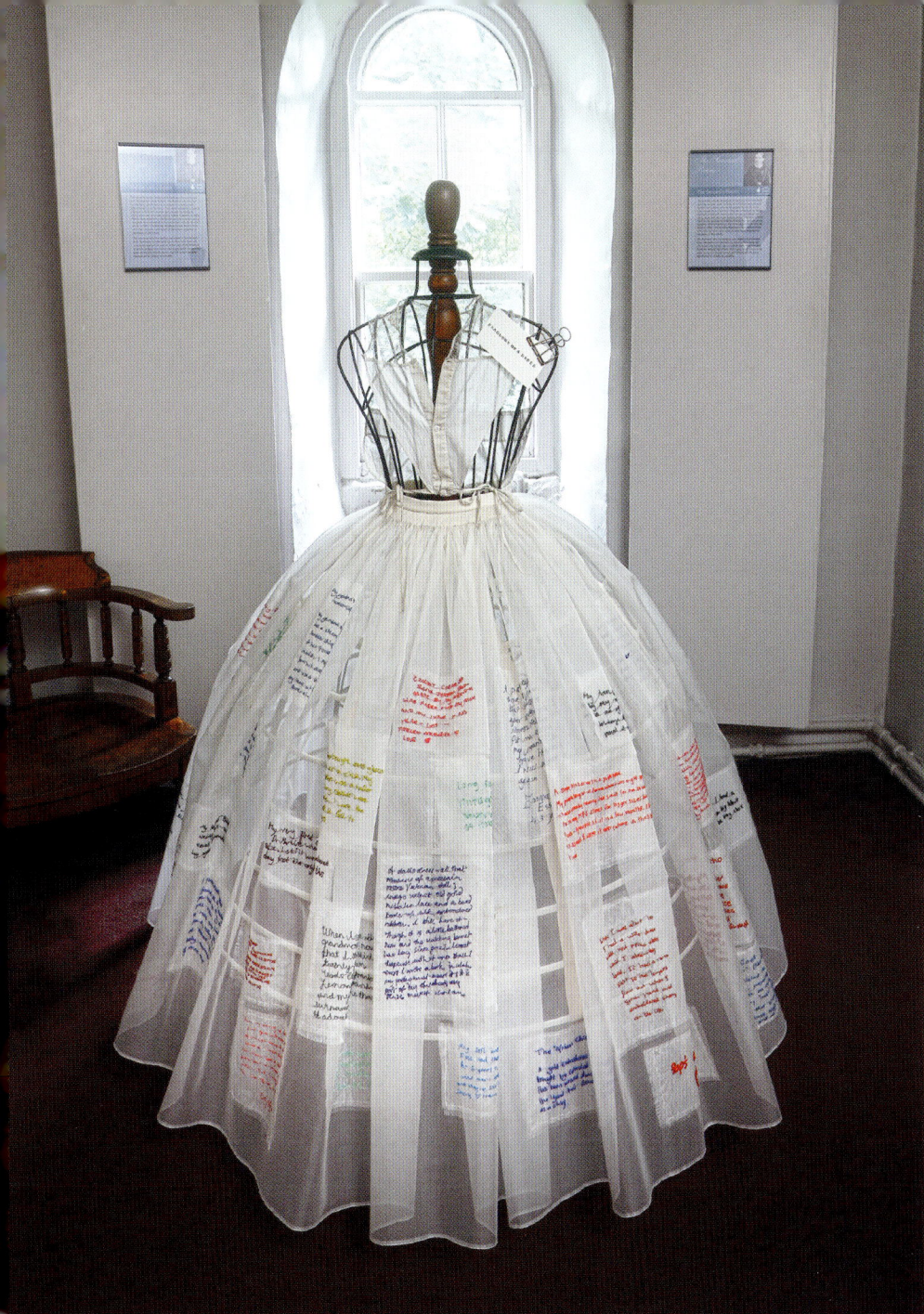

LEFT Fragment of a Dress *(2022)* by Hannah Lamb. Installation view at Brontë Parsonage Museum. Hand and machine embroidery on silk.

When planning artwork for a heritage setting, it is important to remember that curators are, first and foremost, tasked with the care of historic buildings and objects. Consideration also needs to be given to how audiences and communities will use the space. Sometimes these different interests within an organisation can be challenging to navigate, so patience, tact and good communication are vital. Try to make sure you get clear agreement from the relevant people at each stage of a project, to ensure everyone is on board.

Working in a heritage space can be daunting. Sometimes we need to reframe the 'problems' as opportunities, to find ways to work with them. Think of it as a series of exciting creative challenges!

MAKING HERITAGE RELEVANT TODAY

History can often feel like a safe, reassuring place to us, where all the bad things happened in the past, and we know how the story ends. In reality, of course, our understanding of times gone by is constantly changing: new discoveries are made and past ideas are questioned, as we look at things through the lens of our own age. This constant reframing means that rather than being stuck in the past, history actually provides great opportunities to explore a range of issues relevant to our lives today.

Historical textiles hold some unique qualities that make them ideal for exploring a wide range of subjects and stories. Textiles touch us all and this intimacy of material objects helps us to feel a deeper connection and relevance to our own lives. Textiles can also tell global stories, connecting the personal with the political.

Incomplete Histories

Incomplete Histories was created for an exhibition titled Connected Cloth: Exploring the Global Nature of Textiles, as part of the British Textile Biennial in 2021. As a white British textile artist I felt the need to educate myself about historical connections between Britain's dark colonial past and its boom years of textile innovation and mass export. I started my research by looking at printers' and dyers' notebooks from the Society of Dyers and Colourists Textile Collection. Filled with handwritten recipes, technical notes and tiny swatches of cloth, they document cutting-edge innovations of 18th- and 19th-century British textile industries. Yet the brief notes provide only glimpses of an immensely complex history.

Punctuating the pages of the dye recipe books are the names of raw materials imported from European colonies and traded across the world. I learnt about the role of the international slave trade in cotton production, including the deforestation in Central America that resulted from heartwood dye production and subsequently grown by enslaved people on Caribbean plantations. I researched the origins of the dyes, the print processes and the fashionable array of 'exotic' motifs, with their tangled origins from around the world.

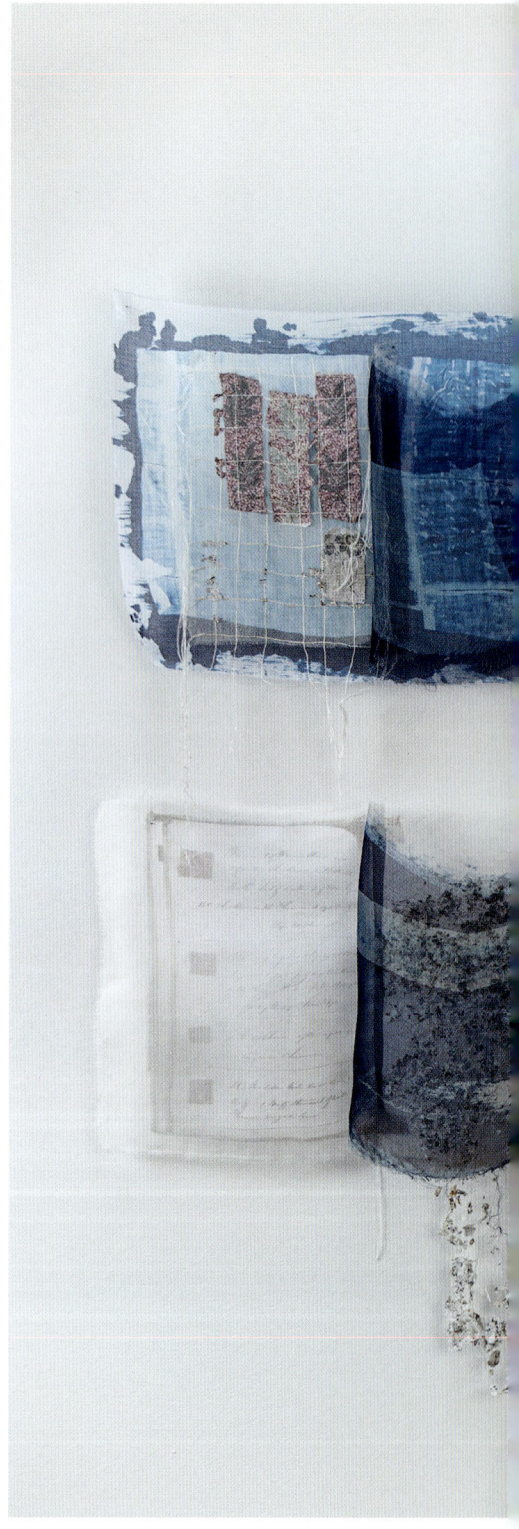

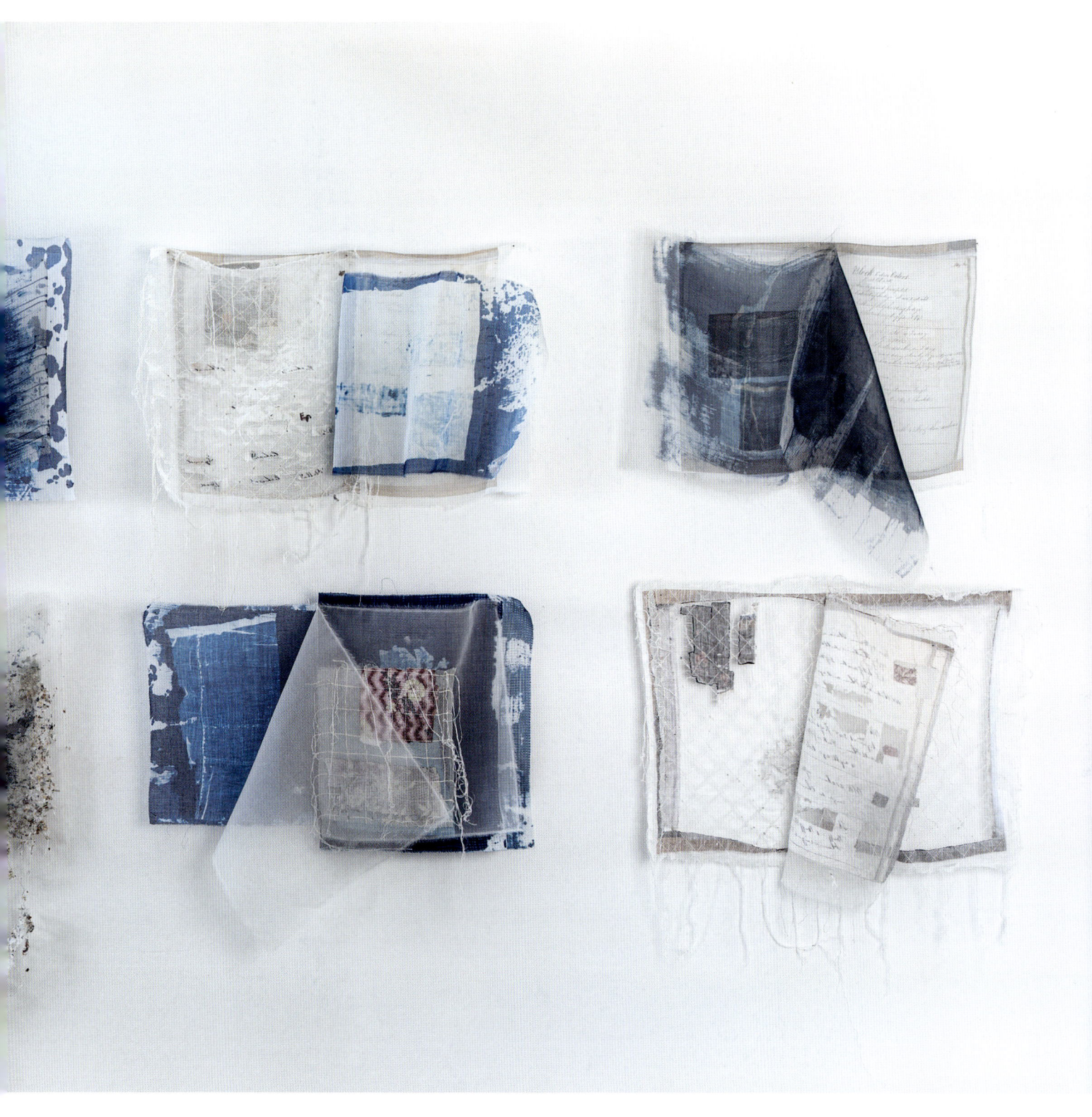

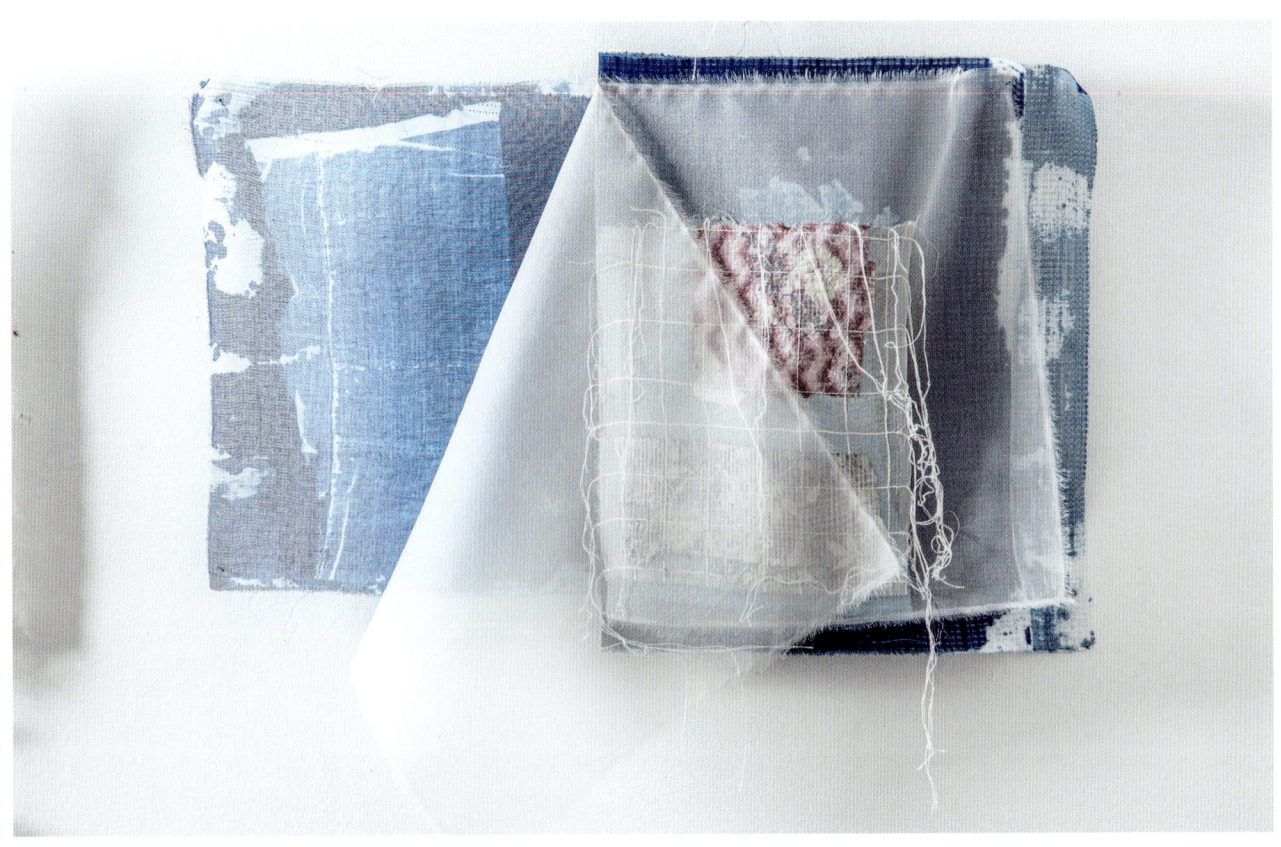

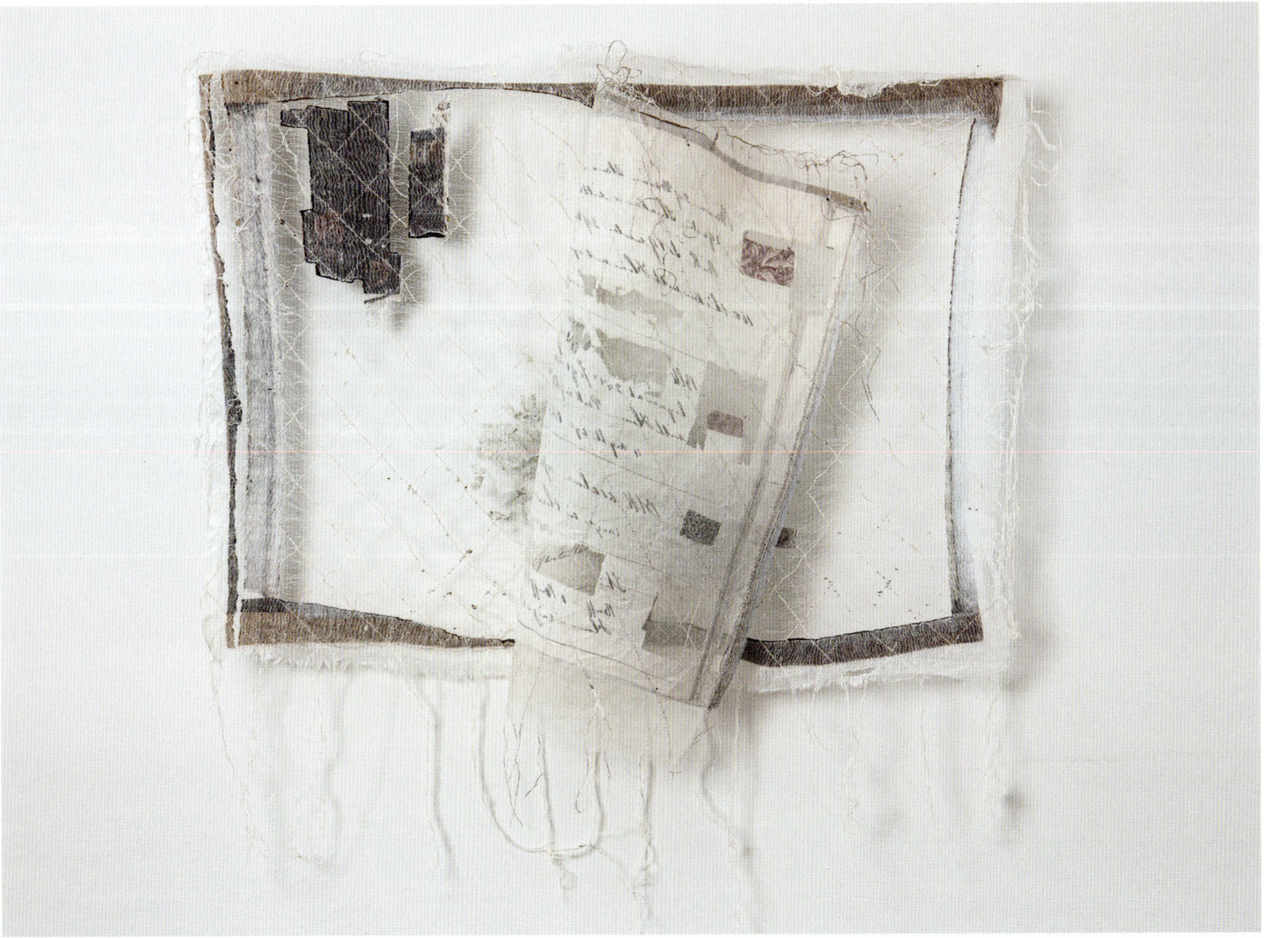

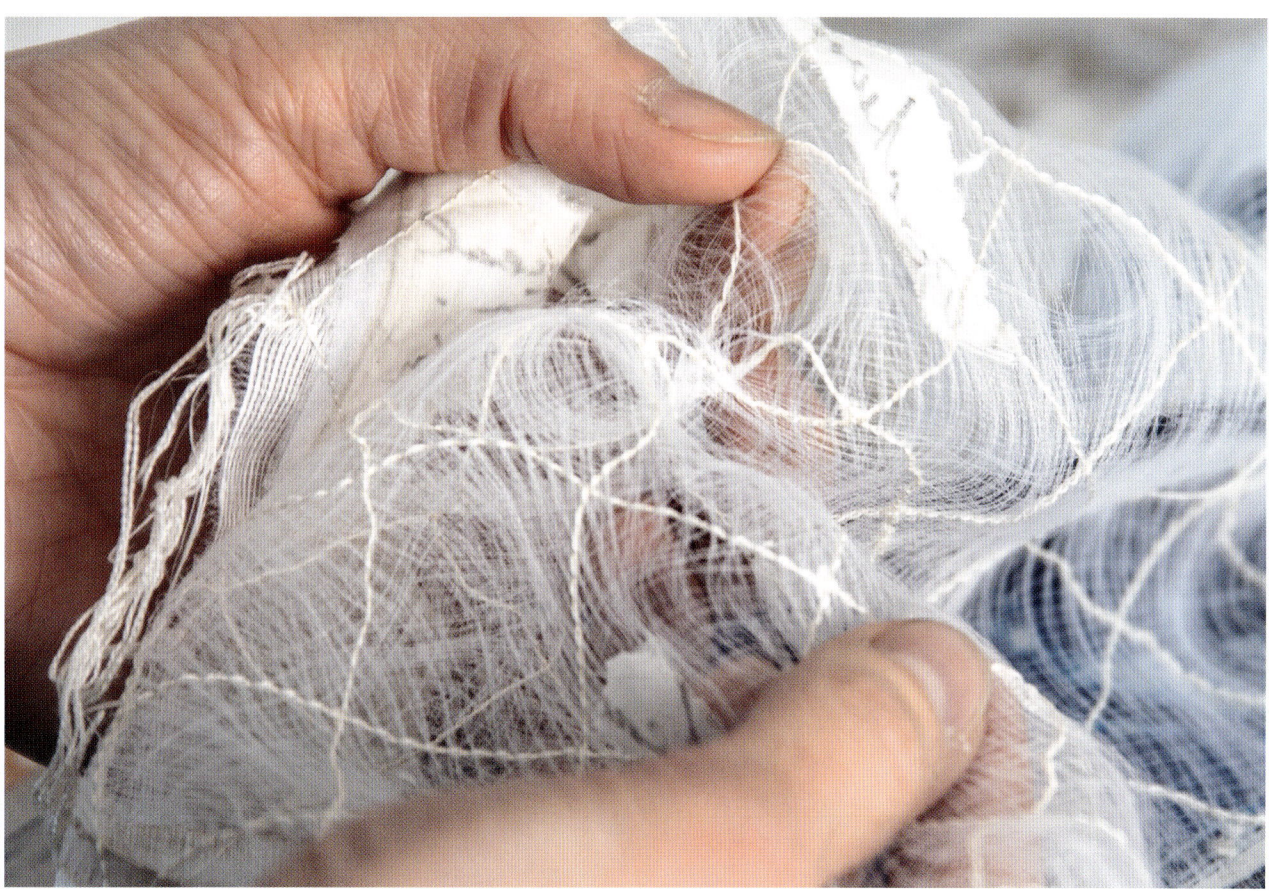

OPPOSITE, ABOVE
*Cyanotype pages
with layers of silk and
fragments of digitally
printed textiles.*

OPPOSITE, BELOW
*Burning away areas
of the facsimile pages
to leave gaps in our
collective memory.*

ABOVE *A wide range
of transparent materials
were layered to allow
glimpses through to the
pages beneath.*

I created a series of textile pages in imitation of the dye recipe books, using cyanotype and digitally printed fabric. I used a devoré technique to burn away areas of the pages, deconstructing and erasing some elements from history, while highlighting others. Although barely scraping the surface with my research, by making this work I started to understand some of the inequalities of the past and how they have contributed to the way we present histories today. I also hoped to encourage others to ask questions about the origins of cloth and clothing, now and throughout history.

Turning the pages of these beautiful volumes, we must remember that the heyday of the British textile industries is a global story, which in many ways is unequal and inadequately represented. The exploitation of people, the pillage of cultural property and the destruction of natural habitats to feed British industry and appetites are all issues that have not gone away.

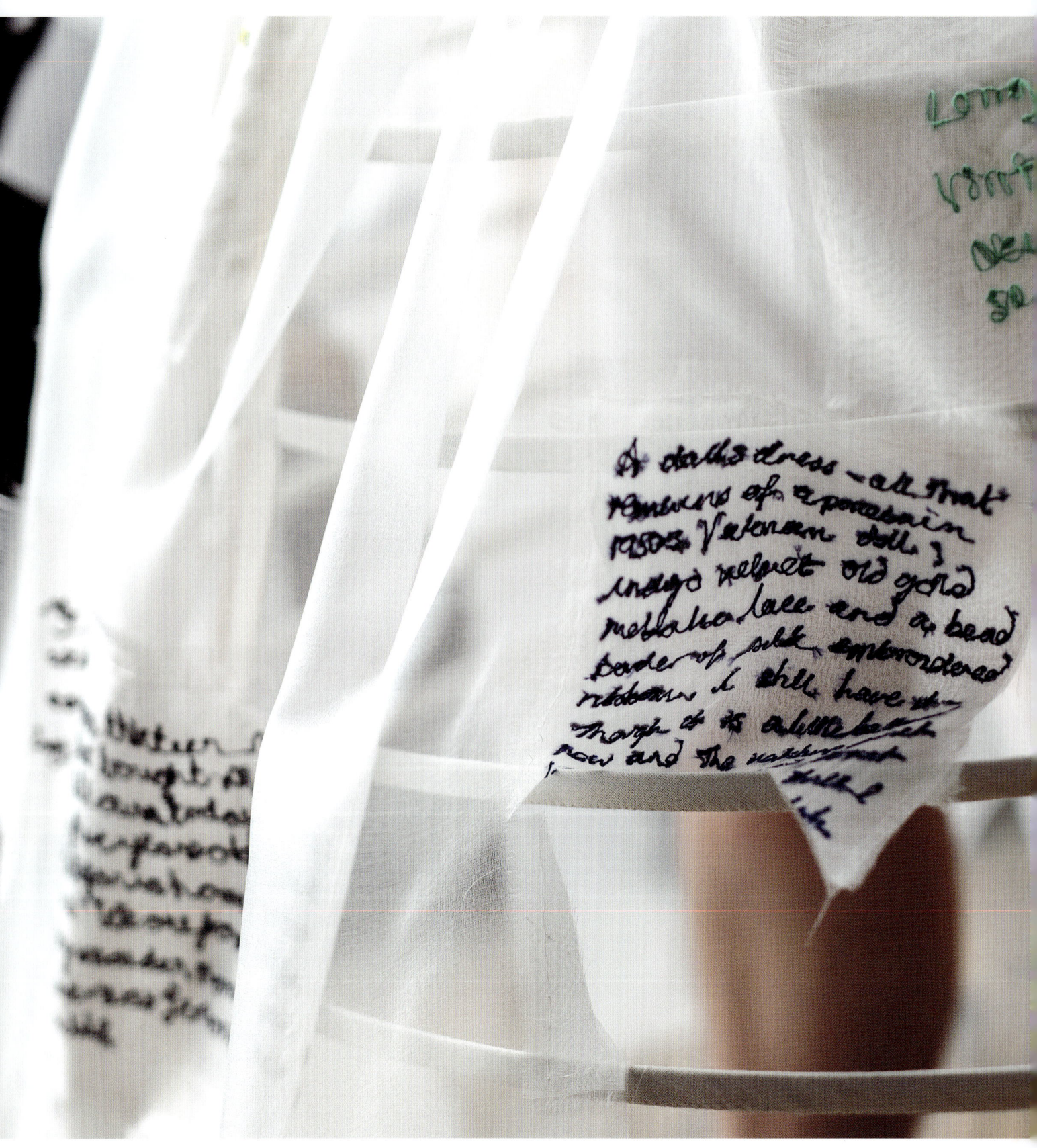

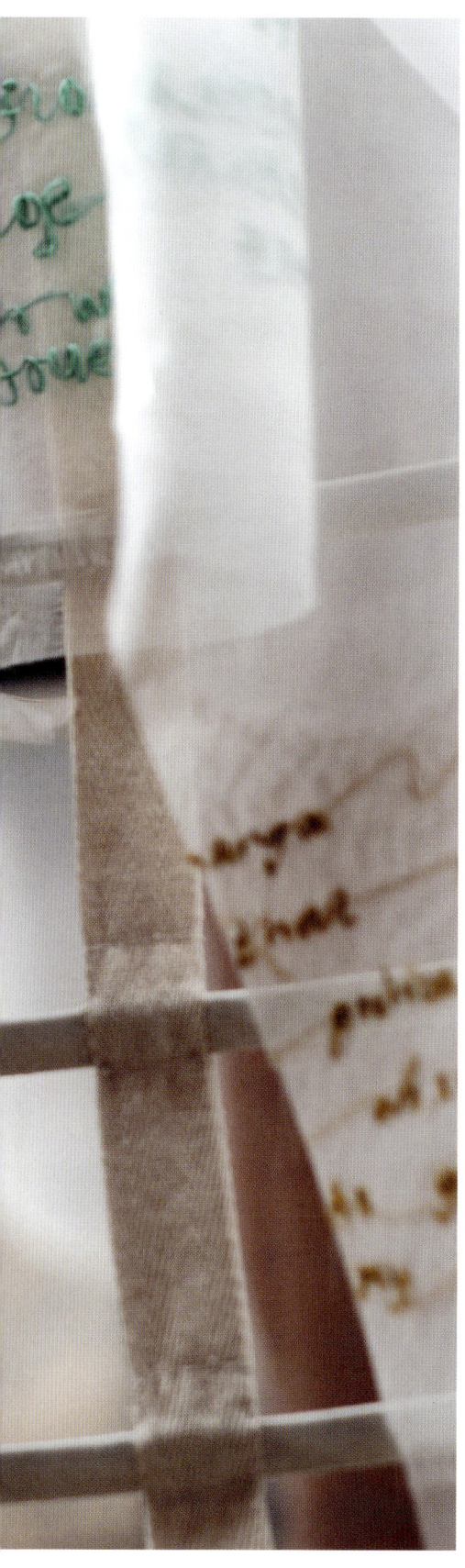

Fragment of a Dress

In 2022 I created another work designed to provoke discussion, this time from a more personal perspective. Approached by the Brontë Parsonage Museum in Haworth, West Yorkshire, I was asked to create a contemporary textile artwork with an interactive element, to accompany an exhibition of Charlotte Brontë's wardrobe. My initial starting point was the digital database, where I browsed the museum collections. Among the beautiful bonnets, parasols and samplers, I noticed a number of small, unremarkable fragments of cloth associated with Charlotte Brontë. These humble scraps intrigued me; were they kept as celebrity souvenirs, family mementos or just part of someone's scrap bag? That led me to think, why do we keep things today? What makes a garment precious and how does it hold memories?

Thinking about how visitors would 'read' the artwork, I wanted to bridge the gap between the historical collections and make them relevant to today's audience. Inspired by the precious scraps of clothing in the collections, I decided to ask people about the clothes that mean something special to them. I invited museum visitors and staff to share stories about significant items of clothing, leaving a handwritten note about their item and what it means to them.

I was really touched by the heartfelt responses, such as 'My mother was a seamstress... I still have a wool coat she wore often. When I wear it, I feel her hugging me.' There were many references to handmade items that have a special resonance, as well as items repurposed and adapted from vintage materials, including a '1920s Chinese silk lounge dress... subsequently refashioned into a short cloak'. Home dressmaking and upcycling or repurposing of materials would have been commonplace in the Brontës' time; but today, despite living in a world of 'fast fashion', many of us still keep garments for the precious memories they evoke. All of the stories were deeply personal and mostly anonymous, offering an intimate peek into the wardrobes (and lives) of strangers.

OPPOSITE Fragment of a Dress *performance (2023). Detail of stitched stories.*

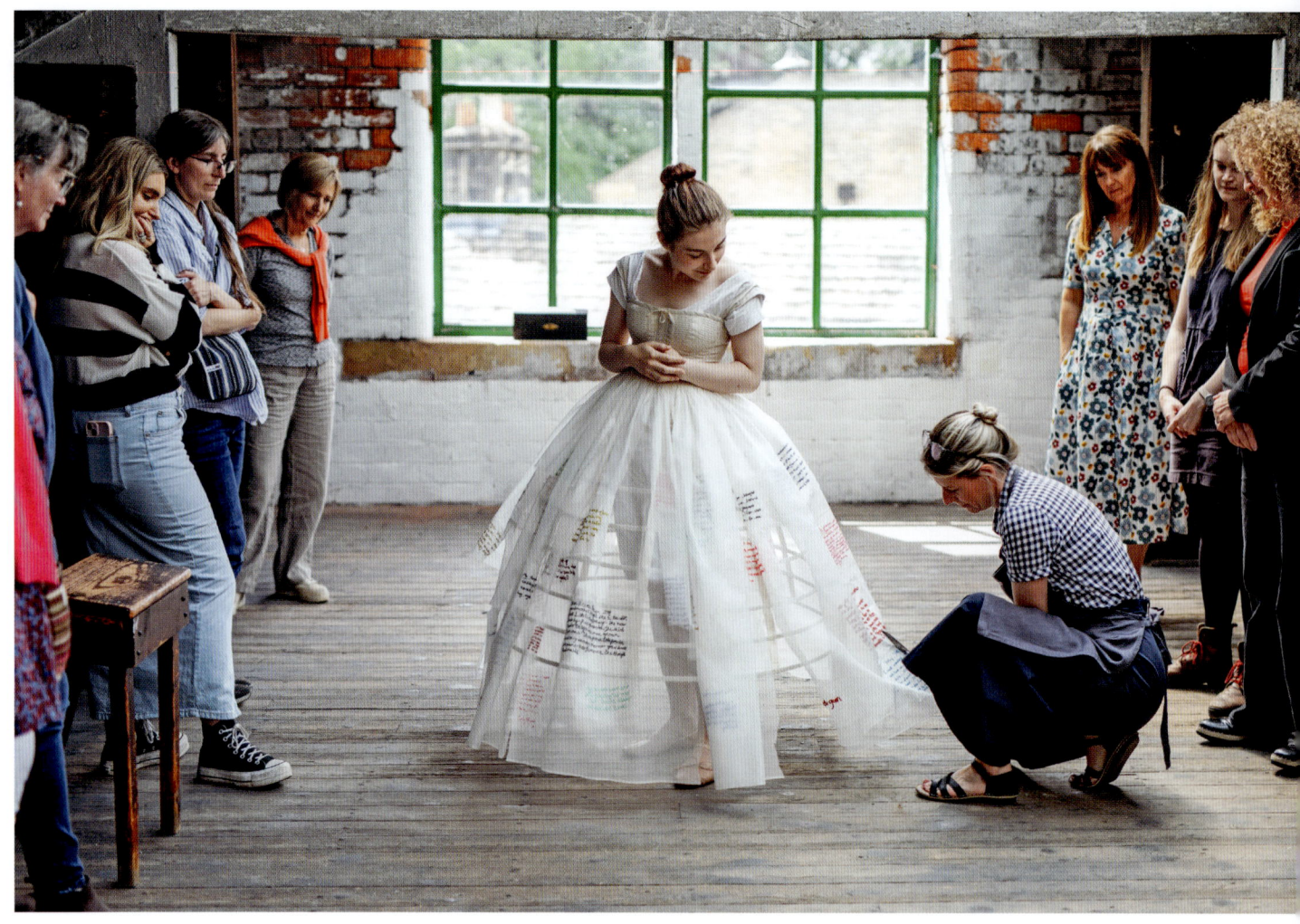

With the help of a group of generous student volunteers, we carefully embroidered the handwritten stories onto silk organza. We tried our hardest to preserve the original style and words of each story, to ensure we represented each 'voice' faithfully. I constructed a skirt from metres of sheer silk and carefully stitched each story to the skirt, overlapping and layering a mesh of memories onto the mid-19th-century silhouette. The final artwork was displayed in the Servants Room at the museum. Placed in front of the window, the transparency of the silk gave an almost lantern-like effect, allowing visitors to read these modern-day love stories about cloth and clothing.

At a later date, a further development of the project involved deconstructing the skirt. I was keen to explore the fragmentary qualities of the original historic textiles and the strangeness (for us today) of cutting up clothes to distribute to souvenir hunters. In a live artistic performance, *Fragment of a Dress* became animated as a costume, worn by performance artist Jenny Skinner. The audience were invited to cut away a fragment of the skirt to keep, leaving the remaining costume in tatters.

ABOVE Fragment of a Dress *performance with Jenny Skinner at Sunny Bank Mill (2023).*

Heritage-informed textile practices

Historical textiles can provide inspiration for diverse projects of relevance today. From sustainability and land ownership, to disability and wellbeing, they allow us to discuss ideas that are personally meaningful and that connect us with others. Textile art projects can be a useful way to engage individuals and groups, providing a chance for people to tell their story, to feel listened to or simply to reminisce about recent history and pass stories to the next generation. As an artist it can be challenging to strike a balance between our own artistic vision and the needs of others, let alone issues of historical accuracy. It is important to consider these different elements throughout a project, and continually question how well we are balancing these factors. Below are some things to keep in mind:

COMMUNICATE INTENTIONS How have you introduced the project to any participants? Try to avoid overpromising and ensure that you can deliver what you offer.

BE TRANSPARENT If you are collecting anything from participants (reminiscences, words, images, objects), be clear about how these will be used. For example, I stated at the outset that *Fragment of a Dress* would be deconstructed.

ARTISTIC VS HISTORICAL INTEGRITY Do your research but consider which historical elements must be accurate, and what can be interpreted through your artistic filter. For example, steel crinoline cages only became fashionable around the time of (or just after) Charlotte Brontë's death, but I decided to use some artistic licence because this allowed me to create the transparent look I wanted.

ORIGINAL VOICES How will you ensure that you maintain the integrity of the project and avoid distorting personal or historical narratives?

CONCLUSION

Throughout this book we have seen how careful observation can reveal clues to stories held within historical clothing and textiles. The first-hand experiences we have with textiles can put us in direct contact with history, one thread removed from historical events, both big and small. But rather than simply looking backwards, I hope that you will have found plenty to inspire future projects. Everyone can find a story to tell through textiles; one that can help us to feel connected through time and place, material and making.

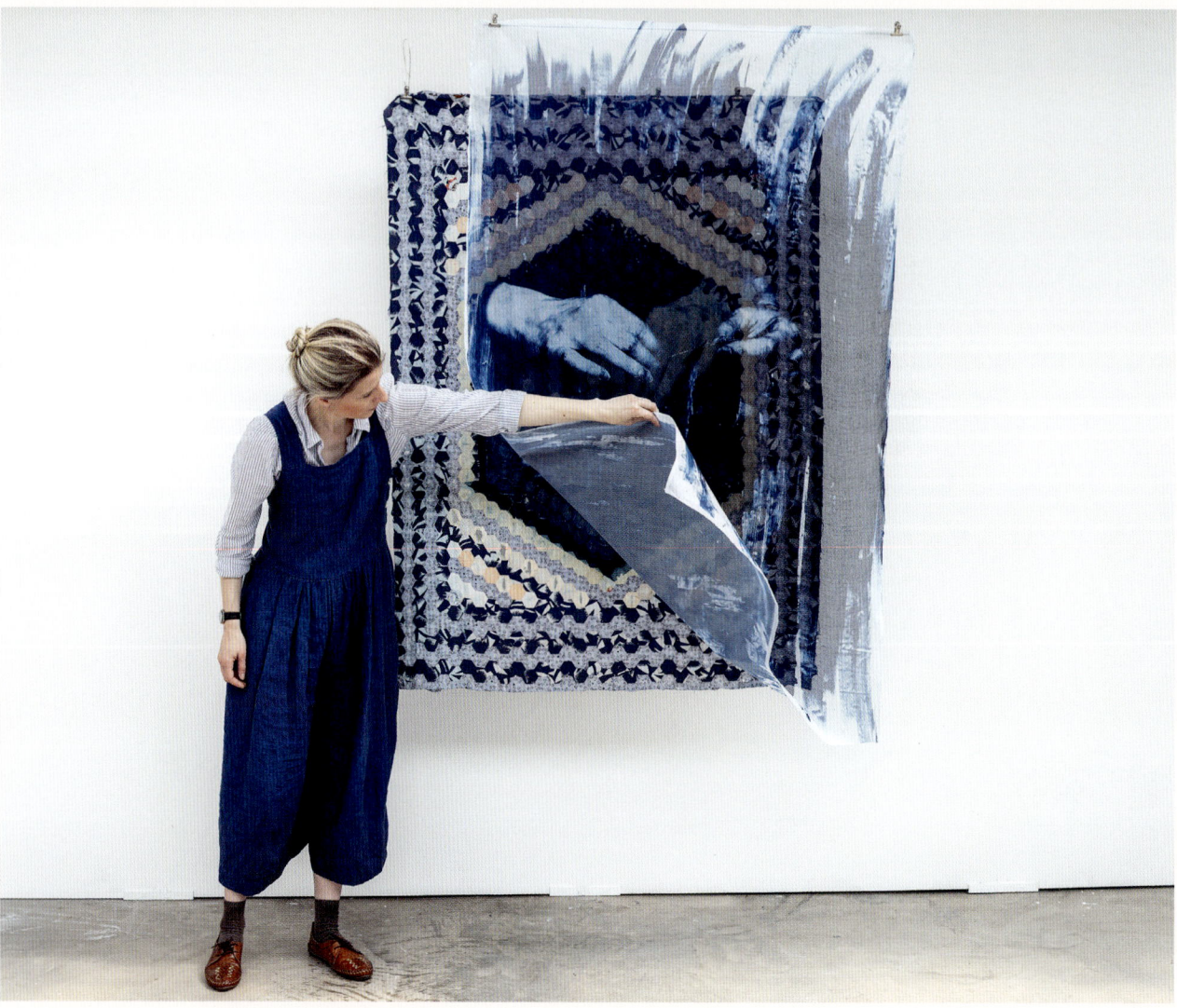

Notes

1. Claxton, Guy, *Wise Up: The Challenge of Lifelong Learning*, Bloomsbury, 1999

2. Mida, Ingrid, *Absent Presence: A Wedding Dress and the Drawings of Sarah Casey* [exhibition catalogue], Toronto Ryerson University, 2019 (Sarah Casey, page 6)

3. Ibid. (Ingrid Mida, page 3)

4. Ibid. (Sarah Casey, page 6)

5. Echavarria, M., 'Origin Sin: Cultural appreciation or appropriation', *Selvedge*: Issue 99, March/April 2021 (page 70)

6. Roberts, Debra, 'Conversation Pieces' [paper presented at Fashioning the Archive: New approaches to materialising textile history], Goldsmiths, University of London, 2014

7. Millar, Lesley (ed.), *Cloth & Memory* 2 [exhibition catalogue], Salts Estates Ltd, 2013 (Lesley Millar, page 17)

OPPOSITE *Hannah Lamb with* Inheritance *(2024). Cotton, vintage patchwork, cyanotype.*

OVERLEAF *Ghost print from* Fragment of a Dress *(2023) by Hannah Lamb. Cyanotype on watercolour paper.*

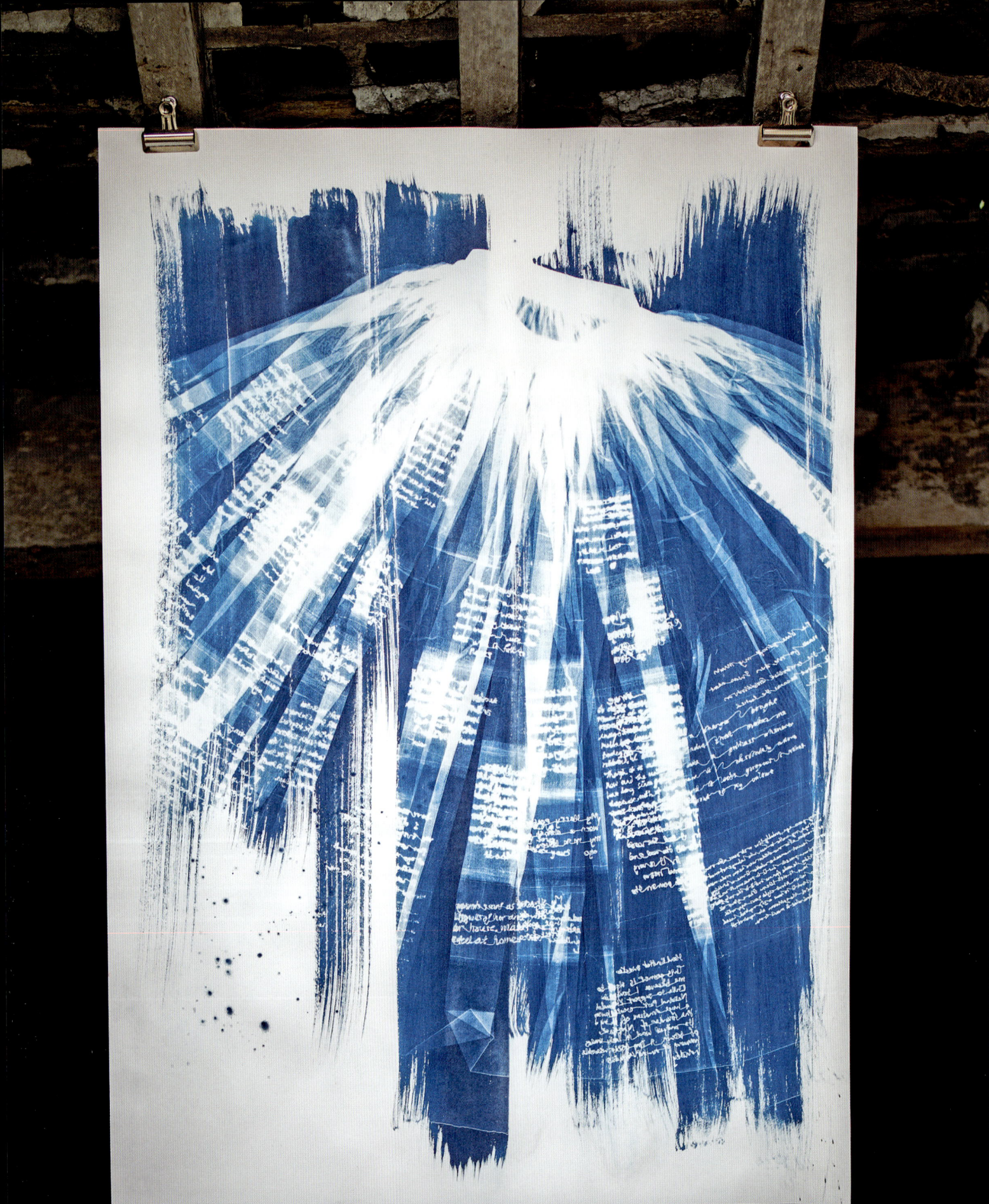

Further reading

Adlington, Lucy, *Stitches in Time: The Story of the Clothes We Wear*, Penguin Random House, 2016

Bowles, Melanie & Isaac, Ceri, *Digital Textile Design* [2nd edition], Laurence King, 2012

Breward, Christopher; Crang, Philip; Crill, Rosemary, *British Asian Style: Fashion & Textiles / Past & Present*, V&A, 2010

Finlay, Victoria, *Fabric: The Hidden History of the Material World*, Profile Books, 2021

Greenlees, Kay, *Creating Sketchbooks for Embroiderers and Textile Artists*, Batsford Books, 2005

Impey, Sara, *Text in Textile Art: Using Lettering and Fonts with Stitch and Embroidery*, Batsford Books, 2013

Kleon, Austin, *Steal Like an Artist: 10 Things Nobody Told You About Being Creative*, Workman, 2012

Koepke, Peter, *Patterns: Inside the Design Library,* Phaidon Press, 2016

Lamb, Hannah, *Poetic Cloth: Creating Meaning in Textile Art*, Batsford Books, 2019

Lynn, Eleri, *Underwear: Fashion in Detail*, V&A, 2010

Mida, Ingrid & Kim, Alexandra, *The Dress Detective: A Practical Guide to Object-Based Research in Fashion*, Bloomsbury, 2015

Millar, Lesley (ed.), *Cloth & Memory* 2 [exhibition catalogue], Salts Estates Ltd, 2013

Nicol, Karen, *Embellished: New Vintage*, A&C Black, 2012

Pattullo, Mandy, *Textiles Transformed: Thread and Thrift with Reclaimed Textiles*, Batsford Books, 2020

Steed, Josephine & Stevenson, Frances, *Sourcing Ideas for Textile Design: Researching Colour, Surface, Structure, Texture and Pattern* [2nd edition], Bloomsbury, 2020

Strasdin, Kate, *The Dress Diary of Mrs Anne Sykes: Secrets from a Victorian Woman's Wardrobe*, Chatto & Windus, 2023

Sykas, Philip Anthony, *The Secret Life of Textiles: Six Pattern Book Archives in North West England*, Bolton Museums & Art Galleries, 2005

Teasdale, Vivien, *Tracing Your Textile Ancestors: A Guide for Family Historians*, Pen & Sword Books, 2009

Wellesley-Smith, Claire, *Resilient Stitch: Wellbeing and Connection in Textile Art*, Batsford Books, 2021

Suppliers

NEW MATERIALS
Cloth House London: www.clothhouse.com
MacCulloch & Wallis: www.macculloch-wallis.co.uk
Whaleys (Bradford) Ltd: www.whaleys.co.uk

ANTIQUE AND VINTAGE TEXTILES
Ebay: www.ebay.co.uk
The Saleroom: www.the-saleroom.com/en-gb
Tennants Auctioneers: www.tennants.co.uk
The Textile Society (twice yearly antique & vintage textile
  fairs in Manchester and London): www.textilesociety.org.uk

ART MATERIALS
Cass Art: www.cassart.co.uk
Fred Aldous: www.fredaldous.co.uk

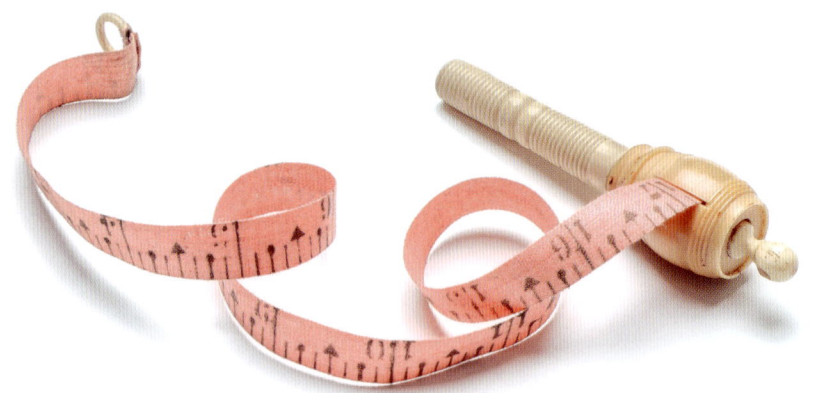

PRINTING AND CYANOTYPE
George Weil: www.georgeweil.com
Handprinted: www.handprinted.co.uk

DIGITAL PRINTING
Contrado: www.contrado.co.uk/fabrics
PrinFab: www.prinfab.com

TEXTILE CONSERVATION
ICON: The Institute of Conservation (conservation register
  for qualified conservators and restorers in the UK and
  Ireland): www.conservationregister.com
Preservation Equipment (archival storage materials):
  www.preservationequipment.com

Resources for research

These lists of resources, while by no means definitive, offer an overview of some useful collections and sites for further study and inspiration.

MAJOR FASHION AND TEXTILE COLLECTIONS

Many of these also have excellent online catalogues that can be searched for free:

British Museum (London, UK): www.britishmuseum.org
Calico Museum of Textiles (Ahmedabad, India): www.calicomuseum.org
Kyoto Costume Institute (Kyoto, Japan): www.kci.or.jp/en/
Metropolitan Museum of Art (New York, USA): www.metmuseum.org
Musée Des Arts Décoratifs (Paris, France): www.madparis.fr/musee-des-arts-decoratifs
National Museums of Scotland: www.nms.ac.uk
Textile Museum of Canada (Toronto, Canada): www.textilemuseum.ca
Victoria and Albert Museum (London and Dundee, UK): www.vam.ac.uk

SPECIALIST COLLECTIONS

Too numerous to include, but here are just a few of my personal favourites in the UK:

American Museum, Claverton Manor, Bath: www.americanmuseum.org
Bankfield Museum, Halifax, West Yorkshire:
  www.museums.calderdale.gov.uk/visit/bankfield-museum
The Bowes Museum, Barnard Castle, County Durham: www.thebowesmuseum.org.uk
Gawthorpe Textiles Collection, Brierfield, Lancashire: www.gawthorpetextiles.org.uk
Killerton House, Exeter, Devon: www.nationaltrust.org.uk/visit/devon/killerton
Manchester Art Gallery: www.manchesterartgallery.org
Pitt Rivers Museum, Oxford: www.prm.ox.ac.uk
The Royal Ceremonial Dress Collection, Historic Royal Palaces, London:
  www.hrp.org.uk/about-us/collections/royal-ceremonial-dress-collection/
The Whitworth Art Gallery, Manchester: www.whitworth.manchester.ac.uk

INDUSTRIAL MUSEUMS

Bradford Industrial Museum, West Yorkshire
Cromford Mills, Derbyshire
Framework Knitters Museum, Nottingham
Helmshore Mills Textile Museum, Lancashire
Quarry Bank Mill, Styal, Cheshire
Silk Museum and Paradise Mill, Macclesfield, Cheshire
Whitchurch Silk Mill, Hampshire

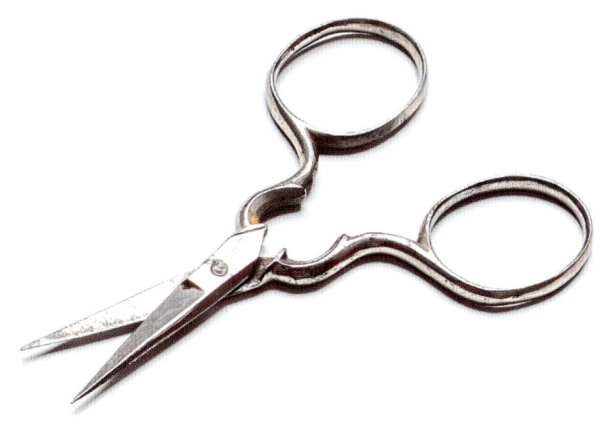

ONLINE COLLECTIONS

The Journal of Dress History: dresshistorians.org/journal/
Lancashire Textile Gallery: www.lancashiretextilegallery.com
National Trust Collections: www.nationaltrustcollections.org.uk
We Wear Culture: artsandculture.google.com/project/fashion

FAMILY HISTORY RESEARCH

The British Newspaper Archive: www.britishnewspaperarchive.co.uk
Genealogy websites: Ancestry, Find My Past
Local studies collections: Ask at your local library

Contributing Artists

Many thanks to the artists included in this book for sharing their time and thoughts:

Sarah Casey: www.sarahcasey.co.uk
Hannah Lamb: www.hannahlamb.co.uk
Hannah Robson: www.hannah-robson.com
Alison Welsh: www.alisonwelsh.com

Thanks

With special thanks to:

The students and staff of Bradford School of Art, Bradford College, the Bradford College
Textile Archive, the Society of Dyers and Colourists Textile Collection, the Brontë Parsonage
Museum, Sunny Bank Mills, Salts Mill and the 62 Group of Textile Artists.

Photo credits

All photography by Michael Wicks, except for the following:

Mark Bentele page 33; Brontë Parsonage Museum/Hannah Lamb
page 111; Clare Dearnaley pages 15, 20, 21 and 107; Rob Ford / Alamy
Stock Photo page 14; Lucy Forrester pages 2, 34–35, 40, 44–45, 50, 51,
56, 80, 82, 100, 104–105, 113, 114, 115, 116, 118, 120 and 122; Paul
Heyes / Alamy Stock Photo page 19; Victoria Hopgood page 32;
Katie Kimber page 108; Hannah Lamb pages 18, 22, 24, 26, 43, 52 and
99; Rikard Österlund page 68; Hannah Robson page 89; Alison Welsh
pages 94 and 95.

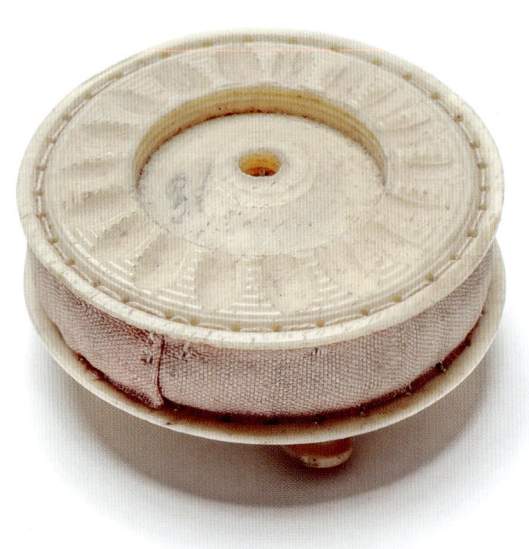

INDEX

First published in the United Kingdom
in 2025 by
Batsford
43 Great Ormond Street
London
WC1N 3HZ

An imprint of B. T. Batsford Holdings Limited

ISBN 978 1 84994 943 9

A CIP catalogue record for this book is available from the British Library.

10 9 8 7 6 5 4 3 2 1

Reproduction by Rival Colour Ltd, UK
Printed by Toppan Leefung Printing International Ltd, China

This book can be ordered direct from the publisher at
www.batsfordbooks.com, or try your local bookshop

Distributed throughout the UK and Europe by Abrams & Chronicle
Books, 1 West Smithfield, London EC1A 9JU and 57 rue Gaston Tessier,
75166 Paris, France

www.abramsandchronicle.co.uk
info@abramsandchronicle.co.uk